World Speed Record Aircraft

Wilbur Wright flying in France, 1908

World Speed Record Aircraft

The Fastest Piston-Engined Landplanes since 1903

Ferdinand C W Käsmann

PUTNAM

English translation © Conway Maritime Press Ltd 1990

First English language edition published in Great Britain in 1990 by Putnam Aeronautical Books, an imprint of Conway Maritime Press Ltd, 24 Bride Lane, Fleet Street, London EC4Y 8DR

First published in West Germany 1989 under the title *Weltrekordflugzeuge* © R Oldenbourg Verlag 1989

British Library Cataloguing in Publication data

Kaesmann, Ferdinand C W
  World Speed Record Aircraft
  1. Aeroplanes. Speed records, history
  I. Title II. Weltrekordflugzeuge. *English*
  629 13334

ISBN 0 85177 844 5

Translated by Keith Thomas
Typeset by The Word Shop, Rossendale, Lancs
Printed and bound in Great Britain by the Alden Press, Oxford

Contents

INTRODUCTION

The history of aircraft speed records spans about eighty years; a period which can be divided into two parts of roughly equal length. Up to the mid-1940s airscrews and piston engines were undisputed masters of the air, but jet propulsion then moved into the lead and stayed there. It was the combination of piston engine and airscrew, or propeller, which first made motorised flight possible in the years around 1900. When the Wright brothers achieved the very first powered, sustained and controlled flights in 1903, 12hp was sufficient for an airspeed of about 50km/h. In 1910 80hp was the power required to exceed 100km/h for the first time. Three years later a doubling of the horsepower to 160 resulted in a doubling of speed, to more than 200km/h. A further doubling in power to 320hp was then necessary to exceed the 300km/h mark in 1920. The speed of 500km/h, achieved in 1928, required all of 1,000hp. In 1939 the 750km/h mark was reached, for which 2,800hp was necessary. Finally the 800km/h record, which was achieved in 1978, required about 3,600hp.

By that time, however, the turbine engine had long since supplanted the piston engine as the power source for high-speed aircraft. Nevertheless, the combination of piston engine and airscrew, in spite of many prophecies of an early demise, has exhibited real staying power as a successful aircraft powerplant, albeit nowadays almost exclusively in the lower realms of performance.

As might be expected, what is known as the 'absolute' world speed record for aircraft is held by a jet-turbine-powered machine. In the course of thirty years the record has been raised from 976 to 3,530km/h, — 3.3 times the speed of sound. Much higher speeds — more than 7,200km/h — have been achieved by pure-rocket-propelled aircraft, but only at altitudes greater than 30km.

Propeller-turbine aircraft have also reached considerably higher speeds than those achieved by aircraft with piston engines. Indeed, it is likely that this will always be the case. It is for this reason that the records set since 1945 by the various types of machine have been registered purely as class records, in accordance with the criteria laid down by the Fédération Aéronautique Internationale (FAI) in Paris, sporting aviation's international governing body. The C-1 class embraces land-based aircraft, the C-2 class water-based aircraft and flying-boats, and the C-3 class amphibious machines. Each class is further subdivided according to powerplant. Group I includes piston engines, group II propeller turbines, group III jet turbines, and group IV rocket engines.

This book provides a detailed portrayal of the fascinating and frequently dramatic history of the 'FAI class C-1, group I', the fastest land-based aircraft powered by piston engine and propeller, from the year 1903 to the present day.

Cologne, June 1990
FERDINAND C W KÄSMANN.

THE PIONEER PERIOD

1903–1914: Up to 200km/h

It is the afternoon of 12 November 1906, in an open field near Bagatelle — a small area of the Bois de Boulogne just outside the gates of Paris. An unwieldy vehicle, resembling an oversized box-kite, rumbles over the grass, steered by a dapper gentleman with a black moustache, correctly dressed in a dark suit: Alberto Santos-Dumont. He stands upright in a narrow wicker basket immediately forward of the rear-mounted biplane wing cellule, with the levers and a handwheel of the controls before him on top of the long forward section of the fuselage, which, like the wings, consists of a wood and bamboo framework covered in cotton fabric. The fuselage sides bear the large number '14bis', while right at the front is a box-kite stabiliser assembly. This is a canard-style aeroplane. The ailerons, octagonal panels mounted outboard between the wings, are connected by cables to a corset worn by the pilot. He moves them by leaning to one side or the other. In the extreme tail of the machine is a 50hp Antoinette V-8 engine fitted with a two-bladed metal pusher propeller. The overall impression of the machine, which has an all-up weight of 300kg, is one of extreme inelegance.

Santos-Dumont 14bis, 1906.

Alberto Santos-Dumont, 33 years old, the son of a Brazilian coffee millionaire, arrived in Paris in 1891, and quickly proved to be an enthusiastic aeronaut/aviator as well as a playboy. He built his first airship, which was 25m long and 3.5m wide, in 1898. It was completely unsuccessful, but Santos-Dumont continued undaunted on the construction of further airships, initially propelled by a 3hp de Dion car engine, then by a 7hp Buchet, and finally by a 12hp aircraft engine of the same make. His sixth version, by now grown to a length of 33m and a diameter of 6m, finally allowed him to fulfil his ambition. On 19 November 1901 he flew round the Eiffel Tower in the machine. This half-hour flight from St Cloud and back won him the Prix Deutsch de la Meurthe, which had been endowed with a prize of 150,000 Francs. To the credit of the Brazilian, he spent part of the prize money on charity, and distributed the rest among his mechanics.

Santos-Dumont continued his work on airships, but at the same time carried out his first experiments with heavier-than-air aircraft. In 1905 he managed a few leaps into the air flying version No 11, towed as a glider behind a high-speed motor boat; on the other hand, version No 12 did not progress far beyond the drawing board. This was a double-rotor helicopter, for which no suitable engine was available.

Santos-Dumont's next machine, the 14bis, appeared at first to be unstable, and he tested its behaviour by suspending it from a tightly stretched overhead cable, and hitching it up to a galloping donkey named Cuigno. Further experiments under his No 14 airship followed. The machine first took off under its own power on 13 September 1906. The hop covered a distance of seven metres, and ended in a rather abrupt landing. On 23 October, after repairs had been completed and the 24hp Antoinette engine replaced by a more powerful unit producing 50hp,

Santos-Dumont 14bis after the fitment of ailerons, 1906.

Santos-Dumont made a short flight lasting seven seconds and covering sixty metres. This achievement netted the courageous aviator a further prize of 3,000 Francs: this was the Archdeacon prize, established in 1904 for the first twenty-five-metre flight in Europe.

Then, on 12 November, barely three weeks later, the enterprising Brazilian prepared to make an attack on the 1,500-Franc prize to be awarded for the first officially measured 100-metre flight, in the presence of official timekeepers of the Aero Club de France (ACF), which had been founded in 1898. He also hoped to use the occasion to establish a number of records. For this attempt the 14bis was

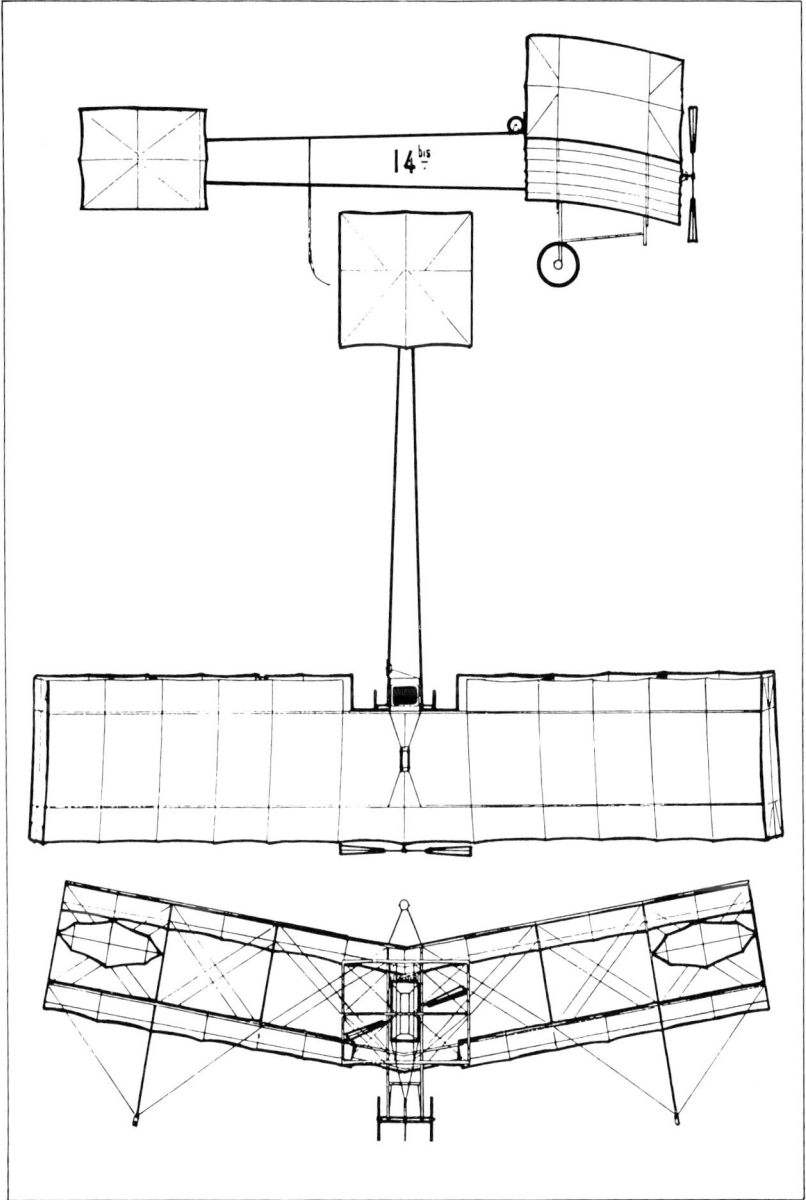

Santos-Dumont 14bis.

fitted with a new type of ailerons. He completed two test flights on the morning of the 12th, but they were not measured. The third attempt, which began at 1609hrs, produced a measured distance of exactly 82.60m, which the aircraft covered in 7.2 seconds. On the fourth attempt, starting at 1645hrs, Santos-Dumont succeeded in keeping his flying machine in the air for 21.1sec, covering a distance of 220m. He had done it: once again he was awarded the prize. The 220-metre flight was recognised as the first French distance record. The maximum speed of exactly 41.292km/h, achieved on the third attempt, was also regarded as the French speed record initially.

One year before these events took place, eight national aero clubs had held a meeting in Paris, the outcome of which was the establishment of an international aviation authority, the Fédération Aéronautique Internationale (FAI). Shortly after Santos-Dumont's efforts, the FAI decided to set up its own list of international records. It adopted all the corresponding French records as the basis of the new record list, and so it was that Alberto Santos-Dumont was included as the first world record holder for aircraft. Unfortunately for the patriotic pride of France, which believed it led the world in aviation, there was one slight fault. It was unjustified.

For some time reports had been reaching Europe of allegedly successful gliding and powered flights carried out by two Americans from the US State of Ohio. However, many other would-be aviators had started rumours of a similar kind, only to be found wanting when their claims were put to the test. Here again, no proof of the claims was offered, or at least none which was accepted by the European experts, ie. the French. Moreover, the excessive secrecy of the two gentlemen from overseas called forth a great deal of scorn and derision in Europe. The 'Flying Brothers' were christened the 'Lying Brothers'.

In fact, Wilbur and Orville Wright had carried out their first four powered flights, the longest of which lasted no less than fifty-nine seconds, on 17 December 1903, three years earlier. The brothers lived in Dayton, Ohio, where they ran a small bicycle business. The site of this historic event was a remote area in Kitty Hawk, North Carolina, known as the Kill Devil Hills, and success had not come by chance. For four years the two Americans had experimented, initially stimulated by the gliding flights and subsequent tragic death of the German Otto Lilienthal, who had also written *Der Vogelflug als Grundlage der Fliegekunst* (Birdflight as the Basis of the Art of Flying). Their first effort was a braced biplane model with a wingspan of about one and a half metres. The Wrights had also studied the experiments made by Octave Chanute, a naturalised American civil engineer, who had made use of Lilienthal's data and had written a study entitled *Progress in Flying Machines*. The two brothers adopted a rigorous and systematic approach to their work, and soon they uncovered inaccuracies, contradictions and errors of logic, with the result that they decided to carry out their own fundamental research, this time in an admirably thorough and logical manner.

One of the greatest problems of the first flying machines, unpowered or powered, was their lack of control. If they could fly at all, they virtually staggered through the air, especially when being turned. It is true that Lilienthal and his student, Alois Wolfmüller, had worked on the idea of wing warping, but they had not succeeded in translating these ideas into practice in a rational manner. In contrast, even the small model built by the Wright brothers in 1899 was fitted with a mechanism for warping the outboard end of the wing trailing edges: they could be twisted up or down. This invention alone solved the greatest control problem.

By September 1900 they had completed their first full-size glider — a biplane with a span of 5.18m. At first they tested it unmanned, then carrying a prone pilot, in a series of tethered and untethered flights over the sand dunes of Kitty Hawk. In 1901 a second glider was produced, and in the Autumn of 1902 the third. They succeeded in completing over a thousand gliding flights with this machine, varying in duration up to 26 seconds and in distance up to 189m.

In the following year, with the experience of this systematic programme of flight testing behind them, as well as intensive tests of aerofoils in a windtunnel, the brothers built their first powered aircraft, the Flyer I, together with the lightweight engine and propellers it required. Just a few months after their epoch-making first flights on 17 December 1903, the Flyer II took off from Huffman Prairie, an expanse of pasture to the east of their home town of Dayton which a friend had allowed them to use. Around one hundred flights followed this first attempt, and eventually they were able to fly turns and complete circuits. The brothers used a monorail system for take-off, and after September 1904 they adopted a form of catapult launch system based on a falling 800kg weight, which pulled the aircraft along the rail via return pulleys. These flights ranged in duration up to five minutes, and in distance up to 4.4km, and it was unfortunate when the engine failed on not one, but two displays laid on for the press. The journalists who had taken the trouble to make the journey were not amused, and wrote embittered reports of the failures in their pages.

In June 1905 the Wright Flyer III was ready. This was a logical development of the first two machines, again controlled by the pilot lying prone on the bottom wing, and again fitted with long skids. This was the first practical aeroplane in the history of the world, and with it the brothers progressively increased their maximum flight duration from an initial eighteen minutes to a marvellous thirty-eight minutes. The latter flight, which took place on 5 October 1905, covered a distance of about 39km.

Encouraged by these successes, the Wrights offered to sell their flying machines first to the American, then to the British and finally to the French government, but all three eventually withdrew from negotiations. In no small part this may have been a result of the extremely rigid, even stubborn attitude of the Wrights, who refused stolidly to show the drawings, far less the machine itself, to any party who might be interested in purchasing it, prior to the signing of a contract — so greatly did they fear the theft of their intellectual property by competitors. The fact that potential customers were disinclined to purchase such an unknown quantity was understandable, even though the contract would have been rendered null and void if the machine had failed to perform as specified. For two and a half years, from

October 1905 to May 1908, the Wright brothers performed not a single flight, nor allowed anyone a single glimpse of their invention. With these facts in mind, it should come as no surprise that their claims of success were not taken seriously in Europe.

Voisin-Farman I(mod), 1907.

Europe, or, to be precise, France, had found its new hero of the air: this was Henry (Henri) Farman, a well-to-do Englishman living in France, who was a motor sport enthusiast. The brothers Gabriel and Charles Voisin, working in the Parisian suburb of Billancourt, had already built crude gliders based on the Wright design, and in June 1907 Farman ordered a powered aircraft from them. This was the third to be built at Billancourt, and proudly bore the name *Voisin-Farman I*. It was similar in general terms to the American machines, but a wheeled undercarriage was fitted and the pilot had a real seat. The powerplant was an Antoinette aircraft engine rated at 50hp. On 26 October 1907, just four weeks after the machine's first flight, Farman made a flight lasting 52.6 seconds and covering 771m at Issy-les-Moulineaux, not far from Paris. The FAI promptly acknowledged this flight as the first official distance record and the second world speed record. A Parisian lawyer named Ernest Archdeacon had donated a prize for the first officially recorded 150m flight, and fourteen days later Farman won it by covering a distance of 1,030 metres in 74 seconds. He subsequently modified the aircraft in accordance with his own ideas, and on 13 January 1908 he completed the first officially observed one-kilometre flight in a closed circuit, which involved flying round a turning point located 500m from the take-off line. This achievement won for him the Grand Prix d'Aviation, worth 50,000 Francs, a series of other prizes, and enthusiastic praise from *The Times* newspaper of London.

At about the same time — February 1908 — the Wright brothers finally signed a contract with the US Army, after months of tough negotiations, and this was followed by another with a French commercial company one month later. In early May, in an effort to polish up their flying skills, the two brothers carried out a series of test flights at Kitty Hawk, including two flights with a passenger, a

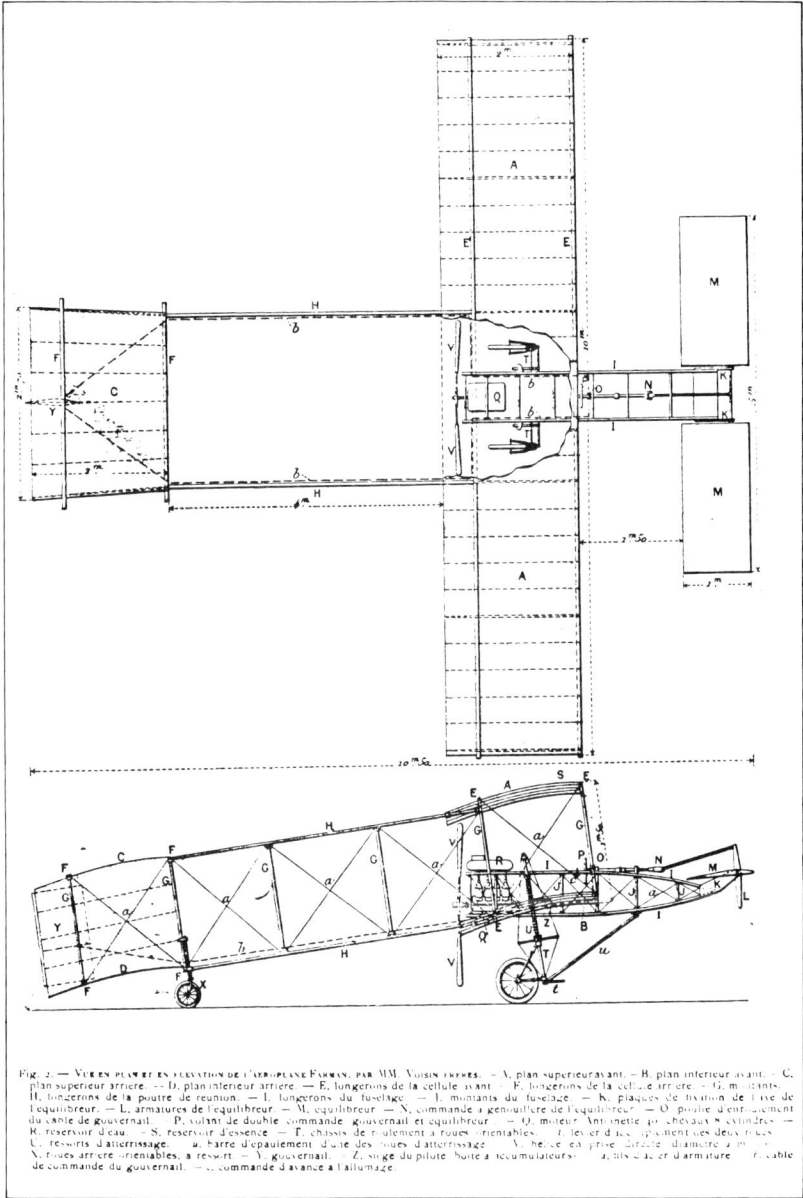

Fig. 5. — VUE EN PLAN ET EN ÉLÉVATION DE L'AÉROPLANE FARMAN, PAR MM. VOISIN FRÈRES. — A, plan supérieur avant. — B, plan inférieur avant. — C, plan supérieur arrière. — D, plan inférieur arrière. — E, longerons de la cellule avant — F, longerons de la cellule arrière — G, montants. H, longerons de la poutre de réunion. — I, longerons du fuselage — J, montants du fuselage — K, plaques de fixation de l'axe de l'équilibreur. — L, armatures de l'équilibreur — M, équilibreur — N, commande à genouillère de l'équilibreur — O, poulie d'entrainement du câble de gouvernail. — P, volant de double commande, gouvernail et équilibreur — Q, moteur Antoinette 50 chevaux 8 cylindres — R, réservoir d'eau. — S, réservoir d'essence — T, chassis de roulement à roues orientables. — t, levier d'orientation des deux roues. U, ressorts d'atterrissage. — u, barre d'épaulement d'une des roues d'atterrissage — V, hélice en prise directe diamètre 2 m. X, roues arrière orientables, à ressort — Y, gouvernail. — Z, siège du pilote, boîte à accumulateurs — a, tirs d'acier d'armature — b, câble de commande du gouvernail. — c, commande d'avance à l'allumage.

Voisin-Farman I(mod), 1907.

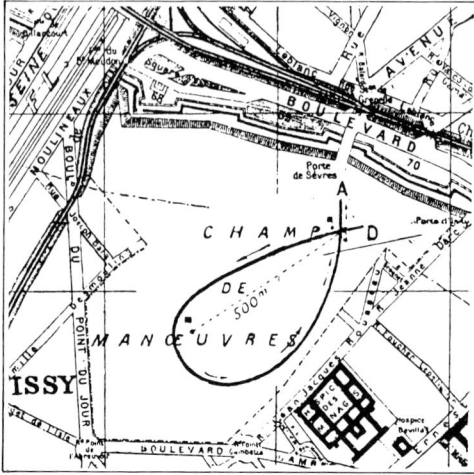

Issy-les-Moulineaux, 1908.

certain Mr C W Furnas. These flights were completed with the modified Flyer III, which could now carry two persons sitting upright. Orville Wright undertook the task of modifying the Model A, which had been constructed in the meantime, to meet the requirements of the US Army. Meanwhile, at the end of May, his brother Wilbur travelled to France, where a Flyer had been in storage at Le Havre since July 1907. This machine was assembled in Leon Bollée's car factory at Le Mans, and on 8 August 1908 the long-awaited first flight of a Wright machine in Europe took place, under the eyes of hundreds of critical, derisive or simply curious onlookers, who had gathered on the small local racecourse at Hunaudières.

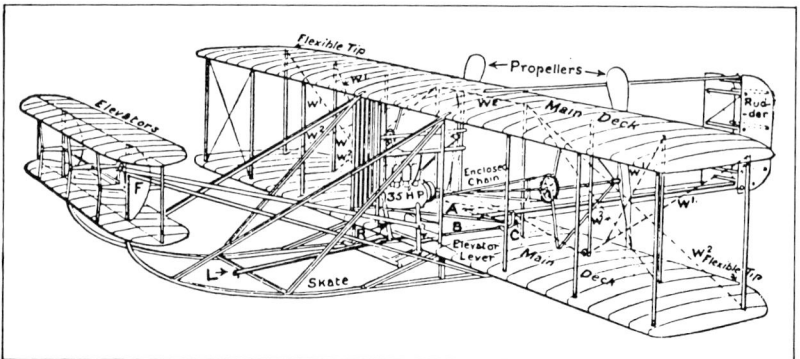

Wright Model A, 1908.

The flight, a catapult-assisted take-off, two full circuits, and a soft landing, lasted exactly one minute forty-five seconds, but it revolutionised the world of aviation. The machine's evident ability to fly under complete control, thanks to the Wright method of wing warping, was a revelation to the Europeans, who had long been extremely sceptical. Leon Delagrange, the successful Parisian sculptor and flight pioneer, expressed the thoughts of many when he said: 'Well then, we are beaten! We just don't exist!'.

One month later, on 3 September 1908, Orville Wright began the official acceptance flights for the US Army, held at Fort Myer, close to the US Capital, Washington DC. On some of the flights the machine carried officers of the US Signal Corps as passengers. These flights were equally triumphant, since they again succeeded in convincing the sceptics. On the tenth flight, on the afternoon of 17 September, the machine suffered a propeller fracture, and the Model A crashed. The passenger, Lt T E Selfridge, was killed, and Orville Wright suffered serious injuries.

The indisputable superiority of the Wright brothers' method of achieving lateral control by twisting the outboard wing trailing edges — a system which was superseded by ailerons — came as a salutary shock to everybody involved in aviation in Europe, where lateral control had been ignored. Every existing and planned flying machine was immediately converted to include this feature. In January 1909 Wilbur Wright moved to a warmer part of France, Pau, where he continued the training of three French pilots as part of his contractual obligations.

Orville Wright's first flight at Tempelhof Field, near Berlin, 1908.

Orville, convalescing after his injuries, followed him later the same month, together with their sister Katharine. In April he carried out a further series of successful demonstration and training flights at Rome, after which he returned home to Dayton.

On 20 May 1909 Paul Tissandier, the first of Wright's French flying pupils, succeeded in setting the first and only officially recorded speed record by a Wright machine, flying at Pau. The Wright brothers had been far more interested in selling their invention than in setting records. The machine flown by Tissandier is known as the Model A (France), and was fitted with a four-cylinder Wright engine

Orville Wright flying at Tempelhof Field.

rated at 35hp, built under licence by the French firm of Bariquand et Marre. Under the attentive eyes of officials of the ACF, the Frenchman covered 57.5km in exactly one hour and two minutes. This gave an average speed of 54.8km/h, and represented a new world speed record for aircraft.

In June and July 1909 Orville flew a slightly modified Model A in a further series of acceptance flights, as required by the US Army. The flights, flown at Fort Myer, were completed successfully. After this he travelled to Germany, where he made many demonstration and training flights at Berlin-Tempelhof. The Model A which he used for this purpose still exists, and is on display in the Deutsches Museum in Munich — the sole example of its breed.

Prize money totalling 200,000 Francs was promised on an elegantly artistic though somewhat technically naive poster which proclaimed the Great Champagne Aviation Week, to be held at Reims over the period 22 to 29 August 1909. Financed by the champagne producers of the area, this event was a complete success in spite of miserable weather. At a time when a single flying machine was a highly unusual sight, no fewer than thirty-eight registered to participate in this, the first flying event. As a demonstration of French dominance in Europe, the firms of Antoinette, Blériot, Farman and Voisin were represented by several machines each, together with no fewer than three French-flown Wright machines. The Wright brothers themselves kept away from the event, true to their principle that the construction and sale of their products had absolute priority over any sporting frivolities. As a result the USA was represented by a single machine, an aircraft designed and built by a hopeful outsider named Glenn Curtiss.

The flying field, named the Aeropolis, was set up on a large field at Betheny, outside the gates of the town. Cloudbursts on the eve of the event caused the site to degenerate into a sea of slippery mud. In spite of this, and the poor weather which

Poster for the Reims Flying Week, 1909.

Reims flying field, 1909.

marred the rest of the week, more than half a million spectators assembled at Reims — an indication of the immense national and international interest in aviation. Among the various prizes on offer, the most attractive in financial terms was the 'Grand Prix de la Champagne et de la Ville de Reims', for the longest distance flight completed at the event. The enticing prize for the fortunate winner was 50,000 Francs.

The second important prize had been donated by the newspaper tycoon James Gordon Bennett, an American domiciled in France, and a man with an extraordinary enthusiasm for sports. His prize, the Coupe Internationale d'Aviation Gordon Bennett, was worth 'only' 25,000 Francs, but it also included an impressive trophy. Both prizes were destined for the pilot who flew two circuits of the ten-kilometre course in the fastest time.

On the opening day of the Grande Semaine, Paul Tissandier, flying his Wright A, beat his own world record, set up three months previously at Pau. However, his new record was soon beaten by another French-Wright pilot, Eugene Lefebvre, who managed a slightly higher speed. Before these figures could be officially notified and recognised, however, they were beaten again. On the second day of the event the American outsider Curtiss recorded an official speed of 69.8km/h, flying his small Reims racer, whose similarity to the Wright machines could not be denied. Curtiss thus became the latest world record holder.

Curtiss Reims Machine, 1909.

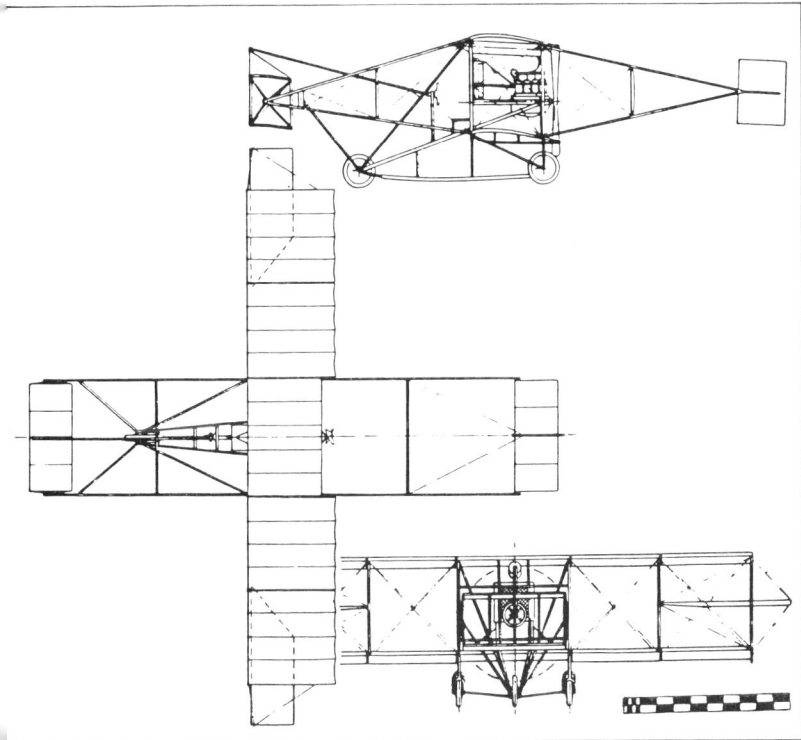

Curtiss Reims Machine, 1909

Glenn H Curtiss had already made his name as a constructor and rider of high-speed motorcycles. In January 1907 he claimed to have swept over the sands at Daytona Beach, Florida, at almost 220km/hr (!). In the same year he became a member of the Aerial Experiment Association founded by Alexander Graham Bell, and in June 1908 he flew his first own-designed aircraft, the *June Bug*. Just fourteen days later, on the propitious 4 July — American Independence day — he won a trophy donated by the journal *Scientific American* for the first officially measured flight in the USA to exceed a distance of one kilometre. The prize had originally been intended as a friendly gesture to the Wright brothers, but they were not interested in competing for prizes. Instead, they eventually sued Curtiss over the lateral control systems which he had used, because the Wrights considered that they infringed their patent and he was exploiting it commercially. The result was a protracted legal battle. For this reason Curtiss abandoned the wingtip control surfaces for his second design, the *Golden Flier*, and also for the Reims machine, in favour of a form of aileron fitted between the wings, but this did not resolve the infringement problems. The engine was also a Curtiss design — a V-8 producing 52hp. The world record flight on 23 August 1908 at Reims also happened to be the maiden flight of the aircraft; there had been no time for flight testing in the USA. But even this world record was destined to stand for just twenty-four hours.

Louis Blériot, a wealthy manufacturer of car accessories, had been actively engaged in the design of flying machines for several years, although the results had been variable and sometimes extremely disappointing. The Blériot VIII, after being subjected to a series of modifications, was the first machine to make a number of significant flights, but his great breakthrough came with the Blériot XI. Flying this machine on 25 July 1909, he succeeded in crossing the Channel between Calais and Dover. He was the first person to achieve this feat, which brought him immense acclaim at the time. He appeared at Reims with various machines, including his Blériot XII, an enlarged variant of the cross-channel

Blériot XII, 1909.

MOTOR

PILOT

—BLERIOT XII—

SECTION OF BODY

0   1   2   3   4
METRES

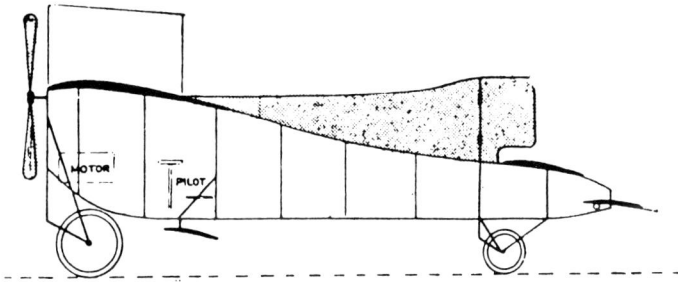

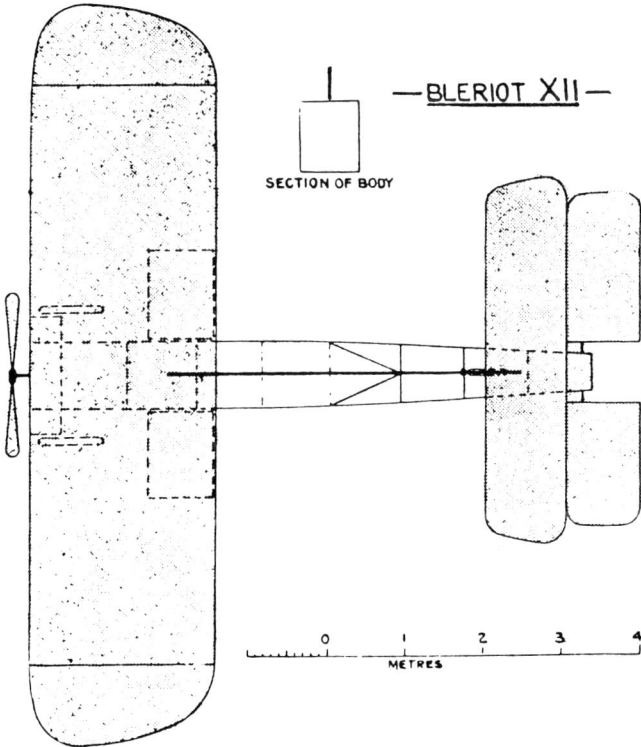

Blériot XII, 1909.

Poster for the Nice Flying Meeting, 1910.

machine with the pilot seated beneath the high-mounted wing. Like the XI, this was a braced monoplane with tractor propeller. It was powered by an eight-cylinder ENV engine producing 60hp. On the third day of the event Blériot beat the American by attaining a speed of 74.3km/h; four days later, with a smaller wing fitted, he raised the record again to almost 77km/h. Thus the world record was firmly in French hands once again. As compensation, Glenn Curtiss had the satisfaction of winning the Gordon Bennett prize in the competition which was held the same day.

Incidentally, Henri Farman won the Grand Prix, flying his own-design Farman III. He covered a distance of 180km in 3hr 4min 56sec. In so doing he thwarted Hubert Latham, who had been considered the certain victor after completing 150km.

This was the third time that the rich Parisian playboy Latham had suffered bad luck. On 19 July 1909 he had made his first attempt to cross the Channel, but had been forced to ditch when his engine failed. Just one week later Blériot made his successful crossing. A few days later, in an attempt to equal Blériot's achievement, Latham ended up in the Channel again, this time in sight of the white cliffs of Dover. His elegant monoplane had been designed by Leon Levavasseur, chief designer of the Société Antoinette. Levavasseur was also responsible for the eight-cylinder engines installed in the machines, and which were also used in a series of other aircraft, including the Santos-Dumont 14bis and the *Voisin-Farman I*. Although Latham had had to ditch the Antoinette IV in the Channel, he was recompensed with second place in the Reims Grand Prix. The next models, the Antoinettes V and VII, were based on the IV, and featured neat, completely enclosed fuselages shaped like racing boats. The structure was mahogany-skinned at the front and fabric-covered at the rear.

Although the Antoinette VII was larger than the Blériot XII and fitted with a less powerful engine, its superior aerodynamics allowed Latham to improve on Blériot's world records early in 1910, albeit by the extremely slim margin of just 0.6km/h. The new world record of 77.56km/h was set on 23 April 1910, the final

Hubert Latham in the Antoinette VII, 1910.

day of the Meeting d'Aviation at Nice, and formed a suitable climax to the event. Latham might well have thought that the organisers of the event had pre-ordained his success. After all, the colourful poster which publicised the meeting featured an eye-catching machine in the foreground — an Antoinette drawn with considerable artistic licence.

Blériot was not to be beaten so easily. His most successful design by far in commercial terms, the Blériot XI cross-channel machine, served as the starting point for a series of aircraft designed expressly for speed. Leon Morane was the first pilot to fly one of these racing monoplanes; at that time he was works pilot at Blériot, but he later found fame as a designer of fighter aircraft.

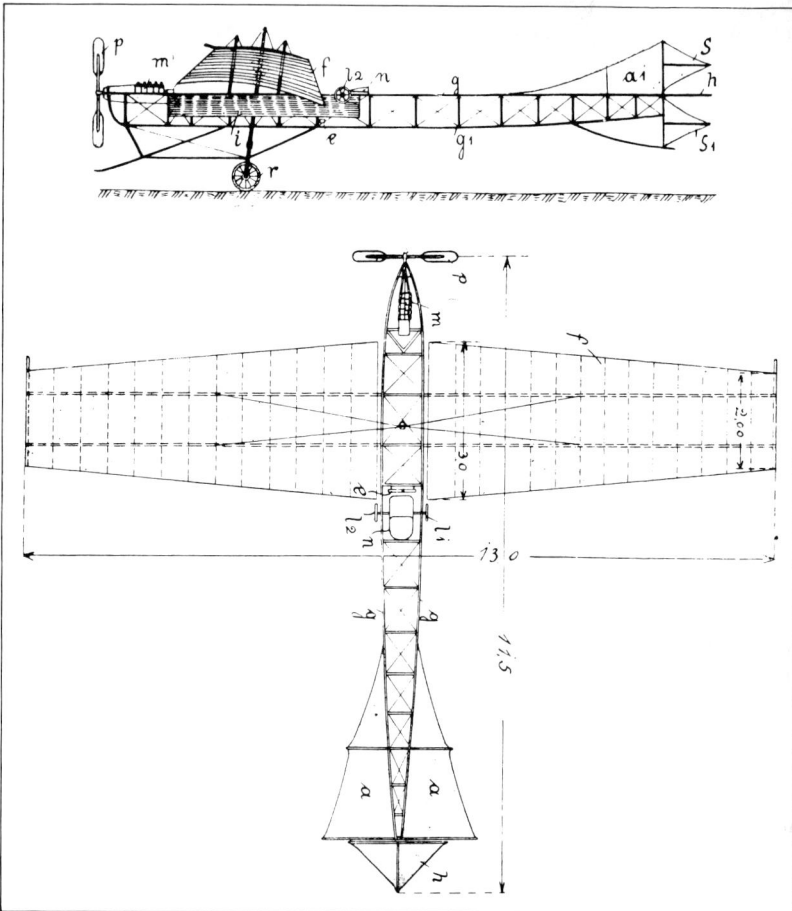

Antoinette VII, 1910.

Antoinette, Blériot and Voisin aeroplanes at the 1909 Paris Salon.

During the second Reims Flying Week, in July 1910, Morane managed to exceed the 100km/h mark for the first time; 106.5km/h was the new world's best performance, although the surviving documents contain some contradictory data. In fact, it is often impossible to check what appears to be erroneous information, as many documents which might have been considered fairly reliable have disappeared irretrievably.

Thus it was that the 100km/h hurdle was finally overcome in 1910. To put this achievement into perspective, it should be remembered that land-based vehicles had reached twice this speed several years earlier. In 1903 a German rail vehicle built by AEG had achieved 210km/h, and in 1906 an American steam-powered car, the Stanley Beetle, had swept across Daytona beach in Florida at more than 205km/h — not to mention the 220km/h which Glenn Curtiss claimed to have reached on his motorcycle at the same site in 1907.

In late October 1910 the FAI decided to relieve the Aero Club de France of the task of measuring and recognising aircraft world records, because the French authority had carried out its duties in a somewhat arbitrary manner. On 29 October 1910, just one day after this decision came into force, the first world record to be established over non-French soil was set. This occurred during the Gordon Bennett races, the first major event of its kind in the USA, held in Belmont Park, New York, and organised by the Aero Club of America. Once again

Advertisement for Latham's flights at Tempelhof Field.

Blériot XI, 1909.

it was a French pilot, Alfred Leblanc, in a French machine, a special Blériot XI, who was the new world's record holder, with just on 110km/h. At the same event Orville Wright, piloting his small Baby Grand racing biplane, seemed to be extremely fast. This latest Wright machine, in contrast to their earlier products, had no canard surfaces, a wheeled undercarriage replaced the former skids, and it was powered by a 60hp V-8 engine. However, Orville did not take part in the record attempts himself.

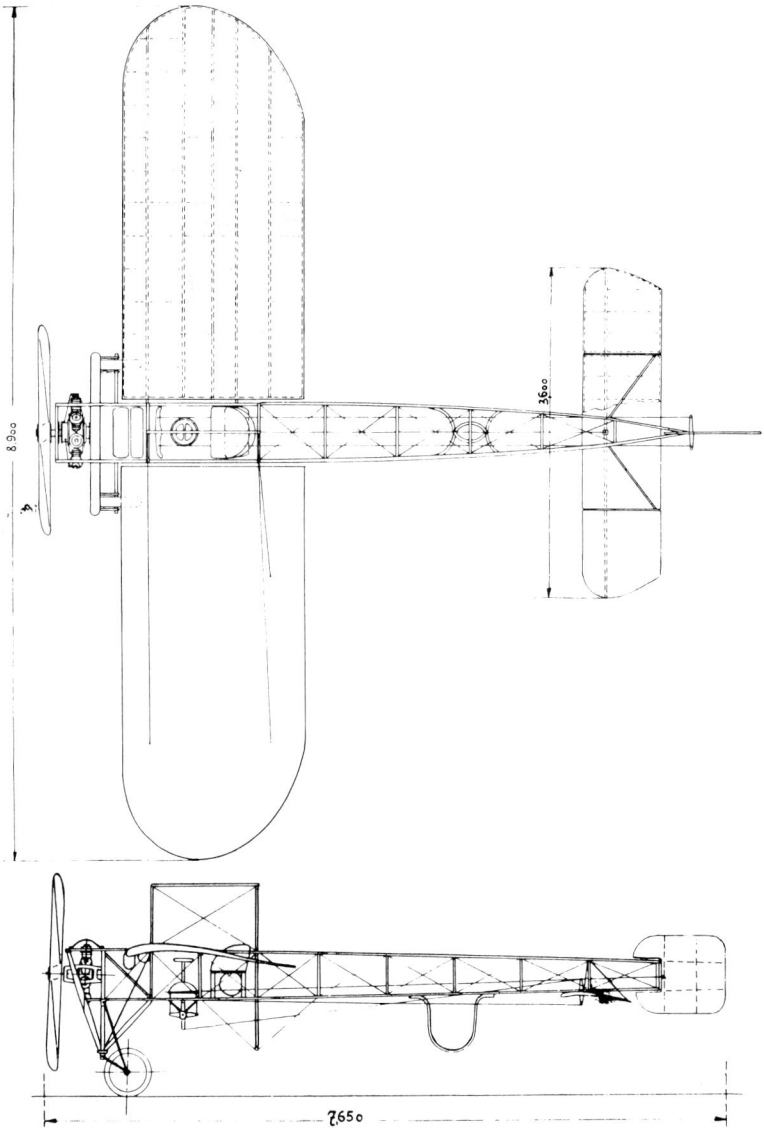

Blériot XIbis, 1910.

Four months after this event, in April 1911, Leblanc managed to push his record a fraction higher, flying the same machine. This time he flew over home ground, at Pau, where Tissandier had set his record two years earlier. Again, two months later, on 12 June 1911, Leblanc succeeded a third time, on this occasion flying a further development of the proven Blériot XI, modified for higher speed. Flying at Etampes, he recorded a speed of exactly 125km/h, but he was destined to hold his new world record for just four days. A new contender had appeared, equipped with a new aircraft and — a crucial advantage — with new ideas.

Edouard de Niéport was the extraordinarily gifted, if somewhat rebellious son of a conservative-minded army officer. It is easy to imagine the dismay of his parents and his teachers when, after studying for several years at the École Supérieure d'Électricité, he suddenly decided to take up professional cycling as a career, and to change his name to Edouard Nieuport. After a few years a heart problem forced him to abandon cycling, and he established a small factory in Suresnes producing electrical goods. Thanks to his extremely inventive mind, his new business was soon thriving. Nieuport had long since taken a great interest in the early attempts at flying made by the original pioneers. Now he mixed more and more with the likes of Farman, Levavasseur and Voisin. It was not long before Nieuport designed his first aircraft, a small monoplane, which he built in 1909. It was based on an open-framework fuselage, which at that time was a standard feature, but Nieuport was all too familiar with the problem of air resistance, which he had experienced at first hand as a racing cyclist. His second design, the Nieuport II, which was built the following year, showed the way forward in terms of aerodynamics. It had a fully enclosed, streamlined fuselage, a similarly well thought out undercarriage with the minimum of struts, and a wing braced with few cables. It was not a sensational machine, but it was a very important one insofar as it showed the logical application of the aerodynamic knowledge which had been gained up to this time. He did not have to wait long for success. After Nieuport had established a series of records with an aircraft of this type, including some carrying a passenger, he decided to attack the absolute speed record. On 11 May

Nieuport IIN, 1911.

Aéroplanes et Hydroaéroplanes

"NIEUPORT"

LIVRE D'OR

1911

Concours Militaire de Reims	WEYMANN.
Coupe Gordon-Bennett	WEYMANN.
Prix Quentin-Bauchart	2ᵐᵉ HELEN.
Critérium de l'Aé. C. F.	GOBÉ.

1912

Circuit de Paris (Coupe Henry-Deutsch de la Meurthe) tenant .	HELEN.
Circuit d'Anjou	ESPANET.
Record du Monde de Distance : Sébastopol, Moscou, St-Pétersbourg	Lieut' DYBOWSKY.
Bombay-Dakar-Saint-Louis (Sénégal)	Lieut' FÉQUANT.

GRANDES MANŒUVRES DU POITOU

HYDROAÉROPLANES

LA PREMIÈRE GRANDE COURSE DE RIVE A RIVE
Saint-Malo-Jersey et retour : WEYMANN

RECORD DE DISTANCE AU-DESSUS DE LA MER
Tamise, Anvers, Calais, Le Havre, Vernon : WEYMANN

GRANDES MANŒUVRES NAVALES

SOCIÉTÉ ANONYME DES ÉTABLISSEMENTS NIEUPORT

Boulevard du Point-du-Jour — Rue Camille Desmoulins

ISSY-LES-MOULINEAUX (Seine)

Téléphone : 7e0-24 — 7e0-25   Adresse Télégraphique : NIEUPORT-ISSY-LES-MOULINEAUX

École de Pilotage à VILLACOUBLAY, près Paris

Ecole d'Aviation maritime : FRÉJUS-SAINT-RAPHAEL (Var)

Nieuport advertisement, 1912.

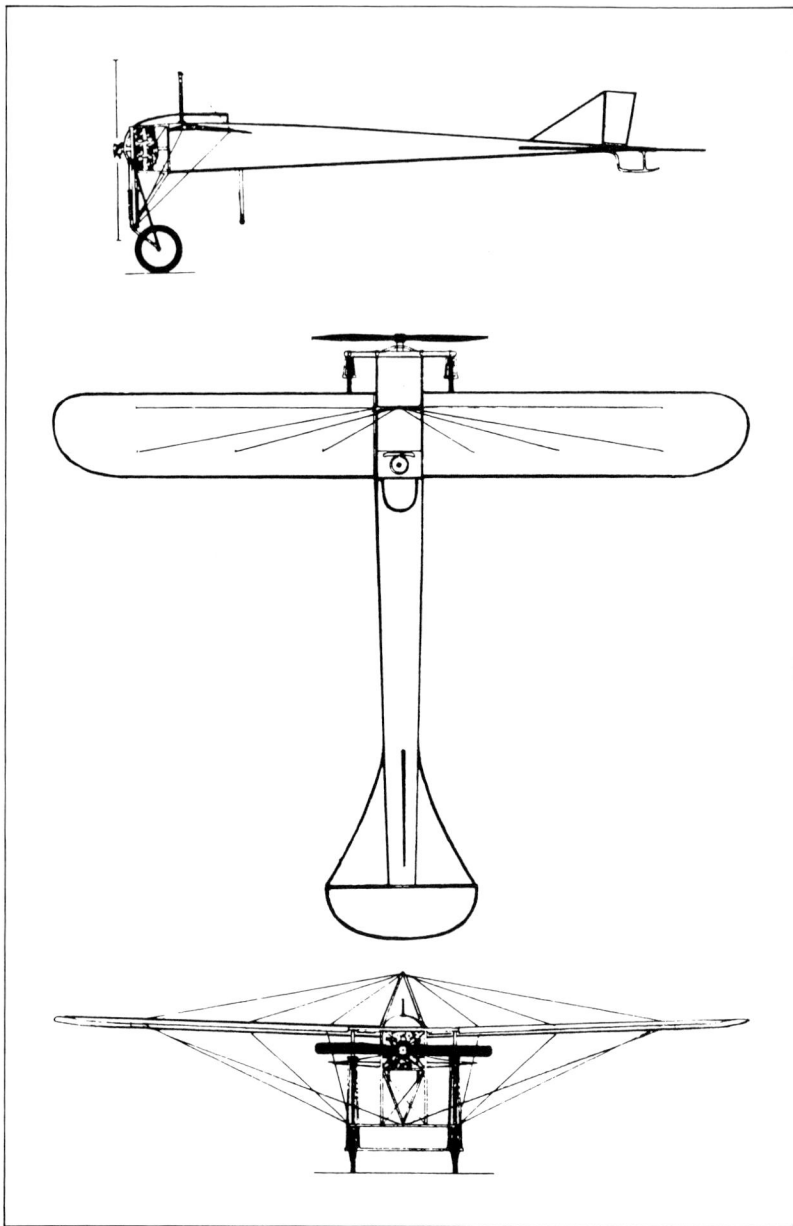

Blériot XXIII, 1911.

1911, flying a Nieuport IIN at Mourmelon, near Chalons-sur-Marne, he completed a 100km flight at a new world record average speed of approximately 120km/h. The extraordinary thing about this record was the fact that the aircraft was propelled by a twin-cylinder Darracq-Nieuport engine which produced only 28hp. It is difficult to imagine a more impressive demonstration of the value of low drag to the speed of an aircraft.

That Alfred Leblanc bettered this in a Blériot XXIII (sometimes known as the Blériot XI Vitesse), fitted with a 100hp Gnome two-row rotary engine, caused Edouard Nieuport little concern. On 16 June 1911, four days later, he made a further attempt to win the speed crown. This time he had fitted his record breaking machine with a similar type of rotary engine, an 80hp Gnome Monosoupape A. He was immediately successful, forcing the record to just over 130km/h; five days later he edged it up again, to more than 133km/h. As far as

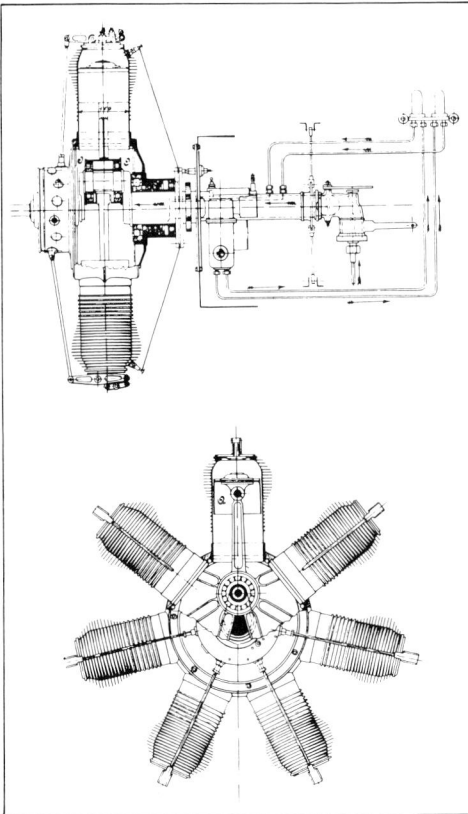

Diagram of the 50hp Gnome rotary engine of 1911.

Nieuport was concerned, Leblanc or anybody else was welcome to try to better this performance. After all, he still had the 100hp engine in reserve to help him regain the upper hand if and when it became necessary. His competitors were realistic in their appraisal of the situation, and did nothing. Three months later, on 16 September 1911, Edouard Nieuport died following a crash during a demonstration flight put on as part of the Concours Militaire.

This event, in which various machines were compared, was organised by the French army, and the aircraft of a new Paris company, founded the preceding spring, turned in an outstanding performance. The company was the Société Provisoire des Aéroplanes Deperdussin, known by the abbreviation SPAD. Armand Deperdussin, the company's proprietor, was a self-assured and charming silk wholesaler, courted by fashionable Paris society, and with wide-ranging interests. When he established his new company he had the good fortune to engage as chief designer a young engineer named Louis Béchereau. His new colleagues included several capable individuals, among them the Dutch engineer Frits Koolhoven, the workshop director Henri Papa and, some months later, the young and inventive master cabinet maker André Herbemont.

The first designs produced by the Béchereau team leaned to a great extent on conventional practice, but very soon they turned to a new constructional method for aircraft, the self-supporting shell, originally invented by the Swiss boatbuilder

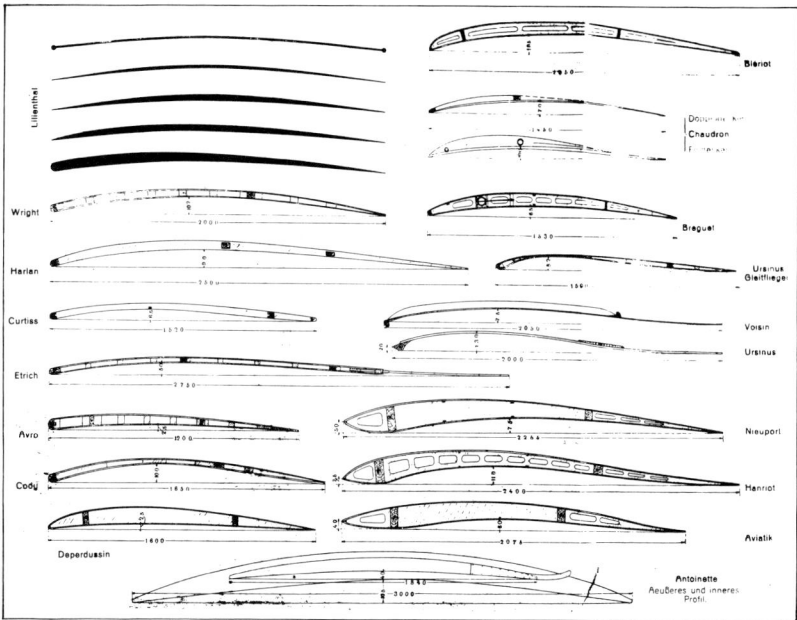

Aerofoil sections, 1888–1912.

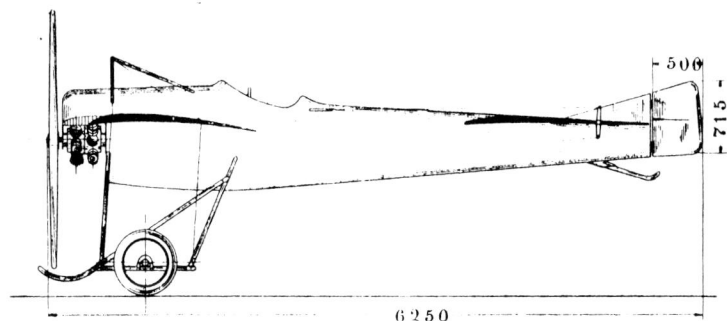

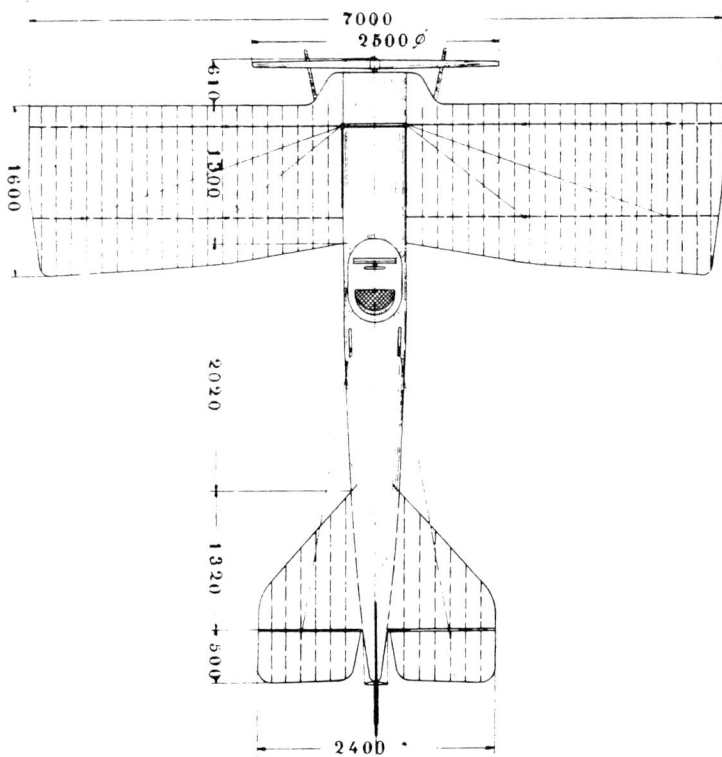

Deperdussin 'Course', 1912.

Eugene Buchonnet. The aircraft's fuselage consisted of plywood half-shells which, when joined, were covered inside and out with fabric and then varnished. This construction superseded the orthodox method, which used a braced timber or metal framework, either open or covered by linen and/or plywood. This new method of construction, which became known as the monocoque system, promised very high strength for relatively low weight, with the incidental advantage of a smooth outer skin. The unavoidable disadvantage was complex and time-consuming construction. At first only the front section of the Deperdussin machines' fuselages were built on the monocoque system, but the self-evident advantages of this method of construction soon led to its adoption for the entire fuselage.

Jules Védrines, the Deperdussin works pilot, was a former car mechanic who showed a natural talent for flying. He made his first record attempt at Pau on 13 January 1912. The fuselage of the first Deperdussin record machine was not constructed entirely on the monocoque principle. Although the top and bottom of the fuselage were curved in the interests of streamlining, the sides were flat. The undercarriage was fitted with a central skid in addition to the two main wheels, and the proven 100hp Gnome Double Omega rotary engine provided the power. Védrines flew round the five-kilometre circuit thirty times, and in so doing he beat every existing record over a range of distances, including the absolute speed

Model of Deperdussin 'Course' in the Musée Nationale des Techniques, Paris.

record, which he succeeded in pushing up to more than 145km/h. But this was just the beginning. The potential of the machine and the pilot would be exploited more effectively with a more powerful engine, a Gnome Double Lambda, producing 140hp. In the following month, February, Védrines returned to the starting line, and once again he set a series of new records. His best speed now rose to more than 161km/h; one week later it was 162.4km/h, the following day 166.8km/h, and the next day, 2 March 1912, just on 168km/h — an amazing and impressive performance.

The rules of the prestigious Gordon Bennett competition stated that each year's race had to take place on the home ground of the previous year's winner. Thus in 1910, after Glenn Curtiss had won at Reims, the venue was to be in the USA. There, in Belmont Park, New York, the Englishman Claude Grahame-White flew to victory in a Blériot XIbis, with the result that the 1911 competition was scheduled for Eastchurch, in England. This time another American, Charles Weymann, won, flying a French machine, a Nieuport IIG. The 1912 event, therefore, returned to the USA, and Chicago was chosen as the location. Naturally it was certain that Armand Deperdussin would send his fast monoplanes to take

Deperdussin 'Monocoque', 1912.

part in this international event. The Béchereau team developed a new model, this time with a full monocoque fuselage and a lower-drag undercarriage. The 140hp Gnome Double Lambda engine was retained, but was now enclosed in a close-fitting, faired cowling which reduced the quantity of castor oil flung out, in addition to reducing drag. During the elimination flights, held at Reims on 13 June 1912, the Deperdussin racers of Jules Védrines and Maurice Prévost, an aspiring pilot of the next generation, proved to be the fastest participants, followed closely by a Hanriot monoplane designed by Pagny and flown by the pilot André Frey. Once again Védrines managed to improve every record over the 10 to 200km range, and the maximum speed recorded was almost 171km/h, a new world record.

In America the Burgess company had announced its intention to build a copy of the Nieuport under the name Cup Defender, to be fitted with the most powerful engine then available, the 160hp Gnome Double Gamma two-row rotary engine.

Burgess 'Cup Defender', 1912.

The pilot, Glenn L Martin, claimed that he would provide the French with real opposition, but the plan got no further than a declaration of intent; the machine did not appear at the start line. So the French team was entirely on its own in Chicago, and, as expected, Jules Védrines scored a comfortable victory. After the actual Gordon Bennett race, held over 200km, Védrines flew three times round the course at maximum speed. A new world record of 174.1km/h was the result: and it was Védrine's seventh in a row. A 'Mona Lisa' painted on the fuselage side below the cockpit may well have served as a lucky mascot.

Although these steady increases in speed are impressive, and demonstrate the abilities of the pilots and the aircraft designers, the contribution made by the new aircraft engines designed by the French Seguin brothers should not be underestimated. In the early years of aviation almost everything depended on the availability of a powerful yet lightweight aero-engine. The wings of early aircraft had a very thin aerofoil section and an arched camber. This necessitated a relatively powerful engine to haul the high-drag flying machine through the air. One flying pioneer produced a notorious comment which is indicative of aircraft design of the time; 'With a good motor even a barn door will fly'. Aircraft manufacturers were slow to incorporate efficient wing sections into their designs.

In 1900 the Seguin brothers had taken out a licence to build a German single-cylinder engine intended for stationary use. This was the Gnom, designed by the Oberursel engine company. Some years later the Seguins began to develop this motor in a rotary form for use in aircraft. In the new Gnome (the French spelling, sometimes spelled Gnôme) the crankshaft was bolted securely to the aircraft, while the crankcase and cylinders, with the propeller attached to them, rotated in the cooling airstream. For this reason these units were known as rotary engines. In spite of the inherently high consumption of the pure castor oil required for their lubrication, these engines very soon gained international recognition for their good power-to-weight ratio and their relatively high level of reliability. Over the years the number of cylinders rose from seven to nine, and later, by adding a second 'star' of cylinders, to fourteen and eighteen. Their power output rose correspondingly from 50hp to 200hp. Among the numerous companies which took out licences to build the engines was the Oberursel engine company.

After Vedrine's victory in the fourth Gordon Bennett race, in Chicago in September 1912, France was clearly the dominant nation in aviation. The French were now determined more than ever to demonstrate their lead as clearly as possible, and to build upon their successes. After all, the British and American pilots who had won the Gordon Bennett races in the preceding years had done so flying French machines. By this time the USA, once the leading player, had long since forfeited its starring role, in spite of the pioneering work of the Wright brothers, their rival Glenn Curtiss and other compatriots. In fact it was the Wright brothers themselves who were to blame for this — at least in part — as they doggedly brought a series of lawsuits alleging infringements of patent, instead of devoting their energies to the further development of their ideas.

In France, in contrast, various companies had developed and built a whole series of new machines for the Gordon Bennett race, due to be run in the Autumn of 1913. Deperdussin had produced two new super-racers, now fitted with 160hp rotary engines of the Gnome and Le Rhône types. These were developments of Védrine's Chicago machine of the previous year, featuring further refinements in streamlining. The propeller hub was now fitted with a larger, almost hemispherical spinner, the motor cowling was of a more elegant shape, and the streamlined

Maurice Prévost in the Deperdussin 'Monocoque', 1913.

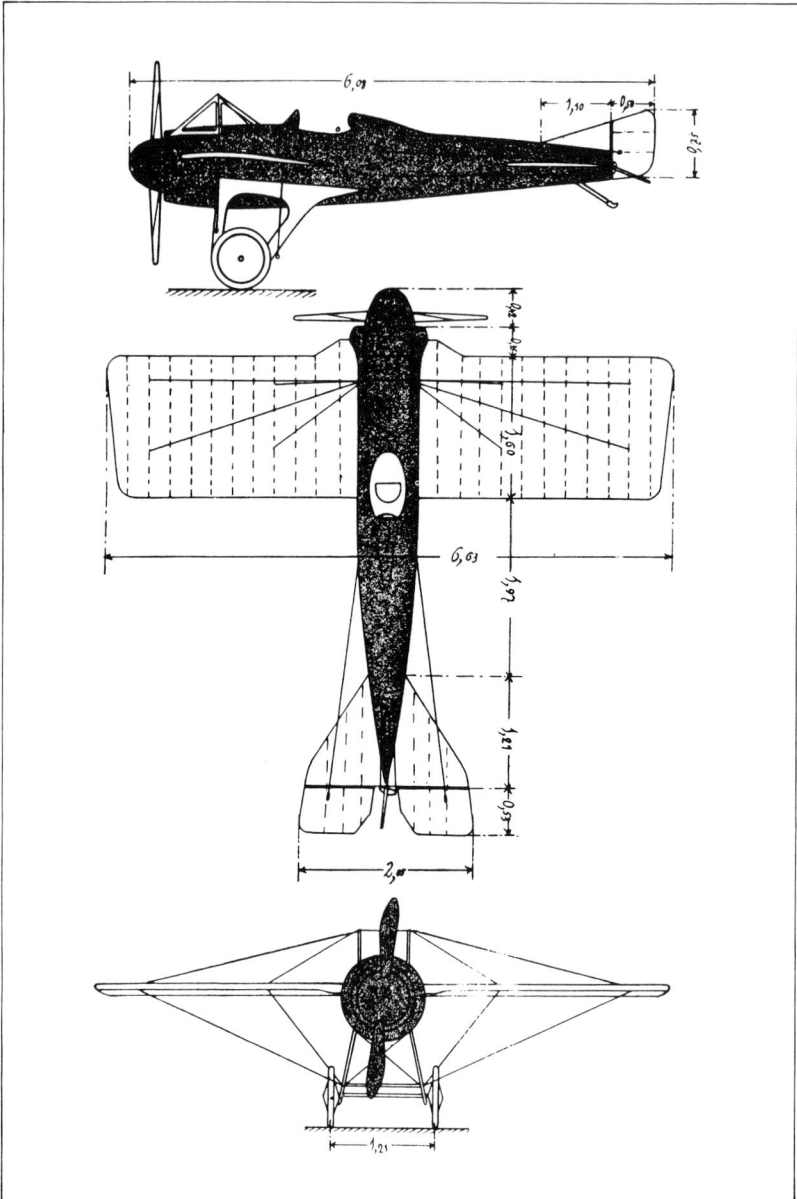

Deperdussin 'Monocoque', 1913.

fairing behind the pilot's head support was designed to reduce drag. In the meantime Armand Deperdussin had purchased the Aérodrome de la Champagne near Reims, and had modernised it at great expense. The first serious test flights of the new machines were held at this site in June 1913. On this occasion Maurice Prévost proved to be the faster, flying the Gnome-powered single-seater. On 17 June he improved on Védrine's record of the previous year, pushing it up by about 5km/h to almost 180km/h. The Aéro Club de France had gratefully accepted Deperdussin's generous offer of the use of his aerodrome for the Gordon Bennett races, and he even offered to donate cash prizes amounting to 100,000 Francs. Many influential individuals suggested that this gentleman benefactor should be recommended for immediate membership of the Legion of Honour. Preparations for the great French aviation event were in full swing when, on 5 August, a scandal erupted. Armand Deperdussin was arrested, accused of being a swindler of amazing dimensions.

Deperdussin 'Monocoque' of 1913 in the Musée de l'Air, Paris.

Gradually it became clear that, by means of embezzlement, lies, financial manipulation and fraud committed over many years, he had procured for himself a total of 28 million Francs, a breathtaking sum at that time. France was shocked. The darling of the Paris establishment, the leading member of the Automobile Club de France, the president of the Aéro Club de France, the Knight of the Legion of Honour, was in prison. Now, the sash of the Legion d'Honneur was to be presented to him in jail. In fact, the promised aerodrome was made available for the races by the liquidator, in spite of various objections, and the prize money of 100,000 Francs was donated by the industrialist Henry Deutsch de la Meurthe.

The great event at Reims was saved, and it took place from 27 to 29 September 1913. The first day was devoted to the elimination flights for the French Gordon

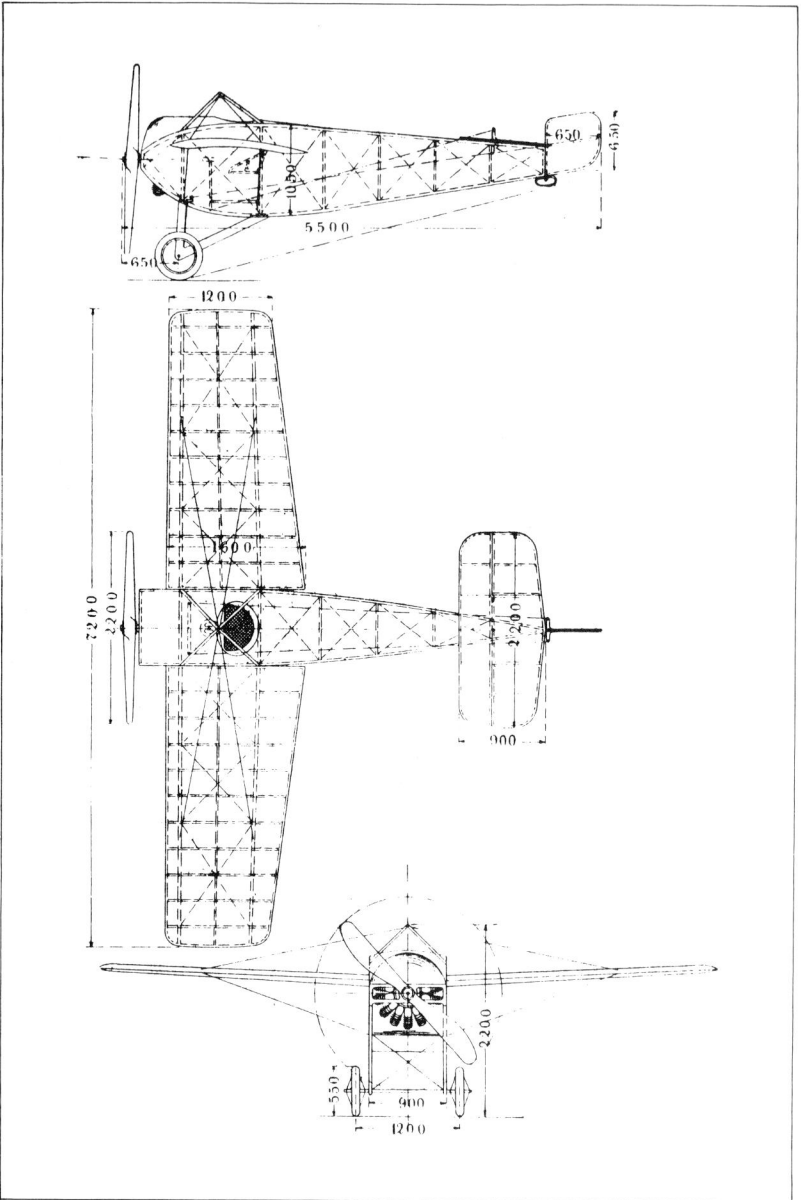

Ponnier Gordon Bennett machine, 1913.

Bennett team. Of the eight aircraft entered — three Deperdussins, two Borels, one Bréguet, one Nieuport and one Ponnier — the two 160hp Deperdussins flown by Maurice Prévost (Gnome) and Eugéne Gilbert (Le Rhône) proved to be the fastest, together with a surprise machine, the Ponnier flown by Emile Védrines, a namesake of the famous Deperdussin pilot. Designed by the former Hanriot designer, Pagny, the small Ponnier monoplane exhibited a clear family likeness to the Hanriot machines, and it was also equipped with the 160hp Gnome. During the elimination flights, Prévost, flying an improved machine, was able to beat his own world record of the previous June, reaching approximately 192km/h. Nevertheless, Emile Védrines was only slightly slower, and was ahead of the Le Rhône-powered Deperdussin flown by Gilbert. These three pilots formed the French team. Their opponents, with the exception of the third Deperdussin fitted with a less powerful engine, did not even appear for the elimination flights.

At Deperdussin (the name had been retained for better or for worse) the alarm bells were ringing out at the appearance of dangerous competition from Ponnier. As the actual Gordon Bennett races were not due to take place for two days — the intervening time was used for other flying competitions — the Béchereau team had time to modify Prévost's machine by replacing the wing, which was already reduced in span, with an even smaller component which André Herbemont had designed. The race results proved him right. On 29 September 1913 Prévost won the Gordon Bennett race flying this machine, and for the first time overcame the 200km/h hurdle. The new world record was almost 204km/h. Védrines, who had taken off after him (flights were made one-up against the clock), also crept over the two-hundred mark, but it seems that imperfect piloting around the turning points cost him victory in the race and the world record, since his small Ponnier was clearly the faster machine. Shortly after the race it was timed unofficially at 230km/h. Gilbert's Le Rhône-engined Deperdussin came third, and the Belgian Crombez, also flying a Deperdussin, took fourth place, well beaten.

France had again underlined its position as the dominant aviation nation: the French were, in fact, far superior to all others at this time. In Germany the heavier-than-air machine had been considered a fruitless line of development, and designers had concentrated on the airship for far too long. But about 1909 patriotic industrialists and major publishers donated valuable cash prizes as an incentive to aviation progress, and the prizes had their due effect. German aircraft designers and pilots began to take up the gauntlet thrown down by the overwhelmingly superior French. The National-Flugspende (National Flight Fund), set up in 1912 by Prince Heinrich of Prussia, the brother of Kaiser Wilhelm II, attracted more than 7 million Marks. These investments paid their dividends, and a whole series of impressive records fell to Germany — but not the speed record. Even the fastest German racing aircraft could manage only 150km/h at best; the top French pilots at Deperdussin and Ponnier still looked unassailable.

A few months later the elite group of the fastest aircraft of the time was joined by a newcomer. This was the S.E.4, built by the Royal Aircraft Factory at Farnborough, in England. It was an aerodynamically refined biplane, equipped

Royal Aircraft Factory S.E.4, 1914.

with the unbeatable 160hp Gnome, and featuring a four-bladed propeller in place of the two-bladed units preferred by the French for their braced monoplanes. Its designers, Henry Folland and Geoffrey de Havilland, had even provided a completely enclosed cockpit for their single-seater, but the pilots refused to fly the machine with the transparent cover in place, complaining of feeling 'locked in'. In June 1914 the aircraft was timed at a speed of 217km/h. However, this achievement met with little acclaim, as major events of greater import than sporting records were in the offing. On 28 June shots rang out in Sarajevo, and on 1 August 1914 the First World War began.

At this point it might be appropriate to record the fate of some of the main characters in the early history of aircraft records. Wilbur Wright, the elder of the two Wright brothers, died of typhoid in 1912, worn down by the bitter patent disputes. Orville remained in the American aviation industry for many years, working in research and as a consultant. He survived the Second World War and died in 1948. The Wrights' main competitor, Glenn Curtiss, turned to the development of naval aircraft in 1910. In 1929 a merger was announced between the Curtiss Aeroplane and Motor Company and the Wright Aeronautical Corporation. The new firm was named the Curtiss-Wright Airplane Company — the fact that Curtiss preceded Wright in the title is not without its irony. Glenn Curtiss died shortly afterwards, in 1930. A number of other designers from the pioneer years of aviation gave their names to successful aircraft companies, including Blériot, Farman, Nieuport, Voisin, de Havilland, Folland and Koolhoven. Alberto Santos-Dumont, after establishing the world record in his flying machine of 1906, built an airship, a hydroplane and a pair of aircraft, of

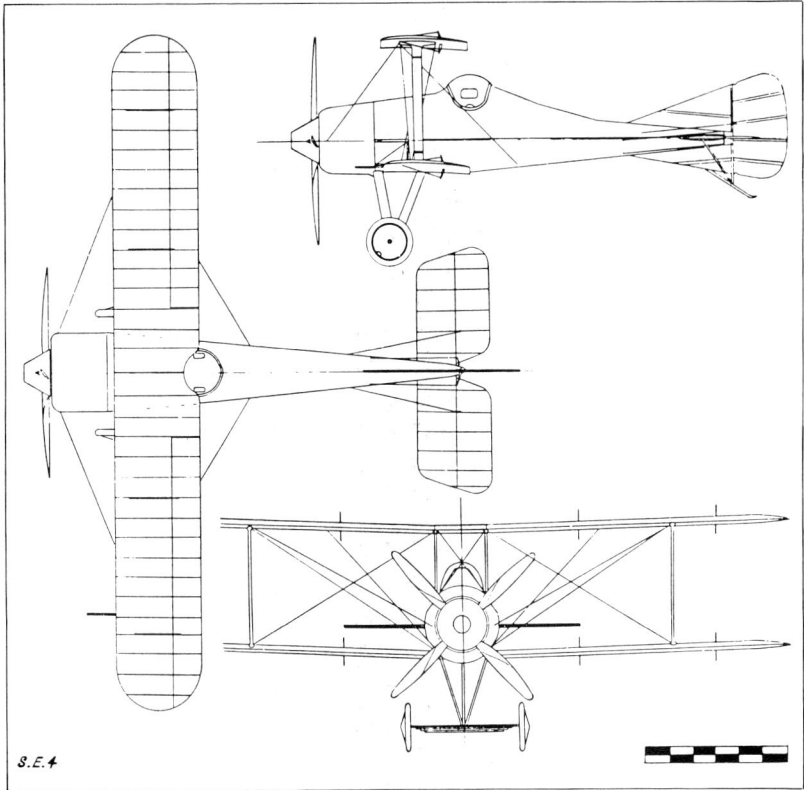

Royal Aircraft Factory S.E.4, 1914.

which only the graceful Demoiselle could be termed a limited success. About a dozen examples of this machine, the forefather of today's ultralights, were built. But by 1910 Santos-Dumont had fallen prey to multiple sclerosis, and withdrew from all public activities. In 1914, in a fit of depression, he destroyed all of his personal documents, and after a further two joyless decades he committed suicide in 1932. Hubert Latham lost his life during a big game hunt in Africa, before the First World War.

As for the fate of the former Société Provisoire des Aéroplanes Deperdussin (SPAD), chief designer Louis Béchereau and his assistant, André Herbemont, continued to run the company, under the overall management of Louis Blériot, after its name had been modified slightly to the Société Anonyme pour l'Aviation et ses Dérivés. The company subsequently produced the legendary SPAD fighter aircraft of the First World War. Béchereau lived to the age of 90, and died in 1970. After his arrest in 1913, Armand Deperdussin had to wait almost four years for his trial, because France, in the throes of the war, had other concerns. Finally, on 30 March 1917, he was sentenced to five years in prison. In fact he was set free shortly after this, probably under the terms of an amnesty, but by then he was a broken man, completely penniless and completely friendless. On 11 June 1924 three lines in the Paris newspapers announced that a certain A Deperdussin had taken his life in a small hotel room in the Rue Saint-Lazare.

THE BIPLANE TRIUMPHS

1918–1927: Up to 450km/h

In the four murderous years of the First World War gigantic strides were made in the development of aircraft technology. At the start of the war most members of the army and admiralty staffs still viewed the aeroplane as a pathetic plaything, devoid of serious military significance, but as the war progressed it became an increasingly potent weapon. Initially both sides in the conflict employed aircraft almost exclusively for reconnaissance, but later they were used in increasing numbers for bombing, for fighting and for infantry support.

For an amazingly long time it appeared that all the knowledge of the importance of streamlining and of designing low-drag airframes, so painfully acquired in the immediately preceding years, had been thrown overboard. No longer was pure speed the fundamental necessity. In the eyes of many of the military, who were now the decision makers, speed in itself was suspect. On the British side, for example, the excellent S.E.4 was considered to be much too fast because of its high landing speed of 84km/h. Stability, duration, reliability and load-carrying capacity were the preferred virtues. Most monoplane designs were turned down because their strength was considered inadequate. One of the few exceptions, at least on the German and Austrian side, was the Taube, designed by the Austrian Igo Etrich. This was an extremely durable and widely copied machine which had a generously braced wing of similar planform to a Zanonia seed. It could barely exceed 100km/h. With this exception, the 'delicate' monoplanes were widely mistrusted. The only monoplanes to see service in significant numbers were those designed by the French engineers Morane and Saulnier, together with the British Bristol M.1 and the German E-series monoplanes designed by the Dutchman Anthony Fokker. The Fokker machines were the first to carry a machine gun synchronised to fire through the propeller disc. Even these few monoplanes eventually disappeared from the skies, and after about 1916 biplanes were virtually the undisputed masters of the air, but for a small number of triplanes produced by companies such as Sopwith and Fokker.

For a while the favoured layout in France and England was the open-framework fuselage with pusher propeller, which allowed a forward-firing gun to be carried. The Germans, however, had settled on an enclosed fuselage and tractor propeller at an early stage — an arrangement which gradually became the norm.

The famous monoplane designers of the prewar years, such as Louis Béchereau, André Herbemont and Gustave Delage, eventually bowed to the all-conquering biplane. It is hardly surprising, therefore, that the top speed of the fastest fighter aircraft was somewhat less than 200km/h, with very few machines exceeding that figure. The handful of machines which eventually exceeded the prewar speed of

SPAD S.XVII, 1918.

the Gordon-Bennett single-seaters of Deperdussin and Ponnier, and the S.E.4, included the French SPAD S.XVII, the Italian Ansaldo S.V.A.5, the British Sopwith 7F.1 Snipe and the American Curtiss 18-T. These were all single-seaters built in 1918, the first three of them being biplanes. A speed of 263km/h was claimed for the Curtiss triplane, but it should be borne in mind that the exceptional speeds which were occasionally claimed seldom stood up to closer examination. For example, the Bullet biplane, designed by the American Dr Christmas, was said to have achieved 281km/h in early 1919, a figure which is all the more amazing since both prototypes (there were no more) crashed on their first flights.

Ansaldo S.V.A.5 'Primo' of 1918 in the Museo Storico, Vigna di Valle.

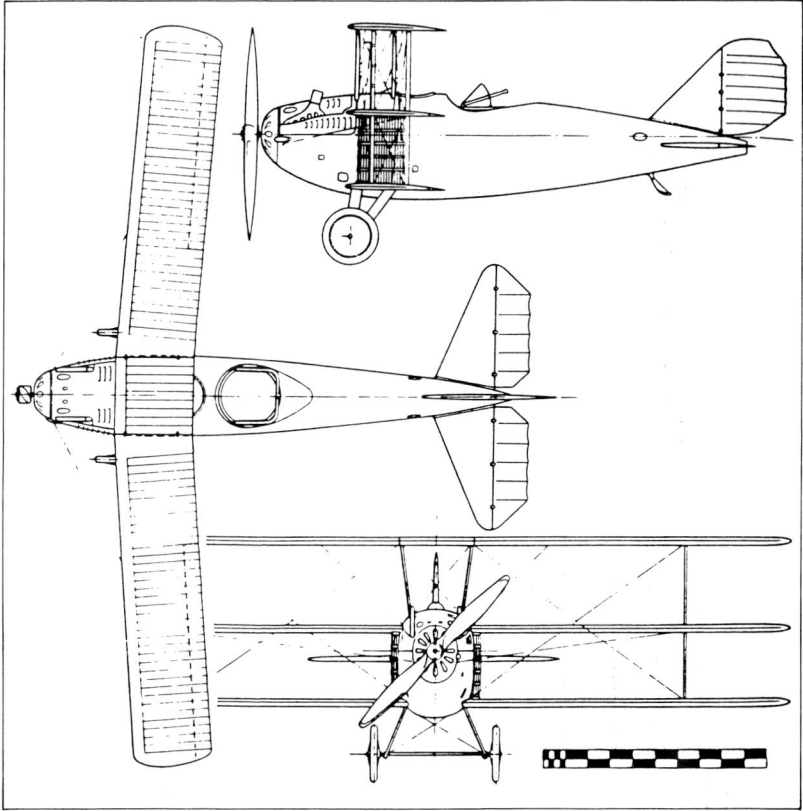

Curtiss Model 18-T Wasp, 1918.

Praiseworthy exceptions were the all-metal cantilever monoplanes designed by the German Hugo Junkers. His sheet iron J 1 and J 2 were followed by several single-seaters and two-seaters utilising a new form of construction using corrugated aluminium as the covering. The prototype of the single-seat Junkers J 9/D 1 fighter, J 9/1, which was produced towards the end of the war, was one of the fastest aircraft of this period. But such major structural advances were undesirable — old prejudices die hard, as we all know — and this racy single-seater appeared too late to see active service.

In contrast, it proved impossible to halt the prodigious progress in aircraft engine development. For technical reasons, the rotary engines which had been completely dominant in earlier years proved incapable of producing significantly more than the 200hp which had been achieved around 1914. The water-cooled in-line engine, followed by its vee-cylindered variant with two rows of cylinders set

Junkers J 9/I(DI), 1918.

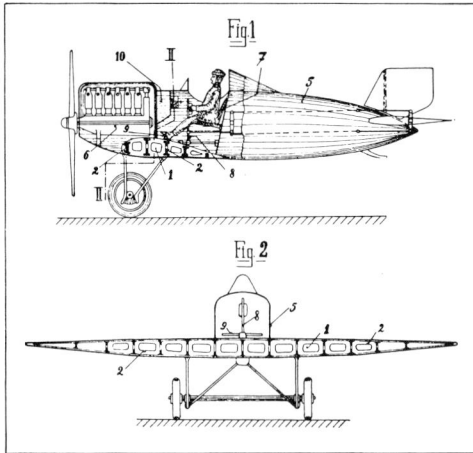

Junkers J 9/I(DI), 1918.

in a V and acting on a single crankshaft, was beginning to take over. By the end of the war production versions of this type of powerplant were already producing more than 300hp in eight-cylinder form, and well over 400hp in their twelve-cylinder versions, coupled with greatly reduced head resistance. Isolated

Fiat BR, 1919.

experimental engines had produced significantly higher power. One of these was the giant Fiat A-14, which in its initial version produced more than 600hp from a total swept volume of 57.2 litres. Later its output was increased to 825hp. Since a monster of this size, weighing almost a tonne, could not be accommodated in a single-seat fighter, a young design engineer at Fiat designed a bomber for it; the Fiat BR. The man responsible was Celestino Rosatelli, who had just abandoned his post as one of three designers at Ansaldo in favour of a top position at Fiat, where he was destined to work as chief designer for many years.

In the summer of 1919 the new bomber achieved a series of record performances, including a top speed of more than 260km/h carrying passengers. The pilot was Francesco Brack-Papa, Fiat's chief test pilot. No official or international recognition of these records was forthcoming. The FAI in Paris was not yet ready to resume the recognition of world records for aircraft, and would not be ready to do so for a further six months. In consequence all the records that were set by impatient record aspirants in 1919 had absolutely no official validity in spite of verified and undisputed measurements.

For the same reason several other potential record-breakers were prevented from making their mark, among them the British Sopwith Schneider with its 450hp radial engine, and another Italian machine, the Savoia MVT. However, the hardest hit by the lethargy of officialdom were the two leading French fighter manufacturers SPAD and Nieuport, whose chief pilots were Sadi Lecointe and Bernard de Romanet. Louis Béchereau, formerly head of design at Deperdussin and later creator of the successful SPAD fighter, had unexpectedly left the company in the summer of 1919 to devote his time to the development of sports and racing aircraft for other clients. His place was taken by André Herbemont, who had been his assistant for many years. Shortly before the end of the war Herbemont had designed the S.XX, an unsophisticated but very fast two-seat fighter. Now that the horrors of the war were slowly receding the French began, albeit hesitantly, to resume their activities in the field of sport aviation. The S.XX, the fastest of all SPADs, was an obvious starting point for further development, and spawned a series of civilian variants, ranging from single-seat racing aircraft to multi-seat passenger machines. Several specialised versions for racing and record

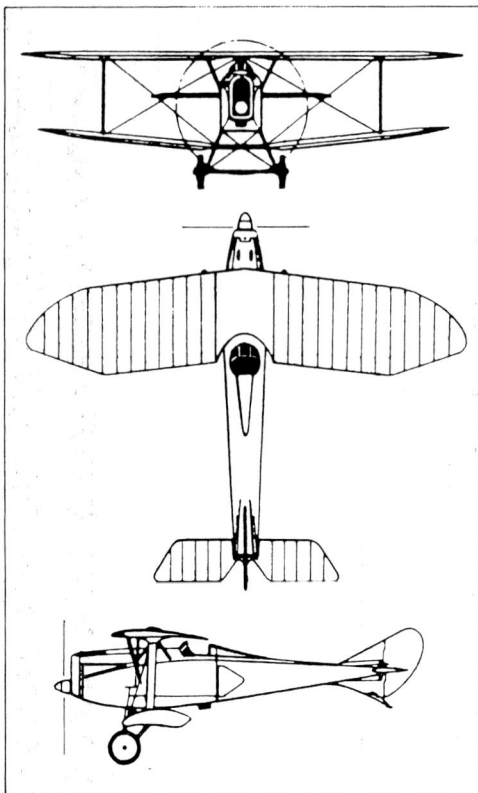

Savoia MVT (Marchetti/Vickers-Terni), 1919.

purposes were produced under the new name of Spad-Herbemont S.20bis, and their maximum speed was steadily improved by continual reductions in drag. The second seat was covered in, streamlined fairings were tested, the wingspan was reduced step by step, and the wings themselves were modified.

Gustave Delage, the chief designer at Nieuport, was heading in a similar direction in the continued development of his Nieuport single-seat fighter. This design also dated from 1918, but was considerably slimmer and more elegant than the Spad-Herbemont S.20bis. Once again, efforts were made to reduce drag by a series of aerodynamic improvements and reductions in wingspan. Both biplanes featured a wooden monocoque fuselage, and both were powered by the excellent Hispano-Suiza Model 42, one of the best aircraft engines of the First World War.

Since 1900 the Geneva engine builder Marc Birkigt had been involved in car design in Barcelona, where he founded his company Hispano-Suiza in 1904. Its high-quality products soon brought the firm worldwide fame. In 1911 he opened a

SPAD-Herbemont S.20bis$_5$, 1920.

subsidiary factory in Paris. In 1914 the company produced its first V-8 aircraft engine, the Model 34, with an initial output of 150hp, later increased to 180hp. The year 1915 saw the introduction of the Model 35, with a reduction gearbox, offering an output of 200hp. The enlarged Model 42 eventually appeared in 1918. It was rated at 280hp, but its power output was later raised to 320hp. The outstanding qualities of this engine can be judged by the fact that no fewer than 50,000 had been manufactured by 1919 in France, England and the USA.

The first major post-war sport aviation event in France was announced in the Autumn of 1919; the competition for the Prix Henry Deutsch de la Meurthe. The original rules, dating from 1912, decreed that the successful pilot had to fly a 200km course and improve upon the existing record by at least ten per cent. The record then had to stand for one year after the first successful challenge. The first winner of the prize, in May 1912, had been the pilot Emmanuel Helen, who clocked 125km/h in his Nieuport. It was won again, in October of the same year, by Eugéne Gilbert, who flew a Deperdussin at 163km/h. Scarcely had the resumption of the competition been announced than Sadi Lecointe flew his Spad-Herbemont S.20bis$_1$ over the prewar course, recording a speed of over 249km/h. Incidentally, he had carried out his first flight in the machine on the previous day, 1 September 1919.

Lecointe had jumped the gun, however, as the rules for the prize competition were not officially announced until four weeks later, and in fact stipulated a new, slightly shorter course. The new regulations were to apply from 13 October 1919 to 31 October 1920. On the first official day the pilot Leth Jensen staked his first claim to the prize, flying a Nieuport monoplane at a speed of just over 200km/h. Thus, any challenger had to achieve at least 222km/h. On 15 October, after a series of training flights with a new S.20bis$_2$ with shorter wings, Sadi Lecointe managed to complete the course at approximately 248km/h, and five days later, this time flying the new S.20bis$_3$ with further reduced wingspan, he raised the mark again to 252km/h, on this occasion carrying his mechanic in the spare seat. Needless to say,

Nieuport 29, 1919.

the Nieuport team was not standing idle, and only two days later the Comte de Romanet flew a circuit of the Paris competition course at almost 269km/h. His machine was the new racing version of the Nieuport 29 C1 single-seat fighter — the 29V, the V standing for *vitesse* (speed). However, his speed was not sufficient to exceed the required 10 per cent margin.

Shortly afterwards, in December 1919, both pilots moved to the opposite camp, evidently believing the saying that the grass is always greener . . .: Bernard de Romanet went to Spad and Sadi Lecointe to Nieuport. On 16 December, on his first flight in the Nieuport 29V, Lecointe was clocked at 307km/h, reaching 364km/h on one downwind leg. Just two and a half weeks later, on 3 January 1920, Lecointe beat his own Prix Deutsch record with a mark of over 366km/h, and this time he could be certain that he had left all his potential competitors well behind.

Finally, on 6 January, the FAI in Paris decreed that the world speed record was open to challenge again, albeit using modified rules. From now on four timed flights, two in each direction, were to be flown over a one-kilometre course, the average speed to count as the record. The aircraft's altitude was not to exceed 50m over the course, nor for a distance of 500m before the first course marker. In addition, the aircraft had to have carried out at least two safe landings shortly before the record attempt, and had to return to its take-off point after the record flight. The final stipulation was that the new record had to exceed the previous speed by at least four kilometres per hour.

On 1st February 1920, at Villacoublay Aérodrome, Sadi Lecointe began his record trials at the controls of his black-painted Nieuport 29V, and achieved a top speed of 274km/h. Just one week later, on 7 February, he made an official attempt, setting a new mark of just on 276km/h — the first official world speed record since the First World War. In fact, the record stood for only three weeks. His opponent,

The Nieuport 29V, which took two world's speed records in October 1920, after an unhappy landing.

in the person of the talented Spad pilot Jean Casale, arrived on the scene with the improved Spad S.20bis$_4$, the wings of which had been cropped to a mini-wingspan of 6.60m. At over 283km/h his margin over the Lecointe-Nieuport combination over the same measured course was barely sufficient, but his record was to stand for more than six months.

Even an exciting series of high-speed flights by the top Italian pilot Brack-Papa came to naught. These attempts were made in the Spring of 1920 with a large Fiat biplane which had originally been designed to cross the Atlantic. The ARF (Atlantic Rosatelli Fiat) was a larger variant of the Rosatelli BR design, which had flown successfully the previous year, and featured the same rugged A-14 engine. On 26 February Brack-Papa reached 261km/h with four passengers on board. On 4 March he achieved 277km/h, this time with two passengers (one of them the poet Gabriele D'Annunzio), and on 5 May he finally reached the 280km/h mark, but it

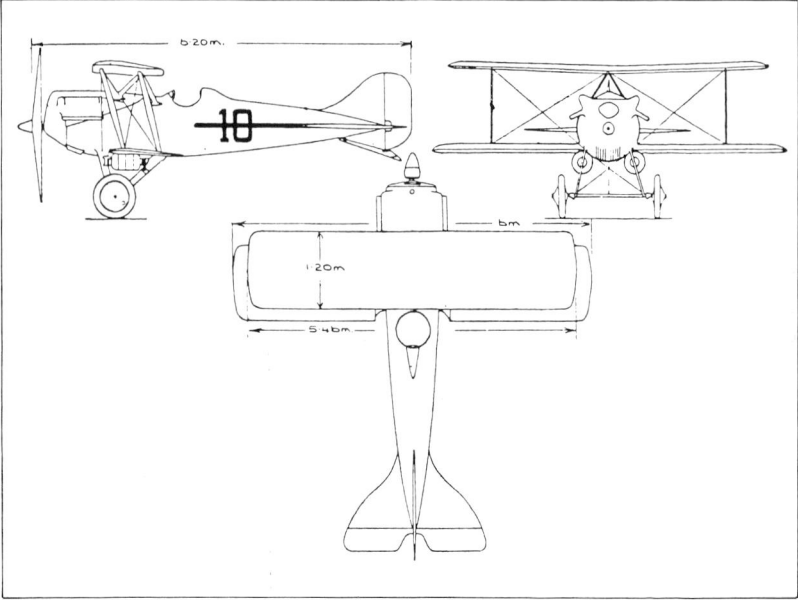

Nieuport 29V, 1920.

Fiat ARF with designer Rosatelli and pilot Brack-Papa, 1920.

was not quite enough for a world record. The same fate awaited the English record attempts which were made at Martlesham Heath, Suffolk. In March the pilot Raynham, flying a Martinsyde Semiquaver, could only manage a best timed speed of just under 260km/h, while in June Leslie R Tait-Cox recorded 268km/h with his Nieuport & General L.S.3 Goshawk.

From the USA came news of an unofficial 306km/h, apparently achieved by pilot Rudolph Schroeder, flying a special biplane known as the Verville VCP-R, but this information was not given general credence. After all, the USA had failed lamentably when it came to building an aircraft which was fit for service in the First World War, and had not even produced a practical aircraft engine. The mighty US automobile industry, scenting lucrative armaments contracts, had claimed for itself the sole right to build aircraft, despite the fact that it understood nothing of the matter. As a result countless dollars were needlessly frittered away, and there were numerous scandals concerning bribery and personal enrichment, but no sensible aircraft emerged. As far as aeroplane powerplants were concerned, a twelve-cylinder engine was developed, claimed to be the solution to every problem, and was christened Liberty. However, it suffered an endless series of failures before eventually being built in considerable quantities — some 18,000 units. By then it was too late for service at the Front, but, since so many had been completed, it came to be used very widely in the post-war years. In the Second World War 6,500 examples built in England powered British tanks.

When the races for the James Gordon Bennett Aviation Cup were announced, to be held in September 1920, the event was seen as the ideal occasion for putting to the test the claims made by the Americans and the British in respect of the superiority of their racing aircraft. With due deference to the competition rules, the USA entered three machines, Great Britain the same, and even Italy announced its intention of sending two Ansaldos to participate, although this entry was immediately retracted. Of the three British machines the first, the Sopwith 107 Rainbow, was also withdrawn owing to the company's financial problems. The second, the L.S.3 Goshawk, missed the entry deadline and was disqualified. In the event the third British machine, the Martinsyde Semiquaver, was forced to make an emergency landing after its first lap, for which it recorded a fast time. Oil pump damage was to blame. The three American machines, fast or not, suffered a similar fate. The first, the Curtiss Texas Wildcat, was completely wrecked on landing at Etampes, the competition aerodrome, after it had been converted at the last minute from a shoulder-wing monoplane to a biplane, in an attempt to remedy its poor handling in the air. The second, the Verville VCP-R, dropped out in the first round of racing when its engine lost power. The third machine, the futuristic Dayton-Wright RB, had to drop out after the first round because of unexplained mechanical problems. This was particularly unfortunate, as the machine included many interesting design features which showed the way forward. It was a cantilever shoulder-wing monoplane with an enclosed cockpit and a retractable undercarriage, a sensational combination for 1920. The wing, consisting of a balsa wood core skinned in plywood, featured articulated sections at the leading and

Dayton-Wright RB, 1920.

trailing edge which allowed the forward and aft thirds of the wing to be lowered over the entire wingspan. The consequent increase in wing camber, and thus lift, was exploited for take-off and landing. Forty years later the world-famous Lockheed Starfighter employed similar high-lift aids. A drawback to the system in the RB was the unfaired mechanical linkage, which caused excessive drag on the upper surface of the wing. Even so, the wing proved to be extraordinarily strong. The two wheels of the main undercarriage could be retracted completely into the fuselage sides by the pilot, with the aid of a large hand-crank on the instrument panel. The process took between twelve and twenty seconds. On a training flight three days before the race, the pilot, Howard M Rinehart, managed a comfortable run of 265km/h with the engine necessarily throttled back, as the directional stability of the silver single-seater was found to fall off alarmingly as speed increased. As for the retractable undercarriage, a similar mechanism had already

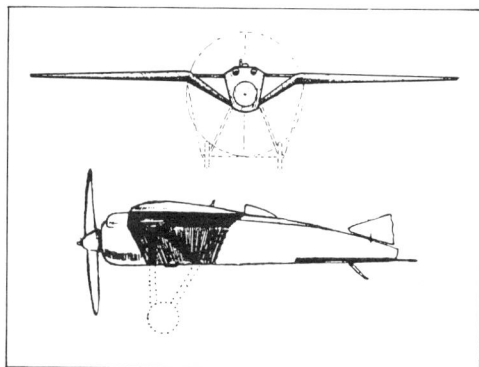

Clement-Moineau racer, 1919.

seen the light of day in a small French racing single-seater, a strutted monoplane built by Louis Clément, at the Paris Aero Salon of the previous year, although this machine never flew.

In the preliminary selection competition held by the French on 25 September for their Gordon-Bennett race team, another newcomer was ruled out. This was the Borel-Boccaccio racing biplane, which was eliminated for technical reasons, even though it had earned its place in the three-machine team as being the third fastest. One former champion was also omitted. Jean Casale had failed to qualify in his Spad S.20bis$_5$, because further reductions in the area of all flying surfaces, including the rudder, had reduced the machine's directional stability to a dangerous level. The same applied to its sister machine, flown by de Romanet. New, even shorter-span wings had been fitted to both aircraft, and the wing gap had been reduced by 20cm, so that the top wing was now at the same level as the top of the fuselage. The two Nieuports 29V which had qualified had also been further refined. Thus, in the event itself, held on 29 September, every entrant was French. The victor was Sadi Lecointe in a white Nieuport 29V bearing the racing number 10, and second was Bernard de Romanet in his Spad-Herbemont S.20bis$_5$, chiefly because he was the only other pilot left in the race. The second Nieuport had dropped out shortly before the end with oiled-up plugs.

Two weeks later, to highlight their supremacy, the French held a record meeting at the Spad works aerodrome at Buc. André Herbemont had fitted one of the Spads with yet another set of wings — an indication of the speed of response which was possible at the time — and had increased the tail surface area. A giant spinner completed the modifications. On 9 October de Romanet pushed the world record up to almost 293km/h with this S.20bis$_6$. His rival, Lecointe, flew exactly one kilometre per hour faster on the same afternoon, but the margin was insufficient for a new record. However, de Romanet was keen to retain his lead, and attacked the course one more time in an effort to improve his own record. During the flight the spinner burst, and then the propeller disintegrated. With a huge effort de Romanet was able to set down the badly handling machine in a

SPAD-Herbemont S.20bis$_6$, 1920.

ploughed field. On the following day Sadi Lecointe rubbed salt into the wound with a new world record of 296.3km/h. Ten days later, in an effort to establish a clear lead, he made a further record attempt at Villacoublay, and became the first pilot to cover the measured kilometre at over 300km/h; 302.5km/h was the new mark.

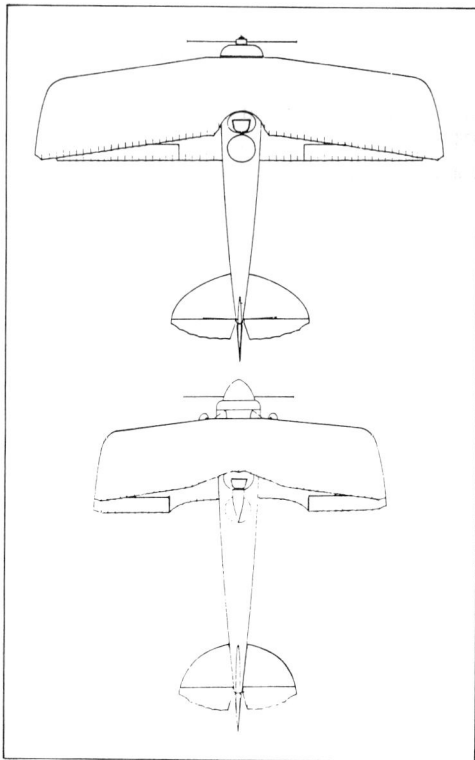

SPAD-Herbemont S.20, showing reduction in wing area.

The de Romanet/Herbemont team did not give up easily. The damaged S.20bis[6] was rebuilt with all haste, now with even smaller wings and an even more powerful engine. On 4 November, again over the works aerodrome at Buc, de Romanet wrenched back the world record with a fine 309km/h, in spite of foggy conditions. Not unnaturally, Sadi Lecointe and Gustave Delage were unwilling to let the world record slip from them. The second Gordon-Bennett machine, No 11, was subjected to further slimming measures. The open cockpit was covered in completely with a canopy over the pilot, who now squatted deep in the fuselage, and the streamlined headrest was also removed. Two tiny teardrop-shaped windows in the fuselage sides had to suffice for the pilot's view, and suffice they did. On 12 December Lecointe swept over the measured course at Villacoublay four times at an altitude of just four metres. His reward was a new world record at 313km/h, and a well-earned gold medal from the Aero Club de France. In 1920 Sadi Lecointe had won the Prix Deutsch, the Grand Prix de Monaco (for float-equipped aircraft) and the Gordon-Bennett Cup, and had also established four world records — a unique achievement.

In the autumn of 1920 the Belgian Viscount Louis P de Monge de Franeau, the inventive and successful manufacturer of the Lumière wooden propeller in the First World War, decided that he would build the fastest aircraft in the world. In the spring of 1921 he produced his Model 5.1, an unusually elegant high-wing monoplane with a completely enclosed cockpit, powered by a twelve-cylinder

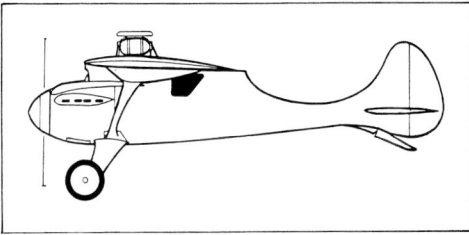

De Monge 5.1, 1921.

Hispano-Suiza Model 42 engine fitted, naturally, with a special Lumière wooden propeller with a large, streamlined spinner. The fuselage was based on a wooden tube core for torsional rigidity, on to which were fitted plywood formers supporting the external fabric covering. The two-spar wing, braced to the fuselage with single struts, was also fabric-covered, in accordance with the standard practice of the time. For initial flight testing the machine was fitted with a removable lower wing. The Comte de Romanet, a friend of the designer and bent on winning back the world record which had been twice wrested from him, was the machine's test pilot, and on the very first flight he achieved 340km/h, although he encountered inexplicable vibration. On 23 September 1921, after various modifications and the removal of the bottom wing, the brown racing single-seater was prepared for further test flights at the Villesauvage Aerodrome, with Bernard de Romanet at the controls. A few minutes after take-off the vibration started up again, and increased in severity as speed increased. De Romanet attempted to bring the aircraft back to the aerodrome and banked the machine into a steep left-hand turn. Suddenly the covering on the bottom surface of the port wing burst, and the machine crashed into a field at high speed from an altitude of about 50m. The aircraft disintegrated, and de Romanet was killed instantly. The cause, not established until some time later, was flutter of the wings and ailerons, which were inadequately braced. The crash also signalled the end of the firm of Lumière.

Yet in the following year de Monge, in collaboration with the furniture manufacturer Buscaylet, managed to bring out a new aircraft, the Model 5.2, an all-metal single-seat fighter which bore a strong resemblance to the earlier ill-fated machine. Although (or perhaps because) it was of very advanced design, this elegant fighter was equally unsuccessful, and was turned down by the State. Later designs by Louis de Monge were also destined to fail, including the racy Bugatti 100P, a world speed record aircraft developed towards the end of the 1930s.

Like Louis de Monge, Gustave Delage, the creator of the successful Nieuport 29, considered that the days of the biplane, with its many drag-inducing struts and wires, were numbered, even though its orthodox layout provided very high

Nieuport-Delage Sesquiplan, 1921.

strength at low weight. It was no surprise, then, that his new design, which appeared in the autumn of 1921, was also a wooden shoulder-wing monoplane with single struts, fabric-covered and fitted with the Hispano-Suiza Model 42. His description of the machine as a sesquiplane was misleading, as the 'half-wing' was no more than a section of wing wrapped round the undercarriage axle. With its monocoque fuselage adopted from the Nieuport 29, the new Nieuport was considerably slimmer than the ill-starred de Monge aircraft. Although the wingspan of the two machines was identical, the wing area of the sesquiplane was a good 25 per cent smaller, and the wing loading was half as high again.

On the aircraft's predecessor, the Nieuport 29, the finned, barrel-shaped Lamblin radiators mounted between the undercarriage struts were an inelegant necessity, but on aerodynamically 'cleaner' aircraft they looked even more out of place. However, compared with the front-mounted, large-area honeycomb radiators fitted to the Spads, they produced the same cooling performance while allowing a considerable reduction in drag, which gave the Nieuport a speed advantage of a good 40km/h. The Lumière de Monge 5.1 had one of these radiators, known as 'casier à homards' (lobster pots), mounted centrally on the top wing; the sesquiplane carried two of them under the fuselage, exactly as on the model 29.

Two examples of the sesquiplane had been built, one red and white (number 6) and one blue and white (number 7). Only two days after Bernard de Romanet's crash, the irrepressible Sadi Lecointe clocked an unofficial speed of 353km/h

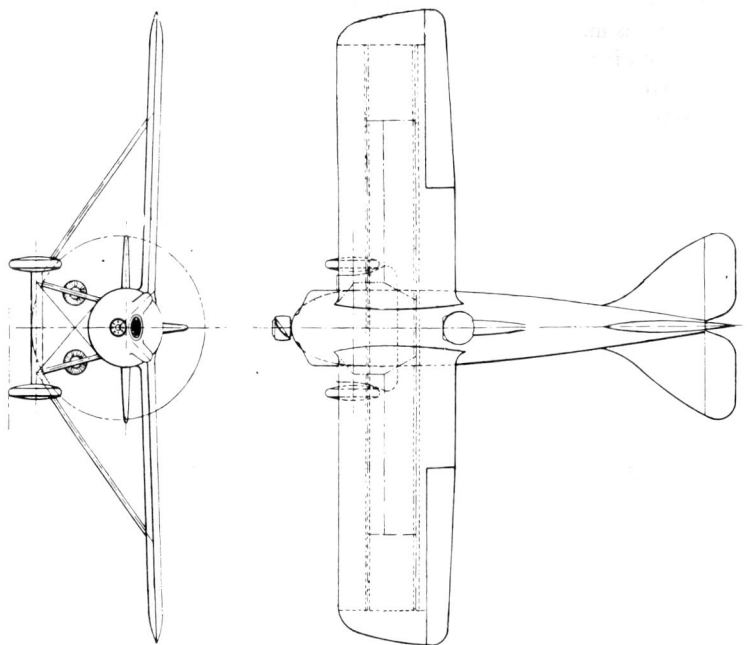

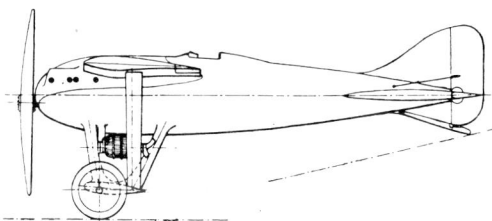

SESQUIPLAN · NIEUPORT
DELAGE

340 HP HISPANO-SUIZA

~ TIPO 'COUPE DEUTSCH' 1922

Nieuport-Delage Sesquiplan, 1921/23.

during test flights with the first of the two new machines, and on the following day, 26 September 1921, he achieved an official record run of over 330km/h, which represented an improvement over his own world record set the previous December. Five days later, however, in the very first round of that year's racing for the Prix Deutsch de la Meurthe, the machine broke up. Lecointe was just able to bring it to rest in a nearby turnip field in a spectacular crash landing, but he suffered serious injuries. The cause was possibly the fracturing of the propeller, but probably wing flutter — a phenomenon with which designers have long since wrestled. The second Nieuport pilot, Georges Kirsch, in the remaining blue and white sesquiplane (number 7), won the race. Second was Fernand Lasne in the 1920 Nieuport 29V, which had been further modified. The other competitors had either been eliminated already or did not even reach the starting line.

The Hanriot HD.22 racer, an all-metal design created by MR Pouit, was an interesting and advanced design. It was a cantilever shoulder-wing monoplane with retractable undercarriage, similar in concept to the previous year's American Dayton-Wright RB. As was the fashion, this powerful machine was fitted with a well-faired Hispano-Suiza 42 in the nose. Although windtunnel measurements predicted a speed of 400km/h for the machine, for a variety of reasons it never flew, although it was completed, albeit with a fixed undercarriage.

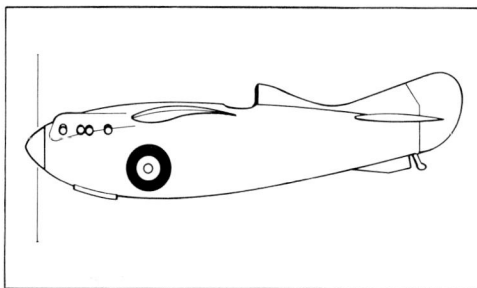

Hanriot HD.22, 1921. It was built with a fixed undercarriage.

Outside France, in Great Britain, Italy, and, particularly, in the United States, serious efforts were being made to catch up. The Germans, who had never been among the 'fastest' of the flying nations, were neither permitted to compete nor capable of competing, because of the restrictions imposed by the victorious powers after the First World War. The situation was not to alter for fifteen years. In the previous November a serious attempt on the world speed record had been made in the USA, although the VCP-R, which had already been flown in the Gordon Bennett races in France, had only been able to manage one run at 299.5km/h because of continual ignition problems with the Packard twelve-cylinder high-compression engine. Curtiss had built the Model 22 under contract to the Texan oil magnate SEJ Cox, and this had been followed by the Model 23, which the US Navy had ordered under the designation CR-1 (Curtiss Racer No 1). Both machines participated in maximum speed and record trials, during which, in late October 1921, the pilot Bert Acosta reached a top speed of 310km/h, flying the Curtiss Cactus Kitten in its triplane form. One month later he achieved 318km/h

Curtiss Cactus Kitten, 1921.

with the CR-1, although the crucial average value of the requisite four passes was only 297.5km/h — nothing like fast enough to constitute a danger to the French.

On the British side, too, energetic efforts were being made to break the French dominance of the record books. In June tests were carried out with a racing biplane, the Avro 539B/1, fitted with the powerful Napier Lion engine. The aircraft was totally destroyed on its first flight in a crash landing. Another potential

Curtiss CR, 1921.

Gloucestershire Mars 1 (Bamel), 1921.

record-breaker, the fast Gloucestershire Mars 1 — better known under the curious name of Bamel (Bear/Camel) — had exhibited alarming signs of wing flutter during the races for the Prix Deutsch, just as had occurred with the Nieuport-Delage sesquiplane. The pilot, James H James, had to abandon the race

Bristol 72 Racer, 1922.

in the second lap when the wing bracing began to come loose. But in December 1921, over home territory, he achieved an average speed of 316.4km/h, which was a British record, but not a world record. It is likely that the Bristol 72, completed in the summer of 1922, was also built with the world record in mind. This was a cantilever mid-wing monoplane with a nine-cylinder radial engine enclosed in a voluminous fuselage, and fitted with a retractable undercarriage. It was hoped that this rather unwieldy looking machine would be capable of speeds greater than 350km/h, but the few test flights were disappointing, even after the wing was given external wire bracing to reduce its evident flexibility. That very year the hopes of the Bristol firm were buried, or rather scrapped. The fuselage was sawn in half, and both ends proved very popular with the children of a Bristol company manager in their new guise of indian teepees.

Some time previously, in April 1922, Bert Acosta had managed a top speed of 335km/h in the Curtiss Cactus Kitten triplane, but no official world record claim was lodged.

Francesco Brack-Papa, the top Fiat pilot, had also taken part in the races for the 1921 Prix Deutsch, but he was eliminated in the second round after a leak developed in the fuel system of his new Fiat R.700. The designer Rosatelli had succeeded in squeezing the gigantic and unusually powerful Fiat A-14 aircraft

Fiat R.700 with pilot Brack-Papa, 1922.

engine, now producing 837hp, into a relatively small racing biplane of conventional construction, which in the hands of Brack-Papa appeared to have the record in its grasp. In fact, the R.700 was faster than all the competition before its enforced early retirement from the race. On 26 August 1922, after thorough preparation, Brack-Papa flew four times over the one-kilometre course at Mirafiori, near Turin, and the officially recorded speed of 336.112km/h was clearly a new world record. Brack-Papa, Rosatelli, Fiat, and Italy were delighted. The episode had a curious end, however. The FAI in Paris never received the flight documents, so official recognition was not granted.

Spurred on by the success of the sesquiplane, Nieuport was busy designing a successor incorporating further improvements. Rumours circulated of a new sesquiplane, which really had one-and-a-half wings, and which was to have an unusually high wing loading of 105kg/m^2 and a 500hp engine which had been built abroad: the twelve-cylinder Sunbeam-Coatalen Matabele. The NiD 41, when completed in the summer of 1922, indeed turned out to be a genuine sesquiplane with a foreign engine, but the powerplant was an American eight-cylinder Wright H-3 developing more than 400hp; the power output was never officially disclosed. The engine was housed deep in the front part of the plump, teardrop-shaped wooden monocoque fuselage, with the inevitable Lamblin radiator located between the undercarriage legs, which were connected at the front by a half-wing. As a racing variant of the Nieuport-Delage 37, which was a high-altitude fighter under development at the time, the grotesque Course machine was a complete failure, despite the fact that it offered the pilot an excellent field of view above, as his head projected out of the centre section of the cantilever, plywood-skinned

Nieuport-Delage 41 'Course', 1922.

mainplane. Even Sadi Lecointe could not manage to get the red and white monstrosity (racing No 6), off the ground. When the carburettor caught fire the trials were halted, and soon the entire project was abandoned. The NiD 37 high-altitude fighter was seen briefly at the Paris Aero-Salon in December 1922 — this time with a strutted top wing — then it, too, sank into oblivion.

In response to the emergency (after all, the Prix Deutsch was imminent) the company returned to the sole surviving sesquiplane. It was fitted with a new, largely plywood-skinned wing of identical span and area but of modified planform and wing section. This was undoubtedly an interim solution, but it was an immediate success. During test flights at Villesauvage, on 10 September 1922, Sadi Lecointe reached 358km/h in the machine, now christened *Eugéne Gilbert*. The proven Hispano-Suiza motor had been tuned to produce more than 360hp. A world record attempt was fixed for 21 September, and this time everything ran

Nieuport-Delage Sesquiplan, 1922.

smoothly. Lecointe increased his record of the previous year by 11km/h to 341km/h.

The race for the Prix Deutsch, which took place ten days later, promised to be the most exotic by far of all these events. Unfortunately most of the super-aircraft which had been entered failed to fly, including the Bristol 72 and the Nieuport-Delage 41, because they were either not fully developed or not completed in time. Two French tailless designs fell into the latter category. René

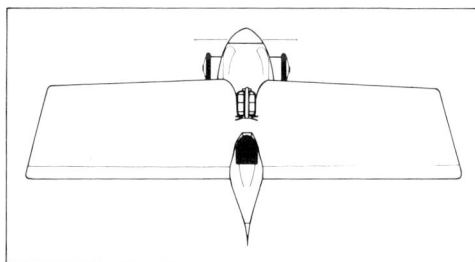

Simplex-Arnoux monoplane, 1922.

Arnoux, a pioneer of the flying wing design, had created a small, robust wooden monoplane with a straight cantilever wing and no tailplane. The powerplant was once again the Hispano-Suiza 42. Unfortunately this interesting and fast machine, known as the Simplex-Arnoux, crashed on landing a week before the race. The second shoulder-wing aircraft, developed by the designers Landwerlin and Berreur, was larger overall, and was powered by a mighty Fiat A-14. The cantilever wing was swept forward 22°, and windtunnel tests had predicted a speed of 450km/h for the machine. The famous pilot Charles Nungesser was to have flown it, but the aircraft was not finished in time and was abandoned completely shortly afterwards.

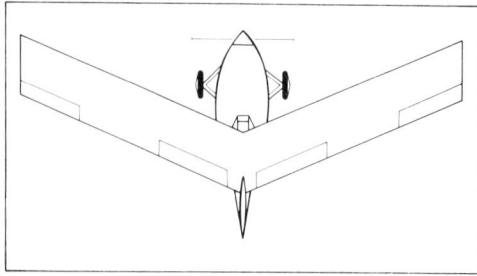

Landwerlin-Berreur racer, 1922.

The aircraft which remained were less exotic but still dangerously fast: the British Gloster Bamel and the Italian Fiat R.700, supplemented by a Spad-Herbemont 58 and, only as a reserve, the obsolete Nieuport 29V which had raced in 1920 and 1921. The racing on 1 October ended paradoxically. During the first lap all of the course maps blew out of the cockpit of British pilot James H James' Bamel, forcing him to give up because he could no longer navigate. Francesco Brack-Papa's first attempt was declared invalid due to a technical error, and in the second lap of his second attempt he was forced to carry out an emergency landing because of carburettor damage. Jean Casale was also forced to give up in the second lap, owing to radiator damage to his S.58. Sadi Lecointe, the hot favourite, had the misfortune to lose one spark plug from his overstressed engine after he had completed a very fast first lap. In the emergency landing which followed the sesquiplane nosed over, fortunately without injuring the pilot. Thus the only remaining pilot was Fernand Lasne in his elderly Nieuport-Delage 29V. Incidentally, Lecointe was granted a new 100-kilometre closed-circuit record with an average speed of over 325km/h, in spite of his untimely accident.

France's international competition, until recently considered to be out of the running, was now making a more concerted effort. Exactly one day later the US Army pilot Russell Maughan, on his first test flight with the second example of the Curtiss R-6 racing biplane, achieved an unofficial average speed of 353km/h over the measured kilometre. Two days later, on 4 October, the British pilot James H James equalled Lecointe's existing world record, which he had set only two weeks before, with a measured run of 341.2km/h. On 8 October in the USA Maughan managed an unofficial flight of approximately 355km/h during training for a prize competition sponsored by the four Pulitzer brothers, American newspaper owners, which was due to take place just one week later. This prize had gained extremely high prestige value in the USA, and Maughan duly won the race. Two days later, on 16 October 1922, he raised his speed again to 373.7km/h on another test flight. To crown this series of successes the world speed record fell to the USA on 18 October with an official run of almost 359km/h, but it was not Russell Maughan who set it. He was on holiday with his wife and son, who had been born during the Pulitzer races. Instead, the record pilot was William 'Billy' Mitchell, brigadier and second-in-command in the US Army Air Service. He became famous for his loudly proclaimed and sometimes unorthodox views. Mischievous tongues claimed immediately that he had exploited his rank on this occasion. Incidentally, it is worth mentioning that 'Billy' Mitchell's world record runs were his first flights in the R-6.

After the exotic and unreliable designs of the previous four years — the Model 18-T, the Cactus Kitten and the CR-1 — Curtiss finally succeeded in producing a real 'winner' in the R-6. The heart of this wooden biplane, which had been

Curtiss R-6, 1922.

designed by the young engineer William Wait under chief designer Filmore, was the high-performance twelve-cylinder Curtiss D-12 engine rated at 470hp. This was the work of the engine specialist Arthur Nutt, and was very neatly accommodated in the nose of the racy-looking machine. Low-drag surface radiators on the top and bottom of both wings completed the performance-enhancing measures. The US Army, spurred on by the successes of the US Navy racing aircraft, also built by Curtiss, insisted that the two machines that they had ordered on 27 May 1922 were to be ready in exactly three months, as the US Army wanted to challenge the Navy in that year's Pulitzer races. Their plans succeeded impressively well. The Curtiss company was deep in the red, but it could now breathe again, as both the US Army and the US Navy had settled on fast Curtiss single-seat fighters powered by Curtiss engines.

Naturally the French in general, and Nieuport in particular, were intent on revenge. The sesquiplane was immediately overhauled under the direction of the Nieuport engineer Mary, and was fitted with a new propeller made by the Regy

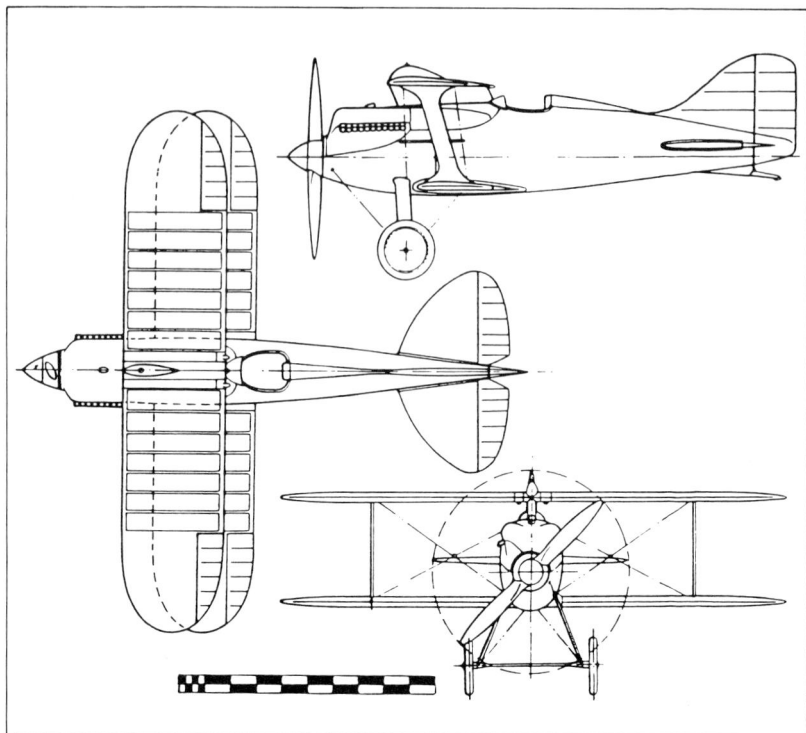

Curtiss R-6, 1922.

Nieuport-Delage Sesquiplan Eugéne Gilbert, *1923.*

company. In accordance with the Pulitzer rules, the landing speed of the Curtiss R-6 had been 120km/h, but that of the sesquiplane was half as high again at 180km/h. Towards the end of 1922 Sadi Lecointe began the test flights at Istres, the French test centre, but the modifications were not enough to set a new record. The inelegant Lamblin barrel radiators were now removed and replaced, following the Curtiss example, by Moreux surface radiators mounted on the underside of the wings. At the same time the Hispano-Suiza 42 was replaced by the Wright H-3 (a development of the Hispano-Suiza) from the abandoned Nieuport 41. This engine was officially described as a 'licence-built Hispano', and in fact the bore and stroke of both eight-cylinder engines were identical. On 15 February 1923 Sadi Lecointe was successful with the modified *Eugéne Gilbert*, and at exactly 375km/h the world record returned to him, to Nieuport, and to France.

Unfortunately for the French their satisfaction lasted only six weeks. The two US Army pilots Russell Maughan and Lester Maitland (the latter had taken second place in the Pulitzer races with the second R-6) were keen to take the world record over one kilometre back to the USA. As of 1 April 1923 new FAI regulations were to come into force which included extending the timed course to three kilometres. This change was made in an attempt to cope with the higher speeds now being achieved, and to reduce any timing inaccuracies. Their attempts began on 12 March, and just five days later Maughan managed a run of 376.4km/h, but this was less than the required 4km/h margin of improvement. On 29 March Maitland flew thirty attempts in succession, and the average of his four best flights was more than 386km/h. Unfortunately Maitland's dedication did not win official recognition, as he had not observed the rules regarding horizontal flight. Thus it was Maughan, taking off shortly after Maitland, who was declared the holder of the new world record with an official timed run of 380.751km/h. Maughan had completed twenty-four attempts. Like Maitland, he had approached the measured course in a dive, to achieve higher speed, but he subsequently succeeded in staying at a

Curtiss R2C-1 with pilot Alford Williams, 1923.

constant altitude over the whole of the prescribed distance. As happened so often, errors were made in the final calculation of the record speed, but the claimed speed was accepted by the FAI and thereby acquired official status, and from then on it could not be corrected. The disappointed Maitland made further attempts in April, but a series of minor accidents prevented success.

As successful as the Curtiss R-6 had been, it now met a superior competitor — from the USA. The US Navy, annoyed by the Army pilots' victory in the previous year's Pulitzer race with their fast R-6, had ordered two even faster machines from Curtiss. Basically a further refined R-6, the new design, the R2C-1, featured a Curtiss D-12A engine with its power output increased to more than 500hp, and a Reed light alloy propeller. The new airscrew alone gave an increase of 16km/h.

Head-on view of the Curtiss R2C-1.

Wright F2W-1, 1923.

Even the two wheels of the undercarriage were of a streamlined cross-section, and the undercarriage suspension system was enclosed in the wheel hubs.

In October 1922 the Wright company had made attempts on the world record with their NW-1, or Mystery Racer, a biplane with unequal-span wings, but it did not prove fast enough. Now the company had built two examples of a new racing biplane, the F2W-1, again for the US Navy, which was similar to the Curtiss R-6. Surface radiators were again fitted to both wings, but in this case the powerplant was the twelve-cylinder Wright T-3 Tornado, producing 760hp.

During trials in September the Curtiss design once again proved to be the faster. In the racing for the Pulitzer prize, which took place on 6 October 1923 in St Louis, Missouri, the two Curtiss machines took the first places, flown by the Navy pilots Alford Williams and Harold Brow, followed at a considerable distance by the Wrights and only then by the Curtiss R-6s of the US Army. An interesting point to note is that the average speed of the two victorious machines, at over 390km/h, was higher than the short-distance world record set only that spring, in spite of the twelve tight turns which this 200km race required.

Williams wanted to attack the official world record in his R2C-1 on the day after the racing, but for administrative reasons the attempt had to be postponed for four weeks. This time the official three-kilometre course was marked out on the Curtiss works aerodrome on Long Island, over which the two pilots Williams and Brow were to fight a friendly speed duel. On 2 November Brow was first to take off, and he achieved an average of 414.3km/h. Williams followed with 416.2km/h, then Brow flew again, reaching 417.6km/h, and this record flight was notified and recognised officially. Strong winds prevented the continuation of the battle on the following day, but on 4 November 1923 Williams raised the figure again to 423.56km/h. Brow countered with 427.3km/h, upon which Williams climbed once more into his racer and was able to wring out a final world record run of 429km/h. He ended his last flight by pulling the Curtiss into a steep climb — into the midst of a formation of Martin bombers, which were on the approach to the neighbouring Mitchel Field. That was enough both for the Admiral in charge and the Secretary of the Navy, who sent a telegram congratulating Williams for his new record and at the same time announced a ban on further record attempts.

In France the breathtaking series of record flights by the Americans was felt as a national tragedy. The Aviation Minister, Monsieur Laurent-Eynac, declared that it was absolutely essential for French designers to attack these records, since they were the best possible advertisement for a nation. He announced two prizes, each of 50,000 Francs, for the designers who produced aircraft which won back the world speed and altitude records respectively. Gustave Delage and Nieuport were the quickest to respond. Their Model 40, basically a Nieuport 29 with increased wingspan, won the prize for maximum altitude with the ever-optimistic Sadi Lecointe at the controls. Their attempt at the speed prize produced the Model 42S, a further developed, slightly larger sesquiplane with the new Hispano-Suiza 51 twelve-cylinder engine. This time the Delage design proved too slow. It proved good enough for a series of long-distance records, but not for the absolute speed

Nieuport-Delage 42S, 1924.

record, in spite of numerous attempts. Sadi Lecointe eventually gave up the quest for records completely. He remained chief pilot for Nieuport for more than twelve years, then became active politically. He died in Paris in 1944.

The second record aspirant was the Société Industrielle des Méteaux et du Bois (SIMB), under the leadership of the entrepreneur Adolphe Bernard. The company was also known under the name of Ferbois (iron/wood). Their chief designer, Jean Hubert, had displayed the prototype of a modern single-seat fighter, the Bernard C. 1, at the Paris Aéro Salon of 1922. The C. 1 was a light-alloy, low-wing cantilever monoplane, but such advanced thinking was greeted with considerable scepticism, and the design methods, in part justifiably, were criticised as crude. The two single-seat racers designed in 1924 by Hubert and his young assistant Bruner bore some similarity to the single-seat fighter, but they were made entirely of wood. The first of these Vitesse models, the V. 1, was fitted with a 540hp Lorraine-Dietrich engine and a wooden propeller. The second, the V. 2, had a 620hp Hispano-Suiza 50 and a Levasseur/Reed metal airscrew. Both engines were twelve-cylinder designs with 'W' cylinder arrangements.

Bernard (SIMB) V. 1, 1924.

Bernard (SIMB) V. 2, 1924.

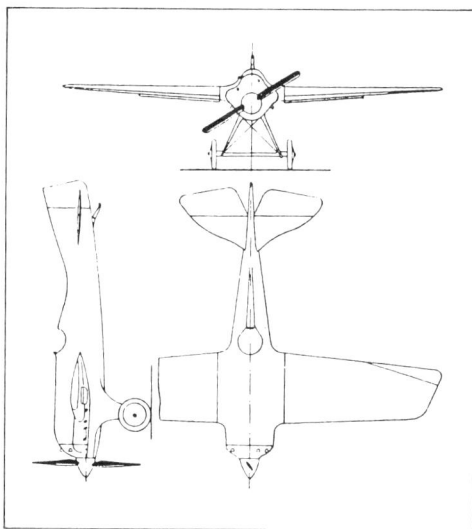

Bernard (SIMB) V. 2, 1924.

On its first flight, in May 1924, the V. 1 proved to be unstable. Its tailplane was far too small, and the aircraft was destroyed on landing. Fortunately the pilot, Florentin Bonnet, was only slightly injured.

In the meantime, the state prize had been raised to 200,000 Francs, of which 140,000 Francs were to go to the aircraft builder and 60,000 Francs to the engine designer. It was no wonder, therefore, that SIMB put immense effort into completing the V. 2. Yet the first world record attempt on 8 November produced an average speed of only some 393km/h. If the machine was to overhaul Alford Williams and his Curtiss R2C-1, the company had to find a ten per cent speed increase. The light blue machine was subjected to a comprehensive course of weight reduction. Its wings were cut down, the air inlets and exhaust stubs were modified, new wheels were fitted, and the machine was polished to a high gloss. On 11 December 1924 the efforts were finally crowned with success. Bonnet flashed over the aerodrome at Istres at treetop height four times, and then the world speed record was back in French hands. The mark now stood at more than 448km/h — a figure which was not to be exceeded by a land-based aircraft (an American machine) until eight years later — not officially, at least.

Aerofoil sections, 1921–1924. Top to bottom: Curtiss R-6, Nieuport-Delage Sesquiplan, Curtiss R2C-1 and Bernard (SIMB) V. 2.

There were plenty of attempts, on the part of the French, the British and the Americans. Even the young nation of Czechoslovakia possessed designers with world-record ambitions, but in 1923 the Letov Š-8 'Osmička' (The Eight) strutted high-wing monoplane, designed by Alois Šmolik, could average only 342km/h over the three-kilometre course. The dogged series of test flights with the fundamentally impotent Nieuport 42S continued right into the autumn of 1925, and at SIMB plans were drawn up for a V. 3 — a further development of the V. 2 with a Lorraine compressor motor and retractable undercarriage, but this machine was never built. In 1925 the British firm of Gloster produced a further development of the famous Bamel, intended specifically for record attempts, under the designation Gloster II Bluebird, also powered by a Napier Lion engine. In June 1925, during the fourth test flight, the tailplane began to vibrate. The aircraft struck the ground at a speed in excess of 300km/h and slid for 150m, shedding parts all the while. The pilot, Larry Carter, was severely injured, and died the following year. On the other side of the Atlantic the Verville-Sperry R-3, an all-wood single-seat racer

Verville-Sperry R-3.

featuring a cantilever low-set wing and retractable undercarriage, had already made vain attempts at higher speeds and records. Another project by this company, dating from 1924, took the form of a low-wing monoplane with two Curtiss twelve-cylinder engines in tandem, but this one never progressed beyond the drawing board. At Curtiss a further refined variant of the R2C-1, the R3C-1, was built, and proved to have a top speed of about 480km/h in the autumn of 1925, but the flights were unofficial.

The interest of the aviation world had shifted to the races for the Schneider Trophy for water-borne aircraft, which had attained vast prestige value in the meantime. The efforts of aircraft designers were also directed towards these highly specialised seaplanes and flying-boats, to the detriment of other forms of aircraft. Versions of the Curtiss racing single-seater were built with floats, and it is a credit to the quality of the basic design that they were successful several times in these competitions. The last, somewhat half-hearted, attempt in the 1920s to improve on the world speed record with a land-based aircraft took place in November 1927.

Alford Williams had asked the former Curtiss designers Booth and Thurston to build a twin-float biplane for the Schneider competition of 1927. This aircraft was powered by a twenty-four-cylinder Packard aircraft engine producing 1,265hp, and was thought to have an excellent chance of victory. However, for a series of reasons the project failed, and the machine was eventually fitted with a wheeled undercarriage. On 4 November 1927 the world record was won officially by Italy for the first time, in the person of the Italian pilot Mario de Bernardi, flying the Macchi M.52 seaplane at a speed of 479.29km/h. Two days later Williams clocked an unofficial speed of 519km/h in his Vespa, but he never undertook an official record attempt.

Kirkham-Williams Vespa with Alford Williams, 1927.

Kirkham-Williams Vespa, 1927.

STREAMLINING PREVAILS

1931–1940: Up to 760km/h

Due solely to an unlikely sequence of events, seaplanes were the fastest aircraft in the world for almost a dozen years.

The reason for this strange circumstance was that the leading aircraft designers in England, Italy and France decided to concentrate their efforts on winning the contest for 'La Coupe d'Aviation Maritime Jacques Schneider' (the Schneider Trophy). This prize had been donated by the French Industrialist Jacques Schneider, and the competition for it was initially held every year, and later every second year. The competition had originally been established with a different purpose, but eventually it developed into a pure speed event in which overall victory, and even participation itself, earned great international prestige. In the autumn of 1927 a highly developed racing single-seater of this type, the Italian Macchi M.52, became the first seaplane to claim the official title of fastest aircraft in the world. Six months later the same pilot, Mario de Bernardi, pushed the world record up to almost 513km/h flying the M.52R, a development of the M.52. Some time later the British Supermarine S.6 and S.6B, and subsequently the Italian Macchi-Castoldi MC.72, all of them twin-float single-seaters, eased the official world record over the 600km/h barrier, and later up to and beyond the 700km/h mark.

Curiously, the extensive theoretical and practical knowledge gained in the

Macchi-Castoldi MC.72, 1934.

development of these high-speed machines was hardly exploited at all in the design of 'normal' aircraft, even when the same designers were responsible for both types, and even when they were asked to design the 'fastest of the fast' — the fighter aircraft which every air force needed. This was because manoeuvrability — the ability to out-turn enemy aircraft in aerial combat — was, and still is, the first priority, as it had been in the First World War. Speed took second place, and the aviation ministry experts of all nations still preferred the biplane to the exclusion of all others, preferably with an open cockpit. Contracts for monoplanes were granted rarely, hesitantly and with reservations, as this type of machine was considered to be 'fragile'. In consequence, monoplane designs were not produced, except in a few unusual cases. For many years the idea of a retractable undercarriage was scarcely considered feasible, in spite of all the knowledge and experience gained from speed competitions.

In the early 1930s the focal points of these competitions were the USA and France. The contrast between the two nations' air races was considerable. At the annual National Air Races in America, the American mentality ensured that the prevailing atmosphere was akin to that of the circus, with a crowd of brightly painted, enormously powerful 'specials' tearing round the course at minimum altitude at breakneck speed. They were flown by insanely brave pilots chasing fat

A THRILL FOR THE NATION !

CURTISS-REYNOLDS AIRPORT --- CHICAGO AUG. 23 TO SEPT. 1

Posters for air races in the USA, 1930–1932.

prizes donated by industry, with a crowd of many thousands of sensation-seeking people in rapt attention. In France racing events were run at a somewhat lower temperature. The Coupe Deutsch competition, of which two series had been held from 1912 to 1919 and from 1920 to 1921, was eventually revived, and a third series ran from 1933 to 1936. The competition consisted of a straightforward flight against the clock, over quite a long course, and attracted the best of the established aircraft designers and pilots. Moreover, the racing was run according to carefully formulated regulations, and there were restrictions on engine capacity.

The Pulitzer races, which were held in the USA every year between 1920 and 1925, and the first National Air Races which followed them, were traditionally dominated by the single-seat fighters of the US Army and US Navy, but military interest in these closed-circuit races gradually began to slacken. Nevertheless, the military authorities did not expect the salutary shock which awaited them in 1929, on the occasion of the closed-circuit race for the newly established Thompson

The Thompson Trophy.

Trophy, which was held as part of the National Air Races that year. The Travel Air Model R, built by a small firm based in Wichita, Kansas, showed a clean pair of heels to all the competing military machines. In contrast to the angular fighters, the red and black 'mystery ship' was an elegant, braced low-wing monoplane with large, streamlined wheel spats and a neat NACA cowling enclosing its radial engine. In the same race in the following year, the Navy pilot Page, rendered semi-conscious by exhaust fumes, suffered a fatal accident in the new Curtiss XF6C-6 navy fighter, and this signalled an end to the participation of US armed forces in these events. American military aircraft seldom took part in other international competitions, and the inevitable result was that they fell further and further behind in terms of technical development, compared with the best products of other nations.

With their main rivals out of the running, the USA's smaller aircraft companies and 'backyard builders' saw their chance to compete in these contests, some of which offered generous cash prizes. The money was particularly attractive in the dire economic situation which then prevailed. Although the racing in these events was spectacular, the speeds achieved even by the winners were still far below the 448km/h recorded by the French SIMB V. 2 back in 1924, not to mention the outstanding speeds attained by the Schneider Trophy racers. For example, the Travel Air R could manage a peak speed of only 380km/h, although this figure was far better than the best achieved by the American single-seat fighters of the time, which was 310km/h.

Even so, other groups of ambitious aircraft constructors were formed, spurred on by the success of the Travel Air team from Wichita, which later formed the core of the Beechcraft company. These new groups then hunted for sponsors for their grand projects. Some were luckier than others, but the most successful were the five Granville brothers from the US state of Massachusetts. Trading under the name of Gee Bee, the brothers built up a reputation locally for their excellent service as aircraft repairers, and they eventually decided to build their own machine. The Gee Bee Sportster was a small, single-seat, braced low-wing monoplane. Its fuselage consisted of a steel-tube framework with plywood formers and fabric covering, while the wings were of wood, again covered in fabric. But there were too many aircraft of this type in the United States, and the number of customers with the money to buy one was small. For this reason the number of Gee Bee machines completed was very low, and there was no question of the enterprise becoming commercially viable.

It was decided that attack was the best method of defence. The closed-circuit races for the Thompson Trophy, which were run as part of the 1931 National Air Races in Cleveland, Ohio, offered a first prize of $7,500, and this money, combined with the publicity which would accrue automatically, was a valuable prize. Bob Hall, a young and very talented aircraft designer and pilot, took on the task of designing a small racing single-seater with a powerful engine which would outclass all of the competing machines. With the plans for this radical racer under his arm, Hall set out to woo potential sponsors, and he succeeded in persuading a

Gee Bee Z with designer Bob Hall in the cockpit, 1931.

number of business people from the town of Springfield in Massachusetts to be shareholders in the newly formed Springfield Air Racing Association (SARA).

The Gee Bee Model Z was a radical but logical development of the preceding model Y, which was a sporting two-seater. The powerplant was to be the popular Pratt & Whitney Wasp Junior nine-cylinder radial engine, tuned to produce 540hp. The unit was loaned by the manufacturer, which hoped for effective publicity from the enterprise. The short, squat fuselage again consisted of a steel-tube frame with plywood formers and fabric covering. The completely enclosed cockpit was located very far aft, and merged directly into the fin. The tail surfaces and wings of this braced low-wing monoplane were of fabric-covered, all-wood construction. The undercarriage legs were fitted with streamlined fairings, and the wheels were enclosed in large, teardrop-shaped spats. The yellow and black machine bore the name *City of Springfield* on the deep NACA cowling which enclosed the engine. It was completed on 22 August 1931, exactly one week before the start of the National Air Races.

Bob Hall wanted to fly his design himself, but the pilot Lowell Bayles had bought his way into SARA with a stake of $500, and had acquired the right to pilot the yellow and black power-packed racer in the most important races, including the Thompson Trophy event. As compensation, Bob Hall test-flew the machine and competed in two minor races in the mammoth Cleveland event, which included a total of thirty-eight different competitions. He won both races with ease. Lowell Bayles was equally successful, winning another race by a margin of more than 80km/h. On one pass of the Shell Speed Dashes, which were included in

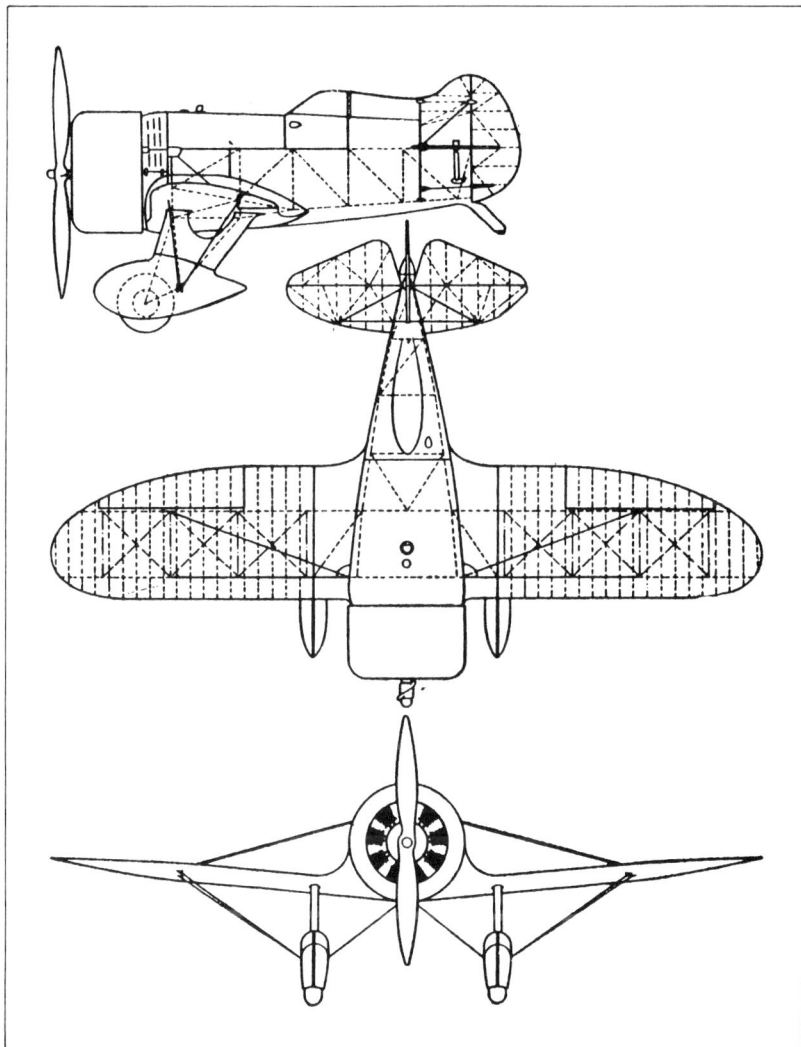

Gee Bee Z, 1931.

the overall event, he was timed at a peak speed of 460km/h, 12km/h higher than the world record for land-based aircraft which had stood for seven years. In the battle for the Thompson Trophy he had to face two serious rivals: Jimmy Doolittle, who was accustomed to winning with his sleek Laird Super Solution biplane, and the imaginative Jimmy Wedell, with his own-design No 44. Both machines were also powered by the 540hp Wasp Junior engine. However, in the races Doolittle dropped out with engine trouble and Wedell could not keep up. Bayles won easily in the Gee Bee Z.

Bayles intended to attack the official speed record for land-based aircraft on the same occasion, but this did not prove possible. Nevertheless, he prepared himself for an attempt on the record. First the aeroplane was fitted with a larger and more powerful Wasp Senior, rated at 760hp. In late November Bayles began his official record attempt, flying over Wayne County Airport, near Detroit. Although he recorded peak speeds of more than 500km/h, he did not complete the four passes required by the FAI regulations, and in the end the measuring camera failed. On 5 December 1931 Bayles made his fourth record attempt. He had just taken off when the fuel tank cap located behind the engine cowling came loose at high speed, smashed through the windscreen, and hit him full in the face. In a reflex movement the semi-conscious Bayles pulled the machine up into a steep climb which overstressed the Gee Bee. The starboard wing broke off, and the aircraft rolled twice to the right at high speed and then crashed and burst into flames. Bayles died instantly. The accident was recorded on film, and excerpts turned up later in several Hollywood cinema films, whenever the storyline called for a spectacular aircraft crash.

Shortly after the Cleveland races Gee Bee designer Bob Hall left the firm, a disillusioned man. The new chief designer, Howell Miller, was given the task of producing an even faster single-seat racer to restore the reputation of the Gee Bee company, which had suffered mightily from the accident. The new machine, the Gee Bee R, proved to be a logical development in the direction indicated by the Model Z. Once more a Pratt & Whitney Wasp Senior provided the power, this version producing an output of more than 800hp. For the first time a two-bladed

Gee Bee R-1, 1931.

controllable-pitch propeller was adopted. The enclosed cockpit was again located immediately forward of the fin.

Initially the top edge of the fin was horizontal, following the line of the canopy, but immediately after the first flight, on 13 August 1932, an extra top section was added, together with a correspondingly enlarged rudder, as directional stability had proved to be extremely poor. The wings of the Gee Bee R were entirely skinned with plywood, but they were still braced externally. Two examples of the red-and-white Super Sportster were built: the R-1 (NR2100) with the powerful Wasp Senior, and the R-2 (NR2101), which, although powered by the less powerful Wasp Junior, could carry a greater volume of fuel. This machine was intended for the long-distance Bendix race.

Fourteen days after the machine's first flight the annual National Air Races in Cleveland began again. In this depressing period of worldwide economic crisis, the event was welcomed as one of the few positive events in a bleak world. Naturally, the Granville team was desperate to win again.

Russell Boardman had been selected as pilot, but he was now recuperating from injuries suffered a few days earlier when a Gee Bee E crashed. Zantford Granville had decided at short notice to hire their competitor of the previous year, Jimmy Doolittle, whose modified Super Solution was in for repairs after a belly landing. Doolittle's first flight in the R-1, on 28 August 1932, took him straight from Springfield to Cleveland. To put it mildly, the machine turned out to be extremely temperamental. In the test flights which followed, Doolittle discovered to his astonishment that any attempt to fly a steeply banked turn immediately resulted in two high-speed rolls, before he was able to resume level flight. Steep turns were therefore out of the question for the fat racer — a characteristic which was not exactly ideal for the two circuits of the Thompson Trophy Race, each of which featured three turning points. In a straight line the Gee Bee R was fast — extremely fast — and for this reason Doolittle exploited the Shell Speed Dashes, which were officially measured, for an immediate attack on the world record. For technical reasons this attempt was not recognised, but on 3 September he was successful. Four times Doolittle guided the powerful single-seat racer over the three-kilometre measured course to claim a new world record for land-based aircraft of almost 474km/h, after a gap of almost eight years. The icing on the cake was a clear victory in the Thompson Trophy Race three days later, despite the fact that he prudently avoided steep turns.

Doolittle's subsequent comments on the aircraft's handling and on the behaviour of the press photographers was anything but flattering. His wife and his sons had been accompanied by the press at every moment during the racing, so that they could get the big picture of their instant reactions should a crash occur. It was just another sign of the usual lust for sensation. After all, at another event spectators had dipped their handkerchiefs in the blood of a smashed pilot, to keep as souvenirs. Doolittle never took part in an air race again.

The remaining history of the Gee Bee Super Sportster can be summarised briefly. The R-1, fitted with an even more powerful engine and an enlarged fuel tank, stalled on take-off in the 1933 Bendix Race with Russell Boardman at the controls, and crashed inverted on the runway from a low altitude. Boardman was fatally injured. The R-2, converted in a similar way, crashed a few months later on landing. The pilot, who was only slightly injured, declared afterwards that the damned machine had constantly tried to bite its own tail. The remains of the two totally wrecked machines were combined to form a new, slightly longer racer: the R-1/R-2 Long Tail Racer, which dug its own grave on its second landing. Repaired and modified again, and fitted with an extra fuel tank in the tail, this machine crashed finally at the start of the 1935 Bendix races, this time killing its pilot. Despite their catastrophic history, and although there were other racing aircraft which were much more successful, these squat Gee Bee single-seaters are remembered to this day as the epitome of the 'brute power racing machine'.

At Cleveland in 1931 Jimmy Wedell, an extraordinarily gifted amateur designer and racing pilot, had proved his ability to fly his Wedell-Williams No 44 extremely

Wedell-Williams No 44 with Jimmy Wedell, 1933.

fast. He had made one unsuccessful record attempt, shortly after Lowell Bayles had done the same. The following year he was beaten by Doolittle in the R-1, but the margin was slim, and he had improved his speed considerably in the meantime. He then fitted his red and black braced low-wing monoplane, which was not dissimilar in design to the Gee Bee Super Sportster, but much slimmer, with an 810hp Wasp Senior, in place of the 540hp Wasp Junior; the same modification that had been applied to the Gee Bee Z. This time, at the National Air Races in September 1933, held at Glenview, near Chicago, he was successful. The official average of the four successive runs was 490.08km/h, a 16km/h improvement; the required one per cent margin. For the first time a land-based aircraft had clearly exceeded 300mph.

The Americans were well satisfied with this speed, and the American media acclaimed the achievement. However, they deliberately overlooked the fact that the absolute world speed record remained in European hands, and was held by a seaplane. That record had been established in April 1933 by the Italian Macchi-Castoldi MC.72, flown by Warrant Officer Francesco Agello. His record speed, set over Lake Garda in northern Italy, was 682km/h; a good 40 per cent higher than the mark reached by Wedell.

A start had also been made in Europe on the renewed development of high-speed land-based aircraft, as the apparently irresistible attraction of the Schneider Trophy contest ended with Britain's outright winning of the Trophy in 1931. To further this development, the French government had offered a prize of half-a-million Francs to the builder of the land-based aircraft which would regain the speed record taken from France in 1933. At the Bernard company, whose elegant V. 2 had set a world record of 448km/h in 1924, the remaining example of the two Type H.V. 120 seaplanes, built for the Schneider competitions, was immediately prepared for a record attempt. There was little time to spare. The

Bernard V.4, 1933.

wooden floats of the mid-wing machine, now renamed the V. 4, were replaced by a massive, strutted undercarriage, and the span of the cantilever wing was reduced. The 1,680hp Hispano-Suiza 18-R, a liquid-cooled eighteen-cylinder W engine, was retained. Surface radiators were fitted to both sides of the fuselage and on both undercarriage fairings, in addition to those on the top surface of the wing. In December 1933 the machine was prepared for flight at Istres, the Armée de l'Air test site, for the record attempt. Technical problems thwarted the attempt at first, and then stormy weather prevented a record flight that year (1933). At the end of

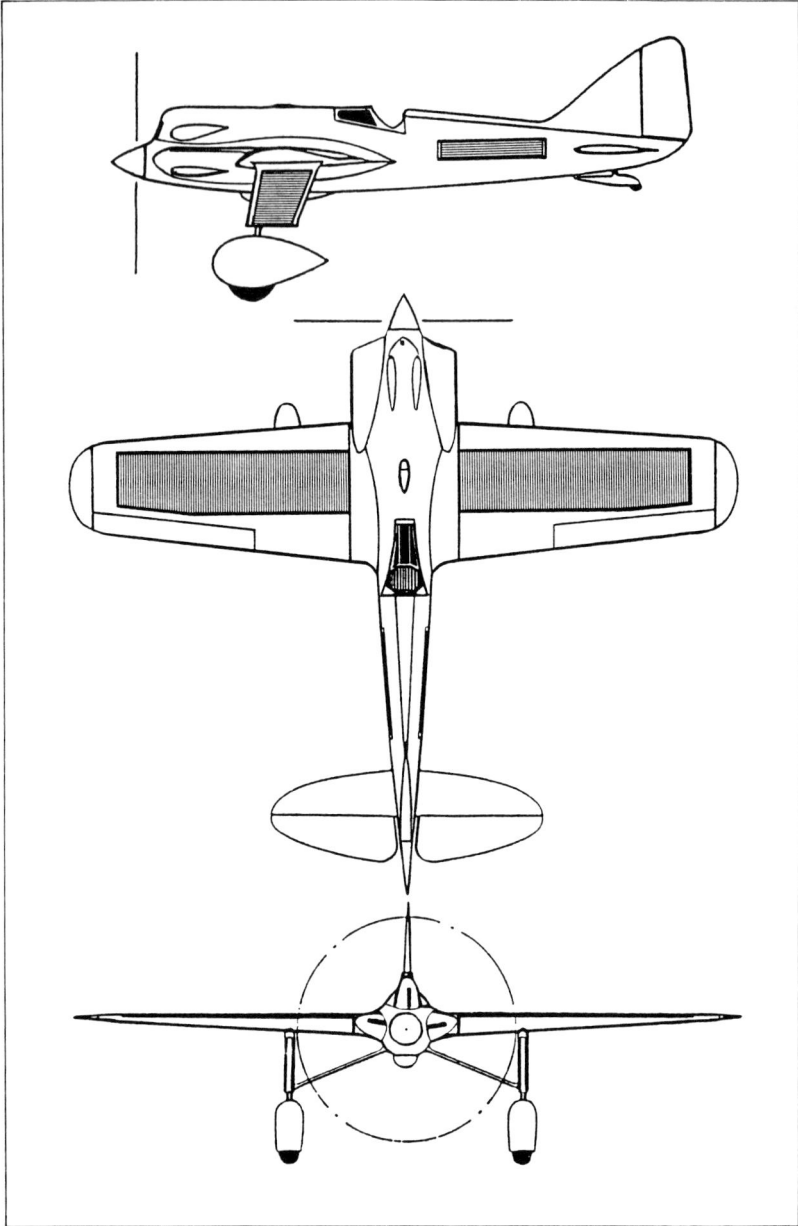

Bernard V. 4, 1933.

the year the prize deadline expired, as did the team's enthusiasm for further expensive attempts. The purposeful single-seater never had its chance.

It was also in 1933 that the famous Coupe Deutsch de la Meurthe was revived in France, this time sponsored by Mlle Suzanne Deutsch de la Meurthe. The race, which was to be held over a distance of 2,000km, consisted of twenty laps of a predetermined course. The course had to be flown in two ten-lap heats, with an intervening pit stop. Engine capacity was restricted to eight litres. Naturally the established aircraft manufacturers entered, but a number of younger designers also aroused interest with several new designs, some of them extremely unconventional. Roland Payen presented his entirely new *Flèche Volante* (flying arrow), with its highly swept delta wing mounted at the rear and unswept stub wings at the front.

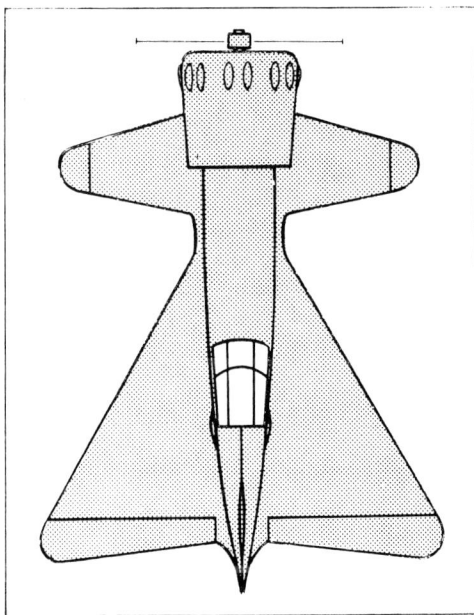

Payen Pa.100 Flèche Volante, 1933.

The Payen Pa.100, built in 1933 and originally intended to have a retractable undercarriage (central wheel and outriggers) and a Regnier in-line engine, was eventually fitted with a fixed undercarriage and a 380hp Gnome et Rhône radial engine. These changes detracted slightly from the racy appearance of the small wooden single-seater, but its predicted top speed of 570km/h made it a potential winner. Unfortunately this extremely interesting machine suffered a hard landing right at the start of flight testing, and had to be written off without fulfilling the hopes of its designer.

In contrast, the new, small and very elegant Caudron low-wing monoplanes proved to be more successful, reaching amazing speeds with their relatively modest engine power. In January 1932 the respected aircraft company owned by the Caudron brothers acquired a new technical director, Marcel Riffard. A few months later he was joined by the young engineer Georges Otfinowsky, who accepted the post of director of the project office. Their first project, the R.300, was purely a design exercise, and the first machine to be completed was the model C.360, of which three examples were built to compete in the 1933 Coupe Deutsch race. Two, designated C.362, were fitted with air-cooled 170hp Renault Bengali four-cylinder in-line engines, and one, the C.366, had a 205hp Regnier six-cylinder engine. These sleek cantilever monoplanes with their fixed single-leg undercarriages were of all-wood construction, and featured a one-piece wing. Particular emphasis was placed on aerodynamic refinement.

To improve weight distribution, the cockpit was located well aft, and the canopy could be moved forward or backward while the aircraft was in flight. The fuel and oil tanks were located between the pilot's seat and the engine, close to the centre of gravity, to avoid major pitch-trim changes. That this overall concept was 'right' is indicated by the fact that most of the Caudron designs produced in the following years showed a very strong family resemblance to the original C.360 design, apart from detail modifications. However, the debut of these blue racing machines was anything but encouraging. Five days before the race was due to start, the Caudron flight director, Arrachart, suffered an engine failure in his C.362 and flew into a high-voltage cable; he was killed in the crash. Two days later the C.366 stalled on take-off and was severely damaged. Nevertheless, the remaining C.362, flown by Caudron chief test pilot Raymond Delmotte, managed to achieve second place in the race, beaten only by a Potez 53 which was over 50 per cent more powerful.

During the next few months the Caudron team began work on a successor,

Caudron C.460, 1934.

which would benefit from their experience with the earlier machines. The fuselage cross-section of the new aircraft was reduced by ten per cent, and a Renault six-cylinder engine producing more than 300hp was installed. Although the wing used the same aerofoil section and planform as before, it was entirely redesigned to allow a retractable undercarriage to be installed. Four examples were built; one C.450 with a conventional fixed undercarriage and three C.460s with a new form of Charlestop retractable undercarriage. Unfortunately the latter proved to be extremely unreliable, and two of the C.460s were modified to have a proven fixed undercarriage. In the second Coupe Deutsch race, held in May 1934, the Caudron company achieved a satisfying triple victory, in spite of several problems. The C.450 came out on top, followed by the restored C.366 which had flown the previous year and the third C.460, with its recalcitrant retractable undercarriage simply locked in the extended position.

Immediately after this race three C.460s were fitted with new retractable undercarriages made by Messier, which proved to be significantly more reliable. One of these machines was also fitted with a supercharged Renault engine increased in capacity from eight to nine and a half litres, which produced up to 400hp. The Caudron team had set themselves the task of finally securing the speed record for land-based aircraft for France, as various Americans had made serious, if unsuccessful, record attempts in April and September 1934, flying single-seat Wedell-Williams racers. Caudron was determined to beat them to it. The first test flights in December, with Raymond Delmotte at the controls, were extremely encouraging, and whispers were heard of speeds greater than 550km/h. On the first day of the Christmas holiday the deed was done. After four perfect flights over a course at Istres the new record was theirs: 505.848km/h. Bearing in mind the relatively low power available, this was an excellent result. On the other hand, only two months previously, Italy's speed ace, Francesco Agello, had raised his own absolute speed record to an astonishing 709.209km/h, piloting another MC.72 seaplane. This was no less than 71 per cent higher than Delmotte's record speed.

France did not have a monopoly of talented aircraft designers, however. Other countries had their gifted individuals, too. In the Soviet Union Nikolai Polikarpov

Bartini Stal-6, 1934.

had developed a number of single-seat fighters, the most recent version of which, a cantilever low-wing monoplane with a retractable undercarriage, exhibited a marked similarity to the American Gee-Bee racers. The prototype TsKB-12 was eventually developed into the production I-16, a machine which was to achieve fame a few years later in the Spanish Civil War, as the Rata. The engineer Roberto Bartini, who had emigrated from Italy to the Soviet Union, had also designed what he hoped would prove to be the fastest fighter in the world. This was the Stal-8, a development of his experimental Stal-6 single-seater. The new machine was an

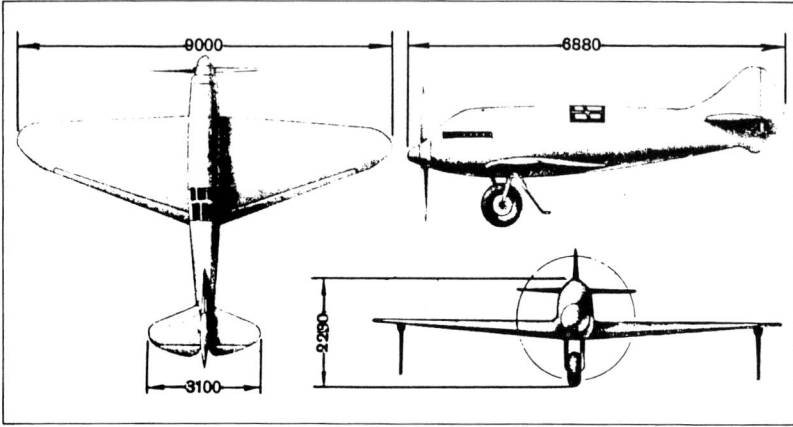

Bartini Stal-6, 1934.

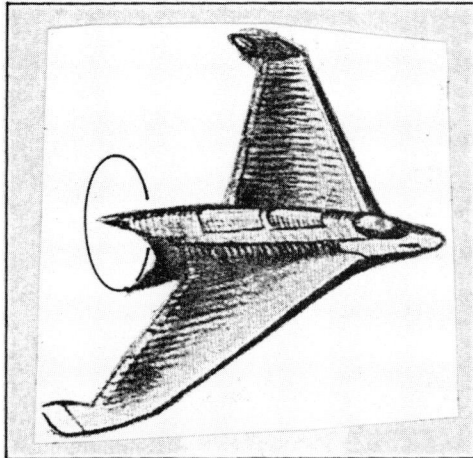

Lippisch project of 1934.

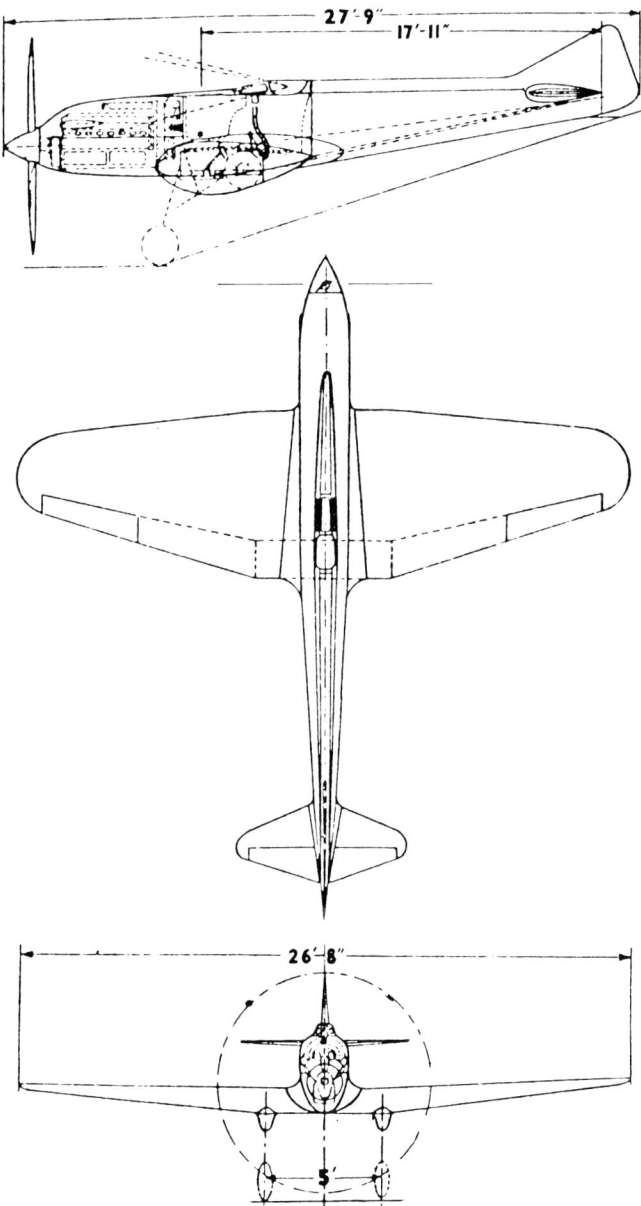

Keith Rider Super-Speed Racer of 1934.

all-metal, cantilever low-wing monoplane with surface radiators and a retractable undercarriage, and was expected to attain 620km/h, but it was scrapped in October 1934, when 90 per cent complete, owing to complete lack of official interest. In Germany Alexander Lippisch, pioneer of the flying wing and creator of the delta wing, suffered a similar experience when he presented his latest project to the German authorities. This was a high-speed, tailless single-seat fighter with a pusher propeller in the tail. The idea was totally ignored. In the USA Keith Rider, a successful designer of fairly small racing aircraft, had exhibited a design for a 750km/h single-seater. This all-metal low-wing monoplane was to be powered by a sixteen-cylinder Miller vee engine producing more than 2,500hp. Finally, John Stack, a NACA engineer, suggested a design for a special-purpose monoplane which was intended to fly at more than 900km/h. It was to feature a retractable or jettisonable undercarriage and a single-blade propeller. None of these projects came to fruition.

In contrast, a private individual in Great Britain did succeed in overcoming the lethargy of state authority. Lord Rothermere, a newspaper publisher like the American James Gordon Bennett before him, commissioned the Bristol company to build him 'the fastest commercial aeroplane in Europe'. The result was the Bristol 142, designed by Frank Barnwell. The 142 was a twin-engined cantilever all-metal low-wing monoplane with a retractable undercarriage. The very first flights, in the spring of 1935, showed that the new machine was exceptionally fast. Once its fixed-pitch four-bladed wooden propellers had been replaced by two-position three-bladed metal units, it attained an astonishing speed of 494km/h during official testing at Martlesham Heath. Fully laden, carrying six passengers, it still reached 458km/h, and was thus exactly 50km/h faster than the Gloster Gladiator, the new single-seat fighter which had just been ordered. The Air Ministry became enthusiastic, and declared that it was interested in evaluating the machine as a bomber. The patriotic Lord Rothermere christened the aircraft *Britain First*, and presented it to the nation. A military variant, the 142M, was developed in short order, and this machine, named the Blenheim, was subsequently built in large numbers.

In the USA another wealthy individual approached the matter in his own way. As sole heir to an extremely successful company which manufactured oil-well drilling equipment, the multi-millionaire Howard Hughes had adequate opportunity to indulge his many and varied passions, which included directing and producing films, playing golf, and piloting aircraft. In 1927 he obtained his private pilot's licence, quickly followed by all the remaining civilian ratings, and he turned out to be an excellent pilot. He was in the fortunate position to be able to procure a whole series of aircraft, each faster than the last. Some of them appeared in his flying film *Hell's Angels*. Among these machines was a modern Boeing single-seat fighter, which he subsequently sent to Douglas and Lockheed for further tuning. While at Lockheed he met a project engineer named Richard Palmer, and one year later, in early 1934, Hughes commissioned Palmer to build 'the fastest aircraft in the world'. In the opinion of many experts the resultant machine, completed sixteen months later, was one of the best-looking aircraft of all time. The monocoque fuselage and cantilever tailplane and fin were built of duralumin, while the one-piece wooden wing was plywood-skinned over two spars. The control surfaces were duralumin with fabric covering. The retractable undercarriage had an unusually wide track. Power was supplied by a closely cowled Pratt & Whitney Twin Wasp double radial engine, the output of which had been raised to around 900hp.

The wing of the Hughes Special 1B was finished in royal blue with yellow registration markings, and the machine was polished to a high gloss. Hughes himself flew the machine for the first time on 17 and 28 August 1935. A fortnight later he prepared to make his official attack on the world speed record for land-based aircraft. The first attempt, carried out on the afternoon of 12 September, had to be interrupted because of failing light. On the following day, Friday, 13 September 1935 (Hughes had many strange habits, but he was not superstitious), he took off from Santa Ana Airport in California and flew the four passes required by the regulations. To be quite sure, he flew a further two passes. By this time the fuel tank was empty, and Hughes had to perform a belly landing in a field of beetroot, which he carried out perfectly. But the flight constituted a new record, which now stood at 567.115km/h. No sooner had the record been officially confirmed than Hughes ordered the 7.59m-span wing to be replaced by a new wing of greater span, 9.75m, to allow an attempt on the transcontinental record. This involved flying the modified machine right across the American

Howard Hughes and his Hughes Special 1B, 1935.

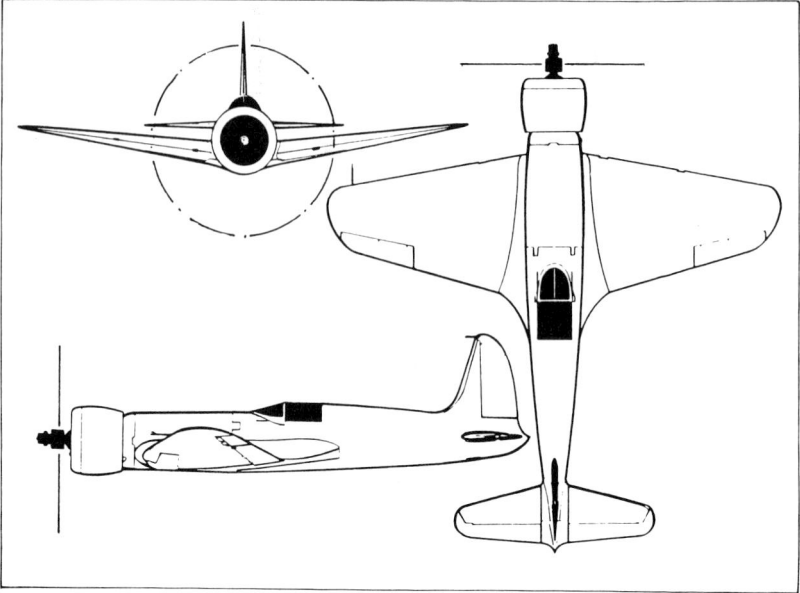

Hughes Special 1B, 1935.

continent. The aircraft was converted to his requirements and fitted with larger fuel tanks and additional equipment and instruments. By January 1937 he was ready. Hughes took off from Burbank, California, and reached Newark, New Jersey, just seven and a half hours later — an average speed of more than 526km/h. The aircraft had fulfilled its purpose, and Hughes never flew it again. It now resides in the National Air and Space Museum in Washington, DC. Attempts were

Hughes Special 1B, 1935.

made to interest the US Army Air Force in a single-seat fighter variant of the record machine, the Hughes XP-2, but to no avail. Another Palmer design dating from 1937, the twin-fuselage Hughes D-2 fighter, suffered a similar fate. Built secretly in 1943, the machine flew only twice before it was destroyed by fire after lightning struck its hangar. A considerably enlarged development of this machine, the XF-11 aerial photography aircraft, crashed on its first flight in June 1946, and Hughes was severely injured. By November he had recovered, and he completed a very short flight in his eight-engined H-4 Hercules flying boat, which was and remains the largest aircraft in the world ever to fly, with its wingspan of 98m. The machine never flew again, and Howard Hughes subsequently devoted himself to other interests.

At that time nobody in the USA seemed to be keen to challenge the various high-speed record holders, neither in the air nor on the surface, apart from the motorboat world record, which had been in American hands since 1932. However, there was one specialist racing aircraft under construction which had been ordered by the racing pilot Frank Hawks. The machine's name was *Time Flies*. Designed

Frank Hawks' Time Flies, *1936.*

by Howell Miller as a development of his Gee Bee R-1, this aircraft was a cantilever low-wing monoplane of wood and metal. The snow-white single-seater was fitted with a 1,160hp Twin Wasp radial engine driving a three-bladed propeller. The undercarriage was retractable, as was the pilot's seat, complete with windscreen. Small teardrop-shaped viewing panels in the fuselage sides allowed the pilot some degree of vision in flight. Hopes had been expressed for speeds far in excess of 600km/h with this machine, and it was intended to be flown in air races and record attempts. The first flight took place in December 1936. However, three months previously the entire US racing elite had been outclassed by one of the three French Caudron C.460s, flown by Michel Detroyat, which in September 1936 won the National Air Races, held near Los Angeles. In spite of its relatively low power (only half the output of the US machines) it was victorious in the Greve Trophy Race (100 miles in 20 laps, for machines with engines up to nine-litre capacity) and also in the coveted Thompson Trophy Race (15 laps, total distance 150 miles), winning by a clear margin. The American pilots, led by Roscoe Turner, protested vociferously against what they claimed was unfair state support for the foreign entry. The fact that they had obtained their super-powerful engines at no cost from US industry was conveniently forgotten. Aggrieved by this curious mutation of fair play — a notorious feature of the USA known as 'home-towning' — the French withdrew all their other entries, and neither they nor any other nation felt inclined from then on to take part in US racing events. For a variety of reasons *Time Flies* never fulfilled its expectations. A hard landing in April 1937 fractured the starboard wing spar. With an eye on a military contract, the aircraft was subsequently converted into the HM-1 two-seat fighter. This turned out to have a very high performance, but it was rejected because of its hybrid construction. During a test flight in autumn 1938 the machine broke up in a dive, and the pilot was only just able to bale out before it struck the ground and was completely destroyed.

This period, 1936 and 1937, saw four European projects for fast special-purpose

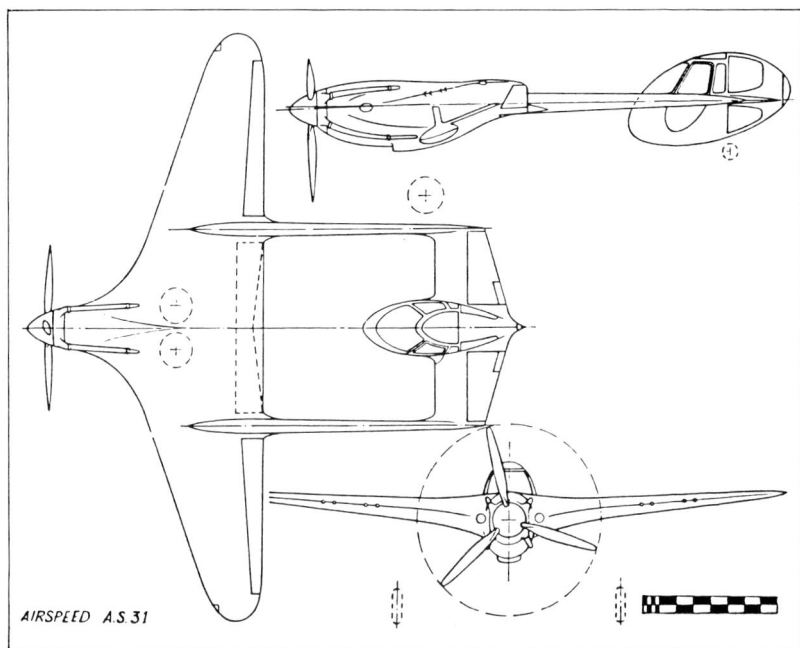

Airspeed A.S.31, 1936.

aircraft which are of great interest because of their exceptionally unconventional design. In Britain, the Airspeed A.S.31 was designed in response to Specification F.35/35, which called for a high-speed fighter. In this single-engined machine the pilot was accommodated in a cockpit mounted on the tailplane, which was carried on twin booms. The company's claimed maximum speed of 725km/h was somewhat optimistic, but in any case the aircraft never left the drawing board.

In Germany Claude Dornier harboured plans for an extraordinarily fast propeller-driven aircraft of equally unconventional form. He had laid the cornerstone of this design in his German State patent No. 728044, dated 3 August 1937. It had tandem engines with one tractor propeller in the nose and one pusher propeller in the tail. This arrangement was a logical development of the ideas Dornier had incorporated in the large Rs IIb flying boat in 1916 — a concept which finally reached maturity in his Wal flying boats. The idea of accommodating the pilot and/or crew between the two engines was new, although this arrangement had featured in a Dornier design for a racing single-seater, intended for the 1927 Schneider Trophy contest. This design eventually saw the light of day two years later in the form of the Italian Savoia-Marchetti S.65. In the new Dornier design the tail propeller was driven by an extension shaft several metres long.

Immediately after this, in December 1937, Dornier produced the DoP 59 design, based on his new patent. The stated object of this special-purpose aircraft was to 'achieve high airspeeds, and permit the study of all related matters'. It was proposed to power the machine with four different variants of the Daimler-Benz DB 601 aircraft engine: two current production engines, each rated at 1,150hp (715km/h at 4,000m altitude); two current record engines producing 1,760hp each (780km/h at ground level); two 2,000hp record engines which had been promised for summer 1938 (815km/h at ground level); and two standard production engines due to be ready in autumn 1938, each producing 1,250hp (755km/h). The single-seat, all-metal low-wing monoplane had an orthodox undercarriage which retracted into the wing, together with a tailwheel in the bottom section of the cruciform tail. The wing had leading-edge slots coupled to the ailerons and flaps, and dive brakes were fitted to the top and bottom of the wing, extending over about half the span. To facilitate take-off and landing, the entire wing could be swivelled down by 14 degrees around the transverse axis passing through the wing leading edge — a principle which was exploited in a similar manner in the Blohm und Voss BV 144 transporter, and later in the American Vought F-8 Crusader jet fighter. But in 1937 the Reichsluftfahrtministerium (RLM, the Reich Air Ministry) presumably considered the project far too advanced, and politely rejected it. Six years later the design was welcomed back, in the form of the Dornier Do 335.

Around 1937 Junkers had also been working on an ultra-fast record-breaking aircraft, but from the outset this was planned to be powered by the jet engine which had been under development at the company, cloaked in the strictest secrecy. The design which evolved, the Rekord-EF, was for a small, single-seat record and experimental aircraft, carrying two of these powerplants mounted on long outriggers forward of the wings. This project, too, found no official favour.

In the Soviet Union the designer Sergei Korolev, working at the Moscow Experimental Rocket Institute (*Reaktivny Nauchno-Issledovatelski Institut*), had produced a design project for a high-speed stratospheric rocket aircraft. His low-wing RP-218, weighing 1,600kg, was designed to be carried up to an altitude of 8,000m by a four-engined Tupolev TB-3. After release it was supposed to be capable either of climbing to altitudes of twenty-five to thirty-seven kilometres — even fifty-three kilometres was mentioned — or of reaching speeds up to 850km/h in level flight. The modest power of the three RM-65 rocket engines, producing 30kp thrust each, would hardly have endowed the aircraft with such a performance, but in any case it was not built. Korolev himself was banished to Siberia as part of the Stalin purges, but he was able to continue his work there. In the 1950s his efforts were finally crowned with success in the shape of the large R-7 rocket, the vehicle which carried the Sputnik and Vostok satellites into orbit.

In France, Caudron's design department had also been active, and had decided to continue on the course which had already proved successful. The first result was two examples of the C.560, a development of the C.460 fitted with a

Caudron C.461, 1936.

Caudron C.561, 1936.

twelve-cylinder engine of eight litres capacity. They were followed by two examples of the C.461, designed by the engineer Maurice Devleiger. This was a refined variant of the C.460, in which the cockpit was completely integrated into the fuselage. Following a similar route, one of the two twelve-cylinder C.560 machines was converted into the C.561. In practice these extremely sleek blue racers turned out to be particularly troublesome, and various problems caused the postponement and eventual cancellation of a number of planned record attempts.

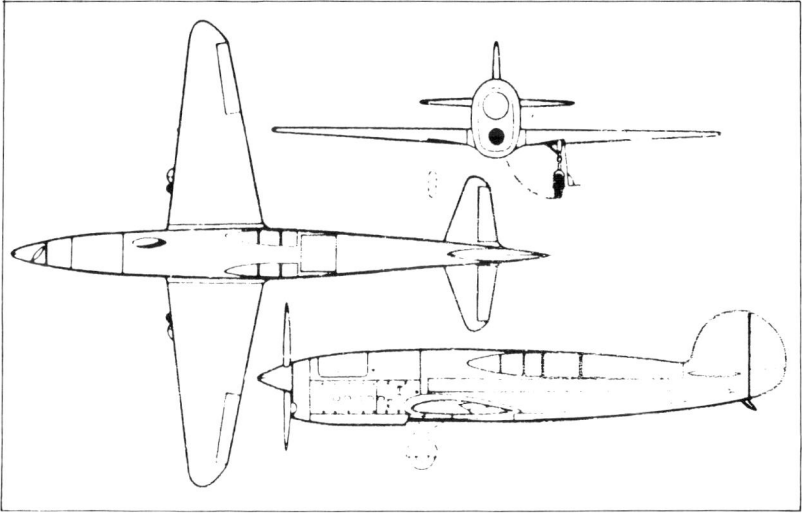

Caudron C.561, 1936.

At the same time Caudron had developed a lightweight single-seat fighter for the Armée de l'Air. This was the C.710 Cyclone single-seat fighter, built on similar principles to the racing aircraft but having a fixed undercarriage, greater wing area, and a larger twelve-cylinder engine. A variant of this design, the C.711, was in fact intended for record attempts, and was displayed at a later Salon de l'Aéronautique, but the project was not followed through because it did not seem certain that the extra margin of speed would be forthcoming. In its place came the C.712, which was an amalgamation of a C.710 fuselage and the wings of the luckless C.561. Its powerplant was a tuned version of the twelve-cylinder engine used for the single-seat fighter. The first record attempts, carried out at Istres in late 1936, were disappointing, as the engine failed to produce the level of power required. Just a few days earlier the French woman pilot Maryse Hilsz had narrowly escaped death when her C.460 disintegrated in the air during an attempt on the women's world speed record; she baled out at the very last second.

The C.712 was then subjected to a series of detail improvements, and the engine brought up to full power. Caudron chief pilot Raymond Delmotte then took off on

Caudron C.712, 1937.

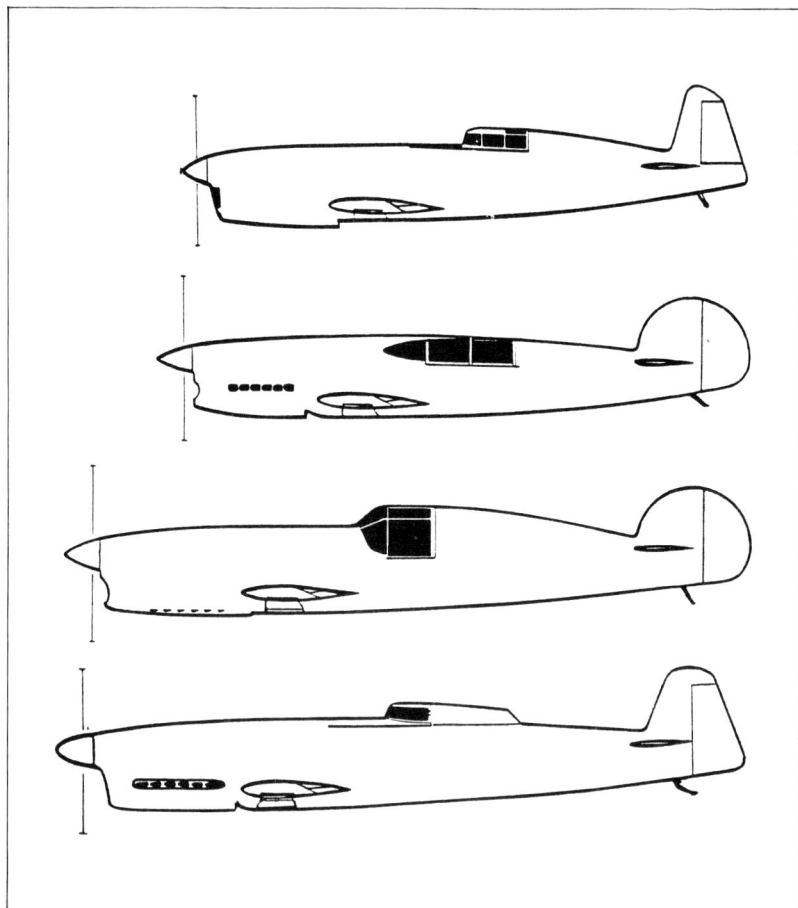

Caudron size comparisons. Top to bottom: C.460, C.561, C.712, C.714R.

29 April 1937 for a further attack on the speed record. After a few test circuits he turned towards the white guideline to begin his first high-speed pass at an altitude of 100m. Suddenly the machine appeared to become unstable, rose up into a steep left-hand turn, and rolled abruptly to the right. Delmotte allowed himself to fall out of the cockpit and pulled the ripcord of his parachute. The aircraft eventually rolled to the left again before striking the ground at a steep angle. The pilot, who suffered only minor injuries, was then handed a piece of the aircraft's empennage by a cyclist. It seems that a stone had been thrown up on take-off and had struck an elevator, which eventually broke off. This accident spelled a temporary end to French record hopes, for now a new record aspirant stepped on to the stage: Germany.

The Fourth Zurich International Flying Meeting, which took place from 23 July to 1 August 1937, gave the German aviation industry the opportunity to display its products to the rest of the world. The show had two stars. One was the Dornier Do 17 V8, a twin-engined bomber, which turned out to be considerably faster than most of the fighters present. Its slim silhouette earned it the nickname 'Flying Pencil'. The other outstanding machine was the single-seat Bf 109 fighter, of

Poster for the Zürich-Dübendorf Flying Meeting, 1937.

which several examples were to be seen. The design was the work of the Bayerische Flugzeugwerke (BFW), and the type monopolised several of the competitions, both individually and collectively. The most significant result was the victory in the climb and dive event of the Bf 109 V13, which was a specially prepared experimental machine, flown by the test pilot Carl Francke from the Luftwaffe test station at Rechlin. He successfully beat off the challenge from nine other pilots from five nations.

The BFW's chief designer, Willy Messerschmitt, until that time known only as a designer of sports and touring aircraft, had designed this advanced single-seat fighter in collaboration with Robert Lusser, the director of the BFW project office. It was based on the Bf 108 Taifun, a four-seat tourer. Early in 1934 the Technical Office of the RLM had released the proposed specification of an all-metal monoplane single-seat fighter. The firms of Arado, Focke-Wulf and Heinkel were approached, and were joined later by BFW, which was considered to be a hopeless outsider in the competition. The respective designs were the Ar 80 low-wing monoplane, the only contestant with a fixed undercarriage; the Fw 159, a strutted high-wing monoplane; the He 112, a low-wing monoplane considered to be the overwhelming favourite; and finally the Bf 109, another cantilever low-wing design. The Ar 80 and Fw 159 were soon eliminated, as expected, but it was some considerable time before the Bf 109 prevailed against the more conservative He 112. Eventually, after a display by the new BFW chief pilot Dr Hermann Wurster in the final comparative flights at Travemünde in autumn 1936, the Bf 109 was selected as the new standard fighter for the Luftwaffe. The design of the Bf 109 was modern, but by no means radical: a light alloy monocoque fuselage, a single-spar wing with automatic slats and split flaps, and a retractable undercarriage; these were all familiar features, but had not previously been combined in one aircraft. An important factor in the Bf 109's favour was its structural simplicity. It would be cheaper to build than its competitor, the He 112, and this was vital, bearing in mind the large-scale production which was planned.

The Bf 109 V13, registration D-IPKY, which had proved so successful in Zurich, was now given a fundamental overhaul at the works and prepared for a serious attack on the world speed record. The engine, a special boosted sprint version of the Daimler-Benz DB 601 twelve-cylinder engine, was now producing around 1,700hp at the higher speed of 2,800rpm. The aeroplane was also cleaned up aerodynamically. A more carefully streamlined canopy was fitted, all slots were taped over — making the use of flaps almost impossible — and the pitot tube was removed. Contradictory information exists concerning the shape of the front section of the fuselage and spinner, and a number of severely retouched photos are in existence. What is certain is that the record machine was polished to a high gloss for the attempt. Early in November 1937 the official three-kilometre record course was set up along the Augsburg-Kaufbeuren railway line.

On 11 November the chief pilot, Dr Wurster, undertook the official record attempt, and it was all over in twenty minutes. Six times he traversed the measured course along the railway embankment; three times in each direction. The four

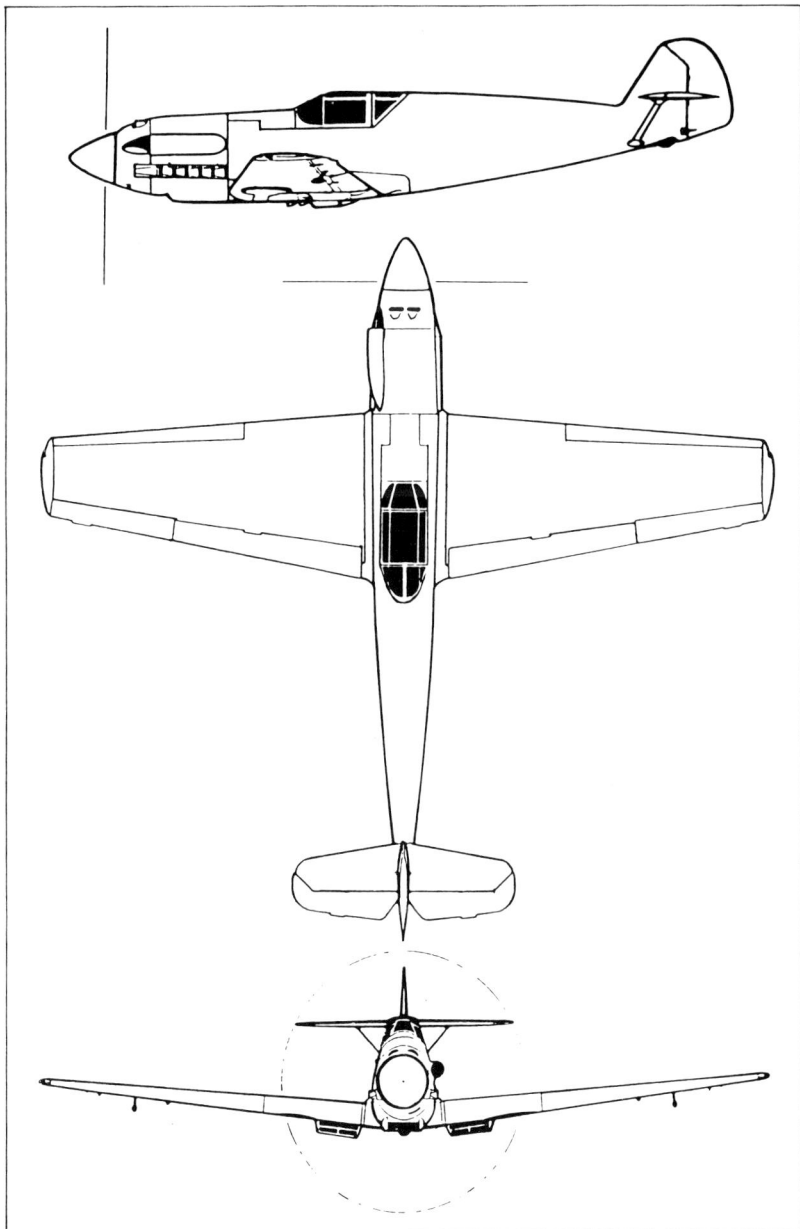

Messerschmitt Bf 109 V13, 1937.

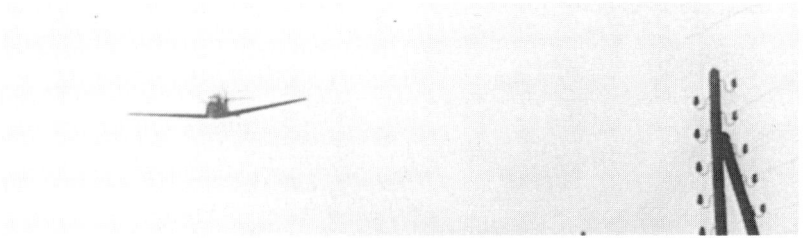

Messerschmitt Bf 109 V13 makes its record flight, 11 November 1937.

fastest contiguous runs produced an average speed of exactly 610.95km/h, almost 44km/h faster than the speed achieved two years before by Howard Hughes. This was Germany's first speed record for land-based aircraft, and the event was celebrated in appropriate style by the media. The *Berliner illustrierte Nachtausgabe* (*Illustrated Berlin Evening Edition*) of 12 November included a report by the pilot, who was in a transport of delight at the achievement. In his opinion: '. . . at high altitude the record machine would easily be capable of speeds around 800

Another view of Bf 109 V13 during its record runs.

kilometres per hour, because of the substantially lower air density' — an extremely optimistic prognosis. For unfathomable reasons the Bf 109 V13 which had achieved this great success was declared officially to be the 'Bf 113', fitted with a DB 600 engine, and even today this ficticious designation still turns up occasionally in lists of records.

In other aviation ministries and design offices around the world the delight in the German successes was understandably less obvious, and work on projects for potential record breakers was duly intensified. In England there was particular annoyance over the fact that a German competitor had stolen the thunder from the new British single-seat fighter, the Supermarine 300 Spitfire, which had been claimed to be the 'fastest fighter in the world'. The successes of the Bf 109 in

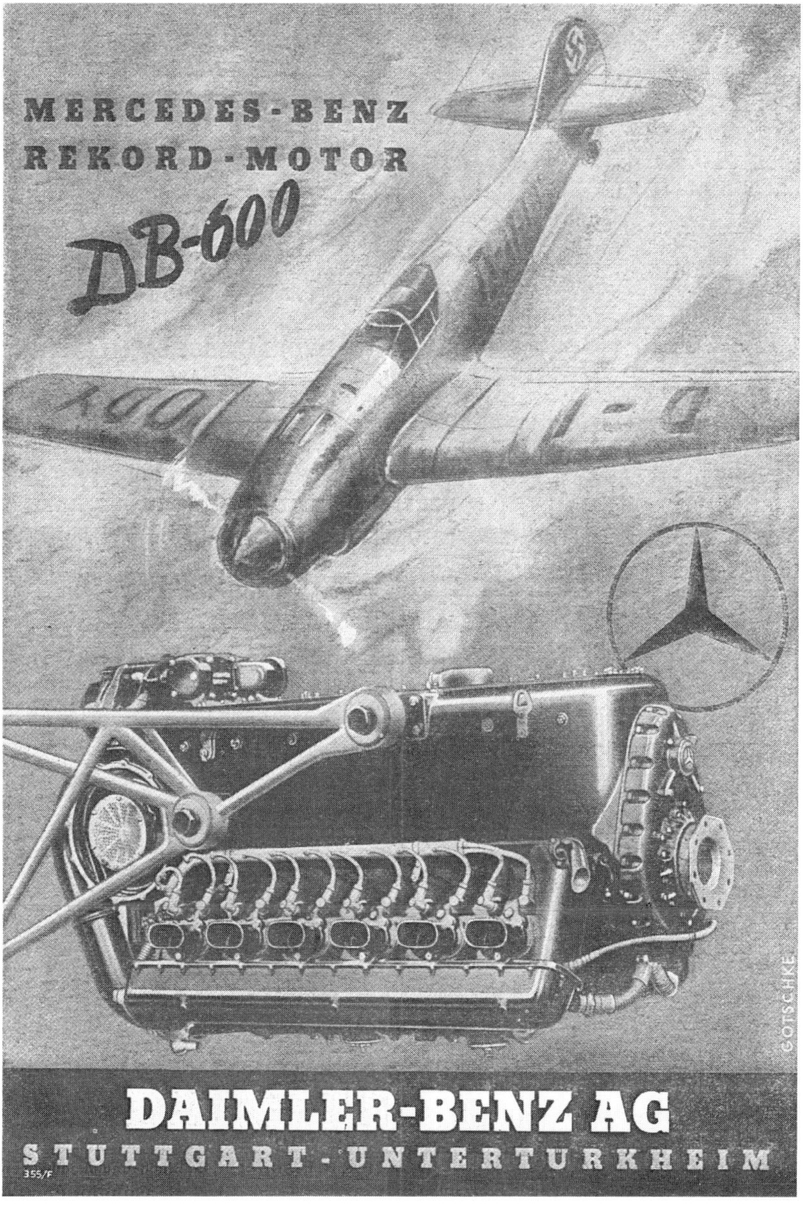

Advertisement for the Daimler Benz DB 600, 1939.

Zurich had already alarmed the British. At Rolls-Royce work began on a racing version of the Spitfire's twelve-cylinder Merlin engine as early as August 1937, and on 7 September a serious discussion took place in the Air Ministry concerning the technical preparations for a record attempt. The record run by the Bf 109 V13 on 11 November 1937 naturally gave this plan even higher priority. Supermarine's chief designer, Joseph Smith, successor to the legendary Reginald Mitchell, who had died shortly before of cancer, was confident of achieving more than 630km/h with a special High Speed Spitfire, fitted with a Merlin which Rolls-Royce promised would produce 2,100hp. This figure would suffice to overhaul the German record of 611km/h. The Spitfire production line was already running, and one airframe was selected to be used for the record attempt, with the designation Supermarine 323. It was decided among other things to shorten the wings and fit a more streamlined canopy. Another Supermarine project of around this time, the twin-engined Type 327 single-seat fighter, was also designed to be very fast. Its planned top speed was 750km/h at an altitude of 6,700m. Development of the type was abandoned, however, after a full-size wooden mockup had been built.

The French were also nettled by the Messerschmitt record, and first thoughts centred on a variant of their most modern single-seat fighter, the Dewoitine D.520, which had just been prepared for series production. The aircraft was to be fitted with smaller wings and a Hispano-Suiza 12Y with its power output raised to

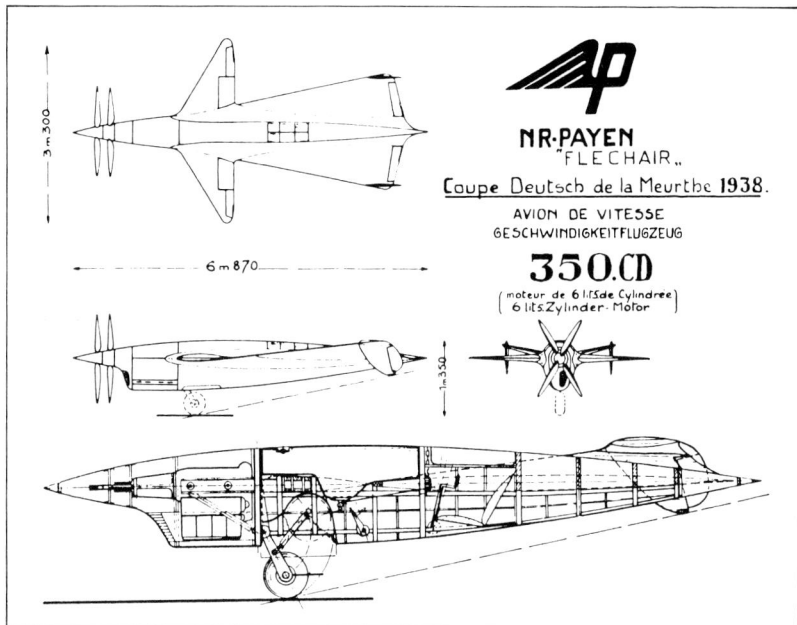

Payen Pa.350 CD, 1938.

1,800hp, the company's intention being that the D.530 speed record machine would be capable of reaching around 624km/h.

Roland Payen, on the other hand, had further refined the tandem-arrow concept which he had first exhibited in 1933 in the form of the unfortunate Pa.100, and had designed a series of futuristic high-speed aircraft, all of which bore the name of Flèchair. His Pa.350.CD, for example, was a single-seater which had been designed initially for the 1938 Coupe Deutsch. A reduced-capacity 6.5-litre engine had been installed, in compliance with the new rules, and contra-rotating propellers had been fitted at the nose. The sweep angle of the leading edge of the forward wing was 33 degrees, and that of the rear delta wing a massive 78 degrees. The intention was that this 'flying arrow' would be fitted with a more powerful engine at a later stage for an attempt on the speed record for land-based aircraft. The Pa.430.CV, however, which was first shown in February 1938, was designed

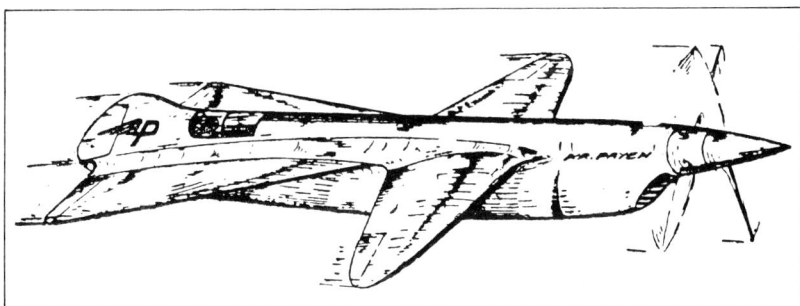

Payen Pa.430 CV, 1938 (twin M-14 engines, 800km/h).

from the outset to wrest back the absolute world speed record for France. Of similar design, but much larger, and fitted with two Gnome et Rhône two-row radial engines, each producing 650hp, this Flèchair was expected to be capable of no less than 800km/h. A fighter-bomber variant, the Pa.400, was also planned.

Finally Ettore Bugatti, the famed creator of fabulous automobiles and engines, had engaged the aircraft designer Louis de Monge to collaborate on the design of a futuristic racing single-seater for the approaching Coupe Deutsch. De Monge had gained a certain fame in the 1920s for his work. The result was the Bugatti 100P, built entirely of wood and powered by two air-cooled Bugatti 3.2-litre engines arranged in line astern in the fuselage. These engines were to drive two contra-rotating tractor propellers. Even the pilot, Maurice Arnoux, had already been selected, and a military variant was also planned, the Bugatti 110P single-seat fighter.

At TSAGI, the Central Aero- and Hydrodynamic Institute in the USSR, the engineer Matus Bisnovat had also begun work on a design for an experimental

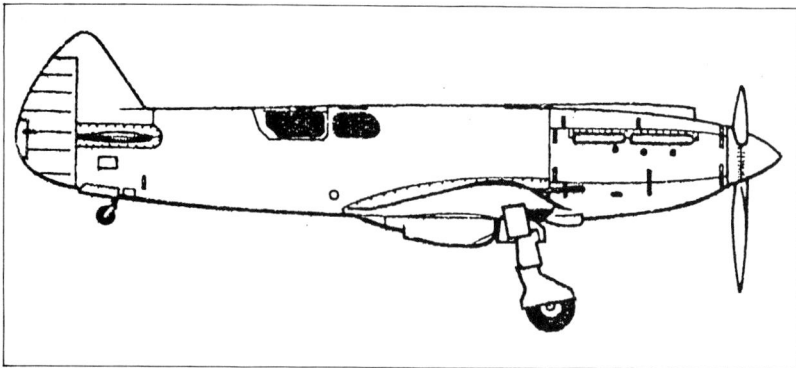

TSAGI SK experimental single-seater, 1940.

all-metal single-seater. This was the SK (*Skorostnoe Krylo*: high-speed wing), which featured a cockpit which could be retracted into the fuselage in flight, reminiscent of the system adopted for the American racer *Time Flies*. Its wings were relatively small, and power was supplied by a twelve-cylinder Klimov M-105 engine rated at more than 1,000hp. This sleek low-wing monoplane was expected to reach very high speeds of up to 680km/h.

In the middle of all these preparations, on 6 June 1938, the news agencies received the astonishing news that the speed record for land-based aircraft had been broken again, and by another German aircraft. In this case the new record had been set over the 100km distance. A modified version of the Heinkel He 112 U single-seat fighter, flown by Maj-Gen Ernst Udet, had recorded an average speed of more than 634km/h on the previous day. There was an uncomfortable feeling throughout the international aviation industry that the Germans had outclassed everyone again. To make matters worse, Ernst Heinkel presented a speech to the Otto Lilienthal Society in Berlin shortly after this achievement, and declared that the He 112 U was just as fast as the current holder of the absolute world record, the Macchi-Castoldi MC.72 seaplane. Since the Heinkel was evidently out of date technically, and clearly inferior to the Bf 109, cynics immediately voiced the inevitable doubts about whether it could possibly have put up such a high performance. After all, only a few pictures were made available, and they appeared to be deliberately unclear. Even so, it was not possible to argue that the record itself was not genuine. Just six months earlier, on 22 November 1937, a different Heinkel machine had established a new international record over 1,000km in a closed circuit, carrying a payload of 1,000kg. The average speed of this bomber, officially designated 'twin-engined combat aircraft, type He 111 U', had been just on 505km/h. There were no pictures, and the mystery grew even deeper when the official FAI announcement referred to the machine as an 'He 606'. In fact, even greater attention would have been paid internationally if it had been known that this mysterious Heinkel machine had a top speed of 620km/h. In any case, the overall result was a degree of uncertainty round the world — an effect which the German government had undoubtedly intended.

Whatever the truth of the matter, the British had to come to terms with the fact that the High Speed Spitfire, which was then under construction, was unlikely to be capable of exceeding this new record by a substantial margin. A further problem then arose when the Merlin IIIM engine specially prepared for this machine failed during a run on the test bench. At this point the decision was taken that the project would proceed, but with a new purpose; general high-speed testing. The aircraft took off on its first flight on 10 November 1938. A series of

Supermarine 323 High Speed Spitfire, 1939.

systematic tests on different propellers and various shapes and types of radiator system were carried out, during which a best speed of 656km/h was recorded in the spring of 1939 at an altitude of about 900m. In July 1939 the silver-blue High Speed Spitfire, bearing the marking N.17, could be admired at the Brussels Aero Salon, albeit minus its belly radiator, and fitted with a three-bladed variable-pitch metal propeller instead of the specially developed high-pitch four-bladed wooden propeller. Testing continued until spring 1940, despite the fact that the war had begun in the meantime. The machine was then fitted with a normal cockpit, a standard Merlin XII and a variable-pitch metal propeller, and allotted to the RAF's Photographic Development Unit. It remained with the unit until June 1946, when it was damaged and subsequently written off. It was scrapped shortly afterwards.

Reactions in France were similar, if less resigned. At Caudron Marcel Riffard had decided to build two further examples of the C.712 as soon as he heard of the Bf 109 V13's record flight. The C.712 had crashed in April that year when the tail surfaces broke up, so the new aircraft were to be fitted with reinforced rear fuelages. The second of these two machines, initially known as the C.712R, was to be fitted with a more powerful Renault engine, and other improvements were to be incorporated. In the summer of 1938, however, when news of the Heinkel record reached France, work on the first of the new 712 machines was halted so that the design team could concentrate exclusively on the much more refined C.712R, from which a world record speed of some 730km/h was expected. The company had also developed a lightweight fighter, the Caudron C.714, which had been test-flown at about the same time. Since great hopes of international sales were vested in this machine, the designation of the potential record breaker was changed from C.712R to C.714R, so that the fighter might benefit from the expected world record, even though it bore no similarity to the other machine in terms of design. France was not the only country to indulge in such public relations trickery, as we shall see.

The Dewoitine team came to a similar decision. Work on the D.530 project was halted, and a completely new project took its place; the D.550. Construction of this high-speed machine started in December 1938. It was designed from the outset to be capable of utilising the most powerful in-line engine available at that time. There were also plans for building a military variant, the D.551, and a smaller racing version, the D.590, intended for the 1939 Coupe Deutsch. In fact this event fell through, just as it had in the preceding two years. Roland Payen also suffered from the cancellation, and his new Flèchair designs were not built. The earlier Pa.100 had suffered landing damage in 1933, and parts of it were used to produce a full-size mockup of a single-seat fighter, the Pa.112, working in collaboration with engine specialist Francois Baudot. However, no government construction contract was forthcoming, as the French aviation ministry considered that the predicted maximum speed of 580km/h for the new machine was unrealistic, in view of the low power output of the two Salmson radial engines mounted in the nose, which were rated at only 100hp each. However, official opinions of the predicted performance of the Bugatti Type 100P single-seater were more favourable. At the time this aircraft was under construction in a Paris furniture factory in the Rue Débarcadère, after the decision had been made to install two larger and more powerful Bugatti T-50B eight-cylinder engines. The main difference between the prototype and the suggested 110P fighter version was the size of the wing. In late 1938 the ministry granted a contract worth 6.9 million Francs to build both machines. If either of the aircraft won back the absolute world record and the 100km record for France, the designer was to receive a further 1.8 million Francs.

Other nations still harboured record aspirations. The USSR continued development work on the fast TSAGI SK, but by now this design was considered primarily as an experimental aircraft rather than a record-breaker. Potential record aircraft were also appearing on drawing boards in various other design offices. England's representative was the Napier-Heston Racer, Italy's the CMASA CS.15 and — a surprise participant — Japan was developing the Ken-3. The stimulus behind all these projects had been the two successful German record aircraft from Messerschmitt and Heinkel, the 'Bf 113' and the 'He 112 U'.

To return to the 'He 111 U/606', this had been designed in 1935 by the Heinkel designers Siegfried and Walter Günter, and was first flown in the summer of 1937.

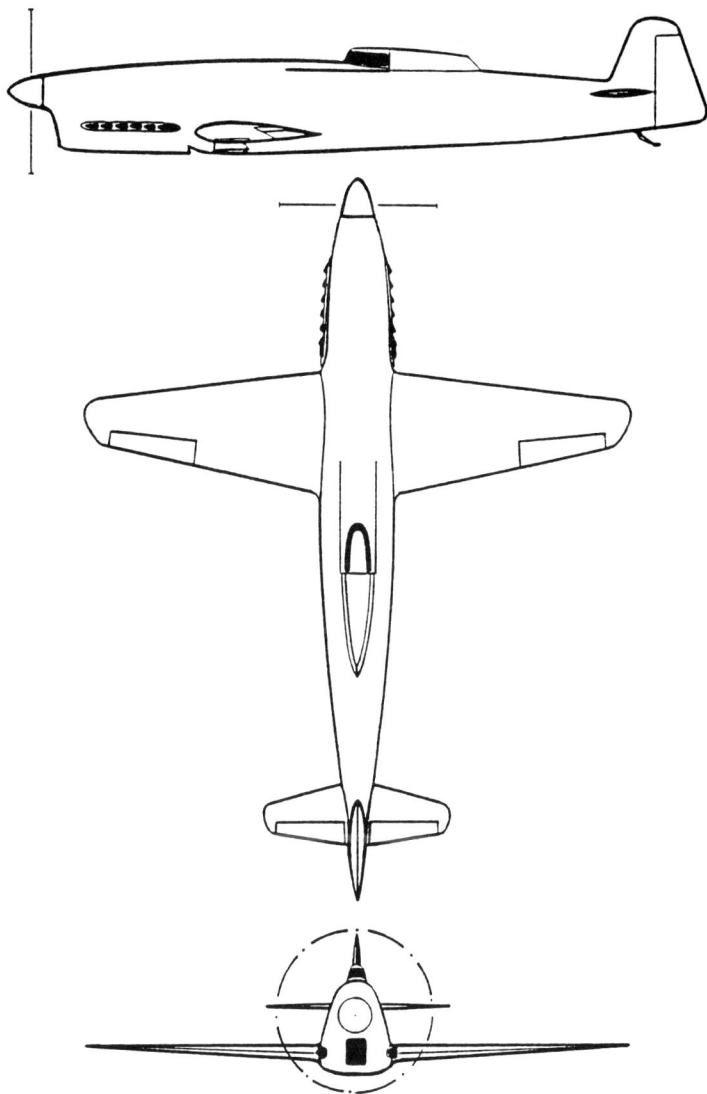

Caudron C. 714R, 1939

Heinkel He 119 V1, 1937.

The He 119, to give its correct designation, was a company project developed by Heinkel without the official sanction of the aviation ministry. It was intended to be an unarmed high-speed bomber and long-distance reconnaissance aircraft, whose superior speed would provide adequate security against enemy interceptors. When the design was presented to the authorities it met with virtually unanimous

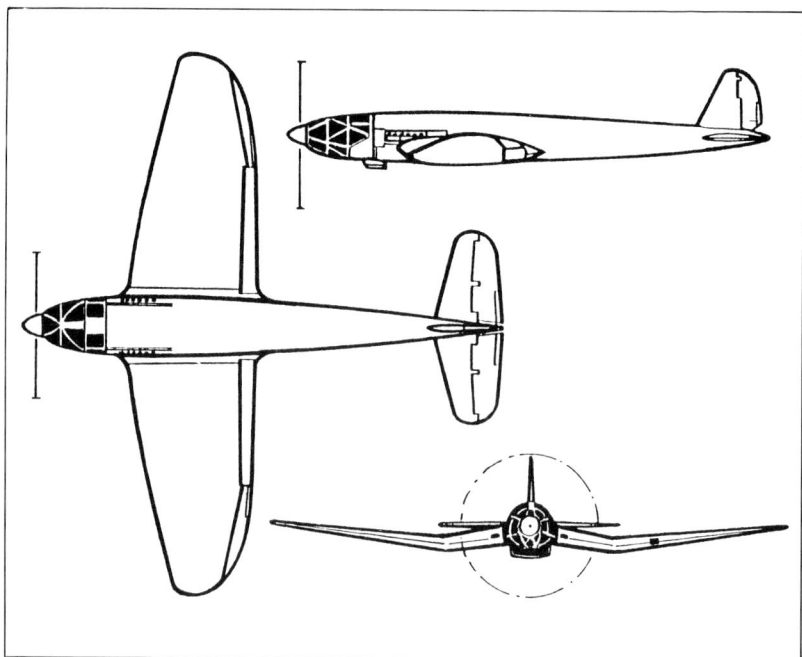

Heinkel He 119 V4, 1937

Daimler-Benz DB 601 aero engine, 1938

rejection, but the concept proved to be thoroughly rational and successful only five years later, in the form of the British de Havilland Mosquito. The Günter-designed, all-metal low-wing monoplane, with its inboard wing panels set at a slight anhedral angle, showed a marked family likeness to the elegant He 70, the 'classic' Günter design dating from 1932, but there was one important difference. It was fitted with two coupled twelve-cylinder DB 601 engines, mounted inside the fuselage forward of the main spar and driving one large four-bladed variable-pitch propeller mounted in the nose via a common gearbox and an extension shaft. Directly behind the propeller was a full-view canopy reminiscent of that used in the He 111. This specially developed Daimler-Benz powerplant, known as the DB 606, produced 2,350hp, but developed such high temperatures that the surface cooling system originally planned for the aircraft proved inadequate, and had to be supplemented by a belly radiator. This was the first indication of a later problem which was to result in catastrophic fires in the He 177 bomber, which had the same engine.

Ernst Heinkel, understandably dismayed by the overshadowing of his He 112 by Messerschmitt's Bf 109, viewed the excellent performance of the He 119 as an ideal opportunity to repair the damage with a few spectacular record flights by the latest Heinkel product. The second prototype, the He 119 V2, which differed from the He 119 V1 mainly in having a semi-retractable belly radiator, recorded a speed of 584km/h at an altitude of 4,500m. Its successor, the He 119 V4 (D-AUTE), was fitted with a completely new wing of different planform, and achieved a speed of 620km/h. Heinkel immediately ordered that it be prepared for an attack on the 1,000km record. Although Messerschmitt had stolen Heinkel's thunder on 11 November 1937, when the Bf 109 V13 broke the three-kilometre record, the record attempt took place as planned on 22 November. The course of the flight was from Hamburg to Stolp in Pommerania and back. Dense cloud cover over Stolp prevented the pilots, Gerhard Nitschke and Hans Dieterle, from recognising the turning point at their optimum cruising altitude of 4,000m. They were forced to descend to 800m, and this substantially reduced their average speed.

Heinkel He 100 V2, 1938.

Nevertheless, the 505km/h they achieved was enough to break the record, even if it only stood for one week. The record was broken again with a new average of 525km/h set by the first prototype of the Breda Ba 88, a high-speed, twin-engined Italian bomber. Heinkel, convinced of the potential of his new design, immediately declared a further record attempt. The flight started with great promise, and the initial average was around 590km/h. Then misfortune struck; a change of fuel tank failed, and the pilots had to make a forced landing at Travemünde aerodrome, which was closed for drainage work. The machine was totally wrecked, and both pilots were injured; Nitschke seriously, Dieterle lightly.

Heinkel already had a new card up his sleeve. The He 112B and C variants of the ill-starred single-seat fighter still failed to make any official impact, in spite of further modifications and improvements, but by October 1937 Siegfried Günter had decided to recalculate project 1035, which his brother Walter had initiated in 1936 (Walter had been killed in a car accident in May 1937), and present it to Ernst Heinkel. The new Heinkel aircraft was an extremely sleek low-wing monoplane with low-drag surface cooling, supplemented on take-off and climb-out by a retractable belly radiator — exactly the system adopted in the fast He 119. It seems that official approval to develop and build ten prototypes and three zero-series machines was granted shortly afterwards by the former aerobatics pilot and new head of the Luftwaffe Technical Office, Maj-Gen Ernst Udet. However, as is the case with many aspects of the He 100 affair, there is contradictory evidence on this point. The detail design was then undertaken by the Heinkel design office under the direction of Karl Schwärzler. At Ernst Heinkel's request, the impressive RLM type number 100 was made available to him for this machine. The number had originally been granted to another company, but it had not been used. Until this time elliptical wings had been the trademark of Günter designs, and this planform had even been adopted by the Supermarine designer Mitchell for his famous

Spitfire, an aircraft which was sometimes termed the 'three-quarters version' of the He 70. However, for the new He 100 Siegfried Günter decided on a trapezoid wing with a straight leading edge, which was much easier to make. In an effort to achieve extra-smooth surfaces, a new method of riveting was adopted. The first prototype, the He 100 V1 (D-ISVR), was completed within three months, an amazing feat for an aircraft of this type, and first flew on 22 January 1938. There were constant problems with the surface cooling, not least with the twenty-two small electric pumps which were used to feed the cooled water back to the engine.

Hans Dieterle prepares to take off in the Heinkel He 100 V1, 1938.

There were twenty-two small warning lamps on the instrument panel — one for each pump. Because of these problems, the He 100 V2 (D-IUOS), which was completed in the spring of 1938, was fitted with a thicker wing skin and also a larger, more angular fin. Power for the first two V-aircraft was provided by Daimler-Benz DB 601A fuel-injection engines which gave 1,100hp at take-off. Once it had been fitted with a slightly more powerful engine and a few other improvements, the first aircraft was designated the He 100 V1/U.

The He 100 V3 (D-ISVR), which was being built at the same time — albeit with a somewhat different purpose — was designed from the outset for an attack on the world speed record; an ambition which Ernst Heinkel had long harboured. It was now redesignated the He 100 V3/UR, and fitted with new wings of greatly reduced

Heinkel He 100 V3, 1938.

span (7.60m instead of 9.42m) and area, a more streamlined canopy, and a racing engine prepared specially by Daimler-Benz, producing almost 2,000hp. It was also given the new registration D-IDGH. The original registration, D-ISVR, was transferred back to the He 100 V1 — a somewhat confusing procedure. Completion of this special machine was delayed, so in the meantime Heinkel decided to carry out an attempt on the 100km closed-circuit record, using the He 100 V2, which was also fitted with a tuned DB 601 for the purpose. (Some sources, however, state that the aircraft was fitted with a standard production DB 601A, No 60008.) The flight was to be undertaken at the most favourable altitude of 4,500m, over a 50km course laid out between the aerodrome of Wustrow and the Baltic Sea spa of Müritz. To maximise the propaganda effect, the wily old fox Ernst Heinkel asked Udet to pilot the aircraft, and chose Whit Monday, 6 June 1938, as the date of the record attempt. Udet covered the course in exactly 9 minutes 27.4 seconds, which equated to a speed of more than 634km/h, exactly 80km/h faster than the previous 100km record, which had been set by the Italian Breda Ba 88 in December 1937 during its 1,000km record flight. After he had landed, Udet mentioned that lights had been glowing continuously in the cockpit. They had bothered him, but he had decided to ignore them. The Heinkel technicians turned pale. They were engine temperature warning lamps, and the pistons could have disintegrated at any moment. The record-breaking machine was officially described as the He 112 U, U standing for Udet. The reasons for this deception are not clear, although it is possible that the intention was to enhance the export sales potential of the He 112.

In spite of this success the RLM intimated repeatedly to Heinkel that there was no possibility of building the He 100 as second fighter for the Luftwaffe, because all the available workforces were to be concentrated on producing the Bf 109 as the standard fighter. Instead, Heinkel was ordered to specialise in building bombers, which did not suit him at all, as he considered himself to be an out-and-out specialist in high speed flight. To make matters worse, the Focke-Wulf company,

Autographed caricature by Ernst Udet, commemorating the record flight, dated 5 June 1938.

which was developing a reputation for progressive thinking, was awarded a contract by the Technical Office to develop a successor to the Bf 109. This was to be powered by an air-cooled two-row radial engine, and eventually emerged as the Fw 190. It seems that the chief designer at Focke-Wulf, Kurt Tank, was favoured with significantly better connections inside the RLM, although he had met with little enthusiasm there for his previous project, an extremely fast twin-engined single-seat fighter. A half-hearted contract for three experimental units had then been awarded, but it provided for the installation of relatively low-power Jumo 210 engines instead of the suggested DB 600 units. Even so, the first prototype, the Fw 187 V1, attained the impressive speed of 525km/h in the spring of 1937. It was not until two years later, in January 1939, that an aircraft equipped with two DB 600 A engines, albeit with a troublesome surface-cooling system, was able to show what it could do. The two-seat Fw 187 V6 recorded 635km/h at ground level. However, further suggestions for variants with even more powerful engines, such as the DB 605 or BMW 801, found no favour. Only nine prototypes were built.

In spite of these setbacks Ernst Heinkel did not cease promoting his company's products. In autumn 1938 the He 100 V4 had been completed. This was the first example of what was known as the B-series, which incorporated a number of constructional improvements. Although it proved capable of attaining peak speeds of about 670km/h at moderate altitudes, the surface-cooling system adopted by Heinkel still proved troublesome. In this system the cooling water, heated to 110 to 130 degrees centigrade under pressure, was passed into the hermetically-sealed, riveted wing, where it turned into steam. The vapour condensed again owing to the influence of the airstream, and was then fed back to the engine by means of the small electric pumps already mentioned. At about this time the He 100 V3/UR was completed, and initial test flights were carried out in August 1938 with Hans Dieterle at the controls. By early September the chief pilot, Gerhard Nitschke, had recovered from his injuries, and he had been selected to make the record attempt. He took off for the final test flight, with the record attempt due to be flown immediately afterwards, but one wheel became stuck during retraction and the mechanism jammed. There was no possibility of landing the highly-tuned record machine on a single leg, so Nitschke had to bale out, and struck the tail in so doing. Nitschke was injured again, and the valuable aircraft was a total loss, bursting into flames on impact.

Heinkel still did not abandon hope, and prepared a further prototype, the He 100 V8, for a renewed record attempt. Just to complicate matters, this aircraft was given the registration D-IDGH from the 'dismantled' V3, though it differed from the latter in certain details. For example, it had a longer, lower canopy and a slightly lower-set tailplane. The oil cooling system was fitted with a new type of heat exchanger, which worked in a similar manner to the surface-cooling system

Heinkel He 100 V8 world speed record aircraft, 1939.

for the engine coolant, but in this case methyl alcohol was the cooling agent and the tail surfaces were the cooling surfaces. The new Daimler-Benz V record engine was finally available, and was rated at up to 2,770hp for short periods, but at the cost of an overall engine life of just half an hour.

Finished in late February 1939, the V8, complete with its crew of twenty-five men, was transferred from Rostock to the Heinkel subsidiary at Oranienburg near Berlin, to take advantage of the more favourable flying conditions there. Hans Dieterle had been selected as pilot for this attempt. The official three-kilometre course was again set up along a railway line, and in mid-March 1939 Dieterle took off for the first record attempt. He was forced to abandon the flight soon after it started, when the fuel pump failed to deliver enough power. A second attempt also failed after two successful passes, this time because of excessive oil temperature. The third attempt, on 30 March 1939, finally met with success. Four perfect passes, followed by a smooth landing, gave a total flying time of 13 minutes, and the new world's record was in the bag: 746.606km/h; Hans Dieterle was the fastest

Heinkel advertisement, 1939.

man in the world. However, as far as the fastest aircraft in the world was concerned, the secrecy and mystery beloved of the RLM remained unchanged. Once again no detailed photographs of the record aircraft were published, and it was described officially as a development of the previous year's He 112 U, powered by a DB 601 rated at 1,175hp.

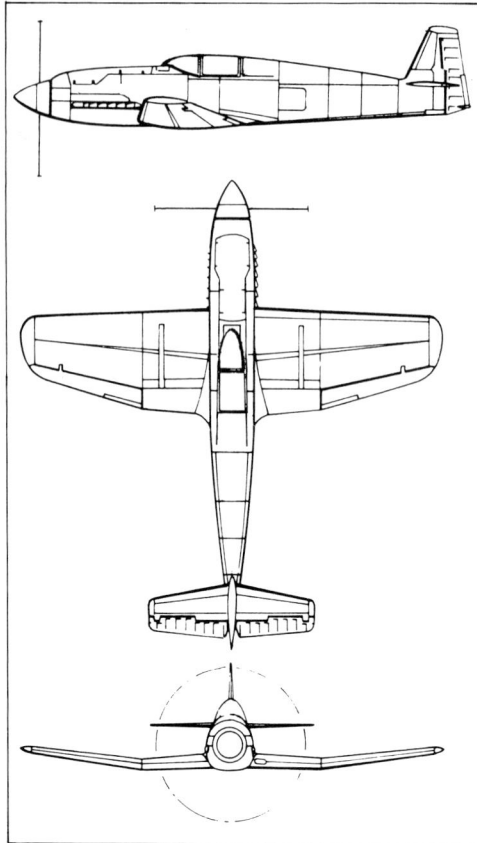

Heinkel He 100 V8, 1939.

Eventually a short film clip was released. Intended for the internationally distributed Pathé Gazette, it showed the He 100 V5, claimed as the world record aircraft He 112 U, complete with strange antenna mast and the curious registration HE+BE.

The engine was indeed a DB 601, but it was by no means the standard 1,175hp DB 601Aa. For several years Daimler-Benz had created specially prepared individual versions of the fuel-injection twelve-cylinder DB 601 engine for record purposes, following the racing traditions of the company. These units featured racing plugs, superchargers, and other non-standard features. They burned special fuel, and could produce peak power outputs at very low altitude and at increased revolutions for brief periods. The 1937 record engine II was rated at 1,660hp at 2,650rpm, the following year's record engine IV produced 2,060hp at 2,980rpm.

and the output of the 1939 record engine V had been raised to 2,770hp at 3,100rpm. Of course, these were test bench outputs, and they were never achieved in practice, even for record attempts. For this reason it is not surprising that power outputs for one and the same engine, as quoted by various sources, often vary considerably. Daimler-Benz built three examples of the record engine V, of which one (DB 601/60021) was used principally for stationary testing. The second (DB 601/M 159) was used in the He 100 V8, and the third (DB 601/V10) was destined for a different world record aircraft: the Messerschmitt Me 209.

Like Ernst Heinkel, Willy Messerschmitt was fully aware of the promotional influence of world records, quite apart from the technical challenges. After the success of his specially prepared single-seat fighter, the Bf 109 V13, on 11 November 1937, Messerschmitt presented a lecture to the German Academy for Aviation Research on 26 November entitled 'The problems of high-speed flight', in which he expressed the following view: 'We need pure experimental aircraft, in the development of which the designer must be completely unfettered; he must not be bound by restrictions, by considerations regarding available tools and equipment, by regulations and preconceptions, by the need for a practical application of the experimental aircraft to an end-user'. Thus it was that Project 1059, launched under Dip-Iing Robert Lusser as Director of the Project Office, was to be a 'motor with a pilot'; a single-seat aircraft which would be as small as possible, and would have one purpose only — to fly as fast as possible. The cockpit of this squat low-wing monoplane was set well aft. The main undercarriage legs retracted inwards, in contrast to those of the Bf 109. The fin extended down below the fuselage, and supported the non-retractable tailskid. Like its competitor, the He 100, the new Messerschmitt was fitted with a low-drag cooling system based on surface and condensation cooling. Soon, however, in response to technical and overheating problems, the designers abandoned the principle of returning the cooling water to the engine after it had been inadequately cooled inside the wings, and instead allowed it simply to fall out of the aircraft at a rate of half a litre per second. This modification necessitated a doubling of the cooling-water tank capacity, from an initial 220 litres to 450 litres. Messerschmitt adopted a conventional oil cooling system, which took the form of an annular radiator located immediately behind the spinner.

This experimental single-seater was allotted the RLM type number 209, and four examples were built, bearing the works numbers 1185 to 1188. Their registrations were D-INJR, D-IWAH, D-IVFP and D-IRND. The Me 209 V1 was flown for the first time on 1 August 1938, and the Me 209 V2 on 8 February 1939. In both cases Dr Wurster was the pilot, but further flight testing was entrusted to the young test pilot Fritz Wendel. In terms of external appearance, the Messerschmitt design had none of the elegance of its Heinkel counterpart, and its flight characteristics left even more to be desired. The fin and wing centre section were soon increased in size, but little improvement was apparent. 'Flying sow's tooth' was one of the milder epithets which pilots bestowed on the machine. The V-series machines were initially fitted with the standard version of the DB

601, rated at 1,175hp. The Me 209 V3, which was still under construction, was selected for the attempt on the world record, which was set for July 1939.

When Heinkel succeeded in breaking the world record on 30 March 1939 with the He 100 V8, he took the Messerschmitt team completely by surprise. Messerschmitt was furious, and ordered the Me 209 V1 to be prepared without delay for his counterattack on the record, by installing the unique and precious DB 601 record engine. Flight testing of the remaining Me 209 V2 was now intensified,

Dr Wurster with the Messerschmitt Me 209 V1 world speed record aircraft.

but a failed piston caused an emergency landing at the works aerodrome, and the machine was so badly damaged that it had to be written off, although the pilot, Fritz Wendel, fortunately escaped without major injury. Even so, it proved possible to move the world record flight forward to mid-April 1939, instead of the originally planned July date. The record course which had been laid out along the Augsburg-Kaufbeuren railway line in November 1937 was prepared for use again. As this course was 450m higher than the more northerly site used by Heinkel, the Messerschmitt team calculated that there was a distinct, if extremely slight, chance of exceeding the 746.6km/h mark set by the He 100 V8 by the one per cent margin required by the FAI regulations because of the slightly thinner air. If the record was to gain official recognition, Fritz Wendel had to achieve an average speed of at least 754.1km/h in the Me 209 V1. Although the Messerschmitt, in its dark blue finish, was completed in the second half of April, the team was dogged by delays. First there were several days of continuous rain. Then a series of technical problems cropped up. For example, on one high-speed test flight along the railway line, a train travelling in the opposite direction created a pressure wave which caused part of the cowling to come adrift. Then there were difficulties with inadequate motor cooling and the aileron attachments. Finally, on 26 April 1939, Wendel completed the requisite four passes at 782, 734, 778 and 728km/h, which

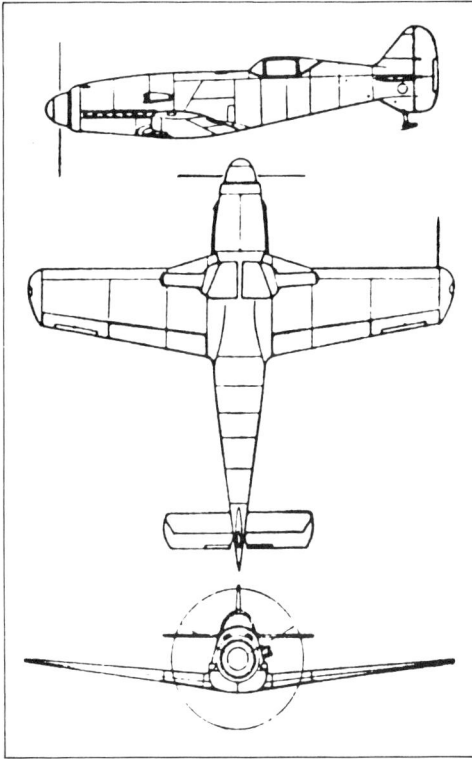

Messerschmitt Me 209 V1.

The Messerschmitt Me 209 V1 makes its record-breaking flight, 1939.

gave an average speed of exactly 755.138km/h — just above the required one per cent margin. A new world record had been claimed for Germany, the second within four weeks, and using an entirely different aircraft. Fritz Wendel, the successful pilot, was promoted to Flugkapitän on the strength of his achievement,

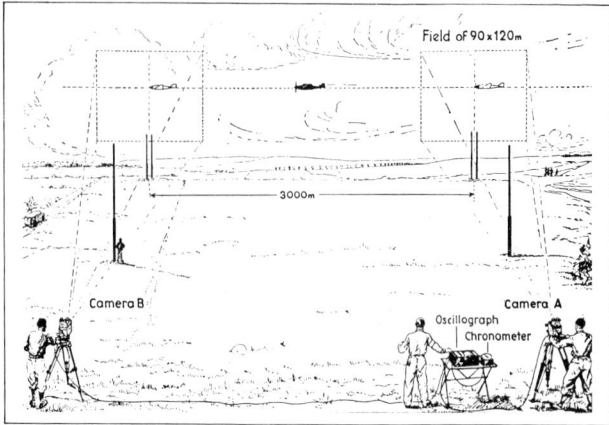

Arrangement of measuring apparatus to determine the absolute world speed record in 1939.

Willy Messerschmitt congratulates Fritz Wendel.

like Hans Dieterle before him. As for the aircraft, once again the Third Reich's propaganda machine chugged into life. The machine was described as the 'Me 109R' fighter, just a variant of the standard Bf 109 Luftwaffe fighter; there was not even a clear photograph.

Now it was Heinkel's turn to rage. He was certain that the difference in altitude of 450m, plus a few small modifications, would make his He 100 V8 about 25km/h faster — around 770km/h — and he decided to repeat the record attempt in south Germany. However, Udet and the RLM made it perfectly clear to Ernst Heinkel that the authorities would by no means be pleased if a fighter which was not in series production should better the performance of the Luftwaffe's standard fighter. In fact, only about two dozen examples of the He 100 were built. In the spring of 1940 six of them were shipped to the Soviet Union, with which Germany still maintained friendly relations. Three pre-production machines (He 100D-0) were shipped to Japan, under the designation He 113, for 1.2 million Reichsmarks, plus 1.6 million Reichsmarks for the licence to build the machines. In neither case did the aircraft go into production. About twelve 'production' He 100D-1 fighters were built. They were given highly imaginative squadron markings and publicised by the German propaganda service in spring 1940 as 'the new He 113 fighter'. In reality they were used only as a form of defence for the Heinkel works, and never fired a single shot. The fuselage of the He 100 V10 was subsequently fitted with the short wings and shallow canopy of the He 100 V8 and put on show in the Deutsches Museum in Munich as the 'He 112U', where it was later destroyed in an air raid.

The few examples of the Me 209 were even less successful. The Me 209 V3, with which it had been planned to attack the 1,000km record, flew for the first time on 26 April 1939, but the Second World War, which began on 1 September 1939, put an end to all record-breaking activities. The Me 209 V4, completed in May 1939, was intended to serve as the starting point for a high-speed single-seat fighter, but in spite of numerous modifications it proved to be entirely unsuitable. The considerably redesigned Me 209 V5 and V6 prototypes were not successful. The Me 209 V1 record breaker was transferred to the aviation museum at Berlin-Moabit at the start of the war. At the end of the war the fuselage, devoid of

Dewoitine D.550-01, 1939.

engine and wings but complete with the remnants of the tail surfaces, turned up again, and is now on show in the Polish Aviation Museum in Krakow.

In spite of, or perhaps because of, the indisputable German successes, by the early summer of 1939 progress had also been made in the development of high-speed aircraft in the design offices of other nations, although the results had been less spectacular. In France construction of the Dewoitine D.550 had begun only in December 1938, but after only six months it was complete. It was flown for the first time on 23 June 1939 by the Dewoitine pilot Marcel Doret. Because of the German record flights, the original target speed of 650km/h no longer applied, but even so the Dewoitine team was not prepared to give up the fight so easily, and work continued even after the outbreak of war. The machine was fitted with a 1,000hp Hispano-Suiza 12Y51 engine in place of the original 900hp 12Y51, and Doret reached a speed of more than 702km/h, albeit at an altitude of 6,000m. The final version of the type HS 12Z engine had already proved capable of 1,200hp on the test bench, and it was confidently predicted that this figure could be increased to 1,300 or 1,400hp in the foreseeable future, at around 2,600 to 2,800rpm. But this engine was never installed in the D.550, and modifications to the radiators and air inlets failed to produce the expected performance increase. The war ensured that the D.550-01 made its last flight on 27 May 1940 at Toulouse. The first flight of the D.551-01, the prototype of the military variant of the record contender, was due to take place that same month, but once again nothing came of it. A similar fate befell the planned developments, the D.552, D.553, D.554 and D.555. Nevertheless, twelve pre-production D.551s were completed. In August 1940 the company expressed a wish to test-fly two of these as unarmed 'D.560 sports aircraft', but the German disarmament commission, which by that time was the regulatory authority in France, refused permission, for obvious reasons.

At Caudron the engineer Georges Otfinovsky had been instructed by Marcel Riffard to press on with the construction of the highly refined C.714R. The characteristic lines of the Caudron racing aircraft were largely retained, with just a few detail modifications aimed at further reducing drag. The airframe of this

Caudron C.714R of 1939 in the Musée de l'Air, Paris.

low-wing monoplane consisted of a magnesium framework skinned with plywood, and power was supplied by the newly developed 900hp Renault 12R Spécial twelve-cylinder engine, fitted with a Ratier three-bladed adjustable-pitch propeller. The fin outline was now trapezoidal, and the extremely narrow canopy was cut off vertically at the rear. As on previous Caudron machines, the tailskid was not retractable. In late August 1939 the aircraft was complete, and stood ready to be transported to Istres for flight testing, but the plan was thwarted by the outbreak of war. Instead the small, rakish single-seater was destined to spend the next five years hidden in the cellar of a house at No 53 Avenue des Champs Elysées, directly under the Renault Exhibition Hall, which was on the ground floor. Today the blue-black C.714R forms one of the most interesting exhibits in the Musée de l'Air at Le Bourget. The predicted top speed of 730km/h (795km/h was mentioned as a possibility) was never realised.

Construction work on the third of the French world speed record candidates, the single-seat Bugatti 100P, continued after the start of the war. Louis de Monge had adopted a series of new solutions to old problems in the design of this all-wood

Bugatti 100P, 1940.

monoplane. For example, the cooling air for the two eight-cylinder Bugatti T-50B in-line engines, which were arranged in staggered line astern in the centre of the fuselage, entered through apertures in the leading edge of the machine's butterfly tail, was deflected forward to the radiators in the rear fuselage, and escaped through the fuselage sides at the rear of the wing root. The forward engine was located on the starboard side of the fuselage, immediately aft of the pilot's seat, and

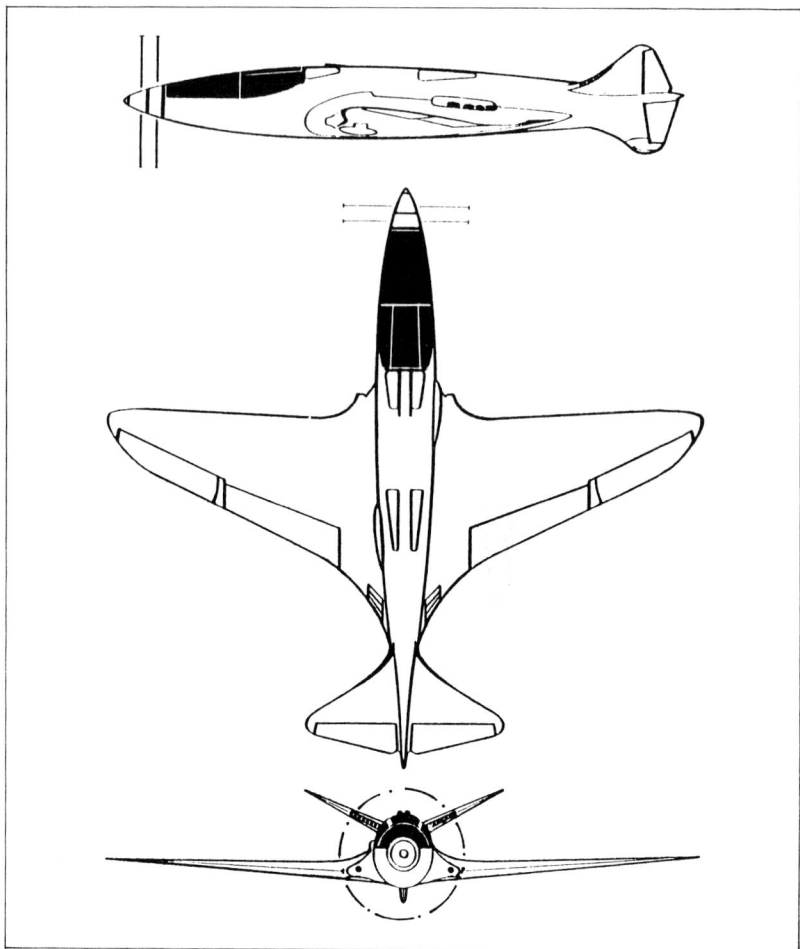

Bugatti 100P, 1940.

drove the rear of the two contra-rotating Ratier two-bladed tractor propellers via an extension shaft, passing the pilot on his right-hand side. The front propeller was powered by the rear engine, which was mounted at a slight angle to the fuselage centreline, via a second extension shaft running to the left of the pilot. Another unique feature was the flap design, which was protected by patents, as were the other special design features of the machine. By the summer of 1940 the slim single-seater was almost finished, but at this point it had to be shipped away on a lorry, fuselage and wings separately, before the German troops marched into Paris.

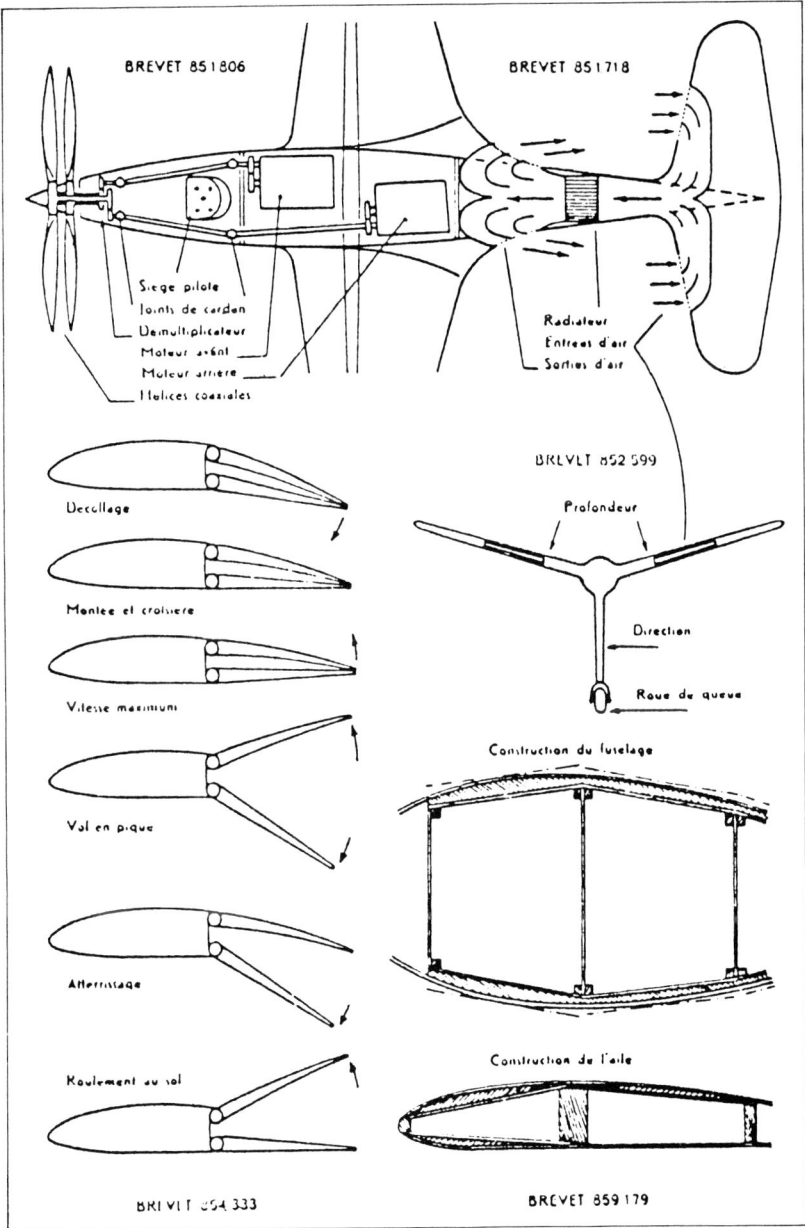

Bugatti 100P design details.

For thirty years it lay concealed in a barn in the grounds of the Chateau d'Ermenonville, north-east of Paris. Then an American Bugatti restorer from Detroit discovered the hidden treasure, shipped it to the USA, and removed the engines from the fuselage. The rest held little interest for him. Another Bugatti enthusiast rescued the now empty airframe and had it restored in Connecticut. As in the case of the Caudron C.714R, one can only guess whether the planned speed of 830km/h would have been attained. The planned Bugatti 110P was never produced.

As far as the record ambitions of the British were concerned, the decision to abandon the High Speed Spitfire as a potential record-breaker may have been eased somewhat by the knowledge that there was another, possibly better iron in the fire. At the Napier engine works an extremely promising twenty-four-cylinder H-type aircraft engine, the Sabre, was under development, and this engine sparked off the idea of building an aircraft for the dual purpose of testing the engine and breaking world records. In the autumn of 1938 the works designer, Arthur Hagg, was commissioned to produce an overall design, and the small Heston Aircraft Company was entrusted with the detail design and the construction of two aircraft. The costs of the undertaking were to be borne by the

Heston Type 5 Racer, 1940.

industrialist Lord Nuffield. In the course of 1939, under the direction of Heston chief designer George Cornwall and Napier 'advisor' Hagg, the Heston Type 5 came into being. It was a small, purposeful low-wing monoplane almost entirely of wooden construction. Only the control surfaces were of light alloy, fabric-covered. A wide-track retractable undercarriage was fitted. The cockpit, covered with a small clear-view canopy, was located roughly in the centre of the squat fuselage, the underside of which housed the inlet of a large tunnel radiator. The radiator outlets were at the tail of the fuselage, on either side of the fin. The engine, rated at more than 2,200hp, drove a large, adjustable-pitch, three-bladed metal propeller

Heston Type 5 Racer, 1940.

made by the de Havilland company. The silver machine was, as usual, polished to a high gloss. The new engine presented teething troubles which were difficult to solve at first — rapid overheating, with consequent piston failure — and these problems delayed the completion of the first of the two aircraft, G-AFOK, until the spring of 1940. The first flight, on 12 June 1940, ended after just seven minutes because of engine trouble, and a crash landing ensued. The second machine, G-AFOL, was to be fitted with a more powerful Sabre engine, and was expected to be capable of more than 800km/h, but construction work was halted. England had greater worries in the summer of 1940.

In the Soviet Union, work on the high-speed SK single-seater had also been delayed, which meant that the first flight was postponed until January 1940. Although flight testing progressed extremely satisfactorily, this sophisticated special-purpose machine, with its high wing loading of more than 220kg/m^2, would have been extremely difficult to convert into a robust single-seat fighter, and for this reason the programme was halted at the end of 1940. At this time no fewer than eleven Russian aircraft design teams were engaged on contracts to create modern, relatively simple fighter aircraft, but only the creations of Aleksandr Yakovlev, Semyon Lavochkin and Artem Mikoyan/Mikhail Gurevich were ever produced in quantity. The others did not progress beyond the prototype stage, and some of them never left the drawing board. This was the fate of the interesting SIG design of 1940, a single-engined single-seater with pusher propellers and twin tailbooms.

For some time the Italians had considered the possibility of producing a successor to the legendary Macchi-Castoldi MC.72 seaplane in which Francesco Agello had set the absolute world speed record in 1933, and in which he managed to push it up again to 709km/h in 1934. In 1938 the head of Fiat's aviation

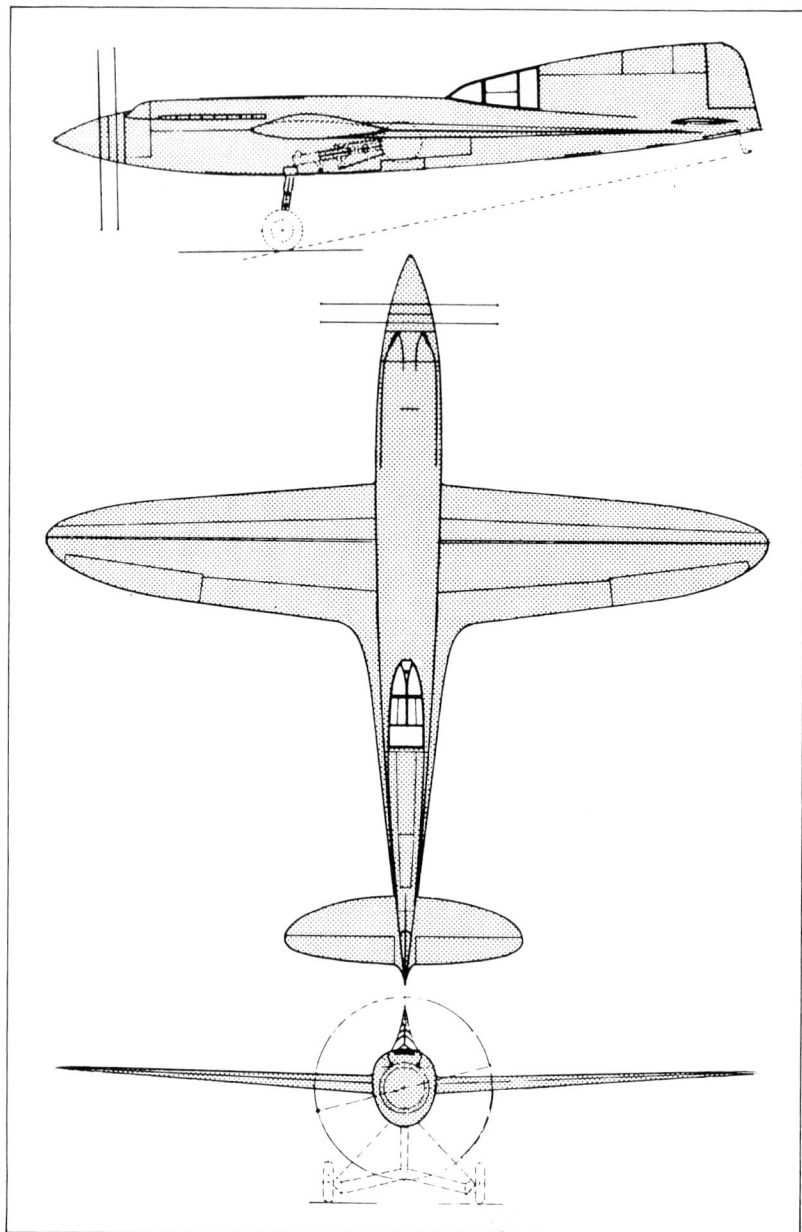

CMASA CS.15, 1940.

department, Umberto Savoia, carried out a feasibility study on this project, commissioned by Fiat president Giovanni Agnelli. It transpired that the two best Fiat aircraft designers, Celestino Rosatelli and Giuseppe Gabrielli, were working at full stretch on other tasks, and so Manlio Stiavelli, the highly talented chief designer of the Fiat subsidiary company Costruzioni Meccaniche Aeronautiche at Marina di Pisa, was awarded the contract. On 10 April 1939, shortly after the success of the Heinkel He 100 V8, Stiavelli presented his CS.15 design (Corsa Stiavelli), an all-metal mid-wing monoplane of low frontal drag, with its cockpit located a long way aft and integrated into the fin. A newly developed Fiat A.S.8 sixteen-cylinder engine rated at 2,250hp was to drive two contra-rotating, two-bladed propellers. The aircraft utilised a low-drag condensation cooling system, in which about 80 per cent of the wing area served as cooling surface. The

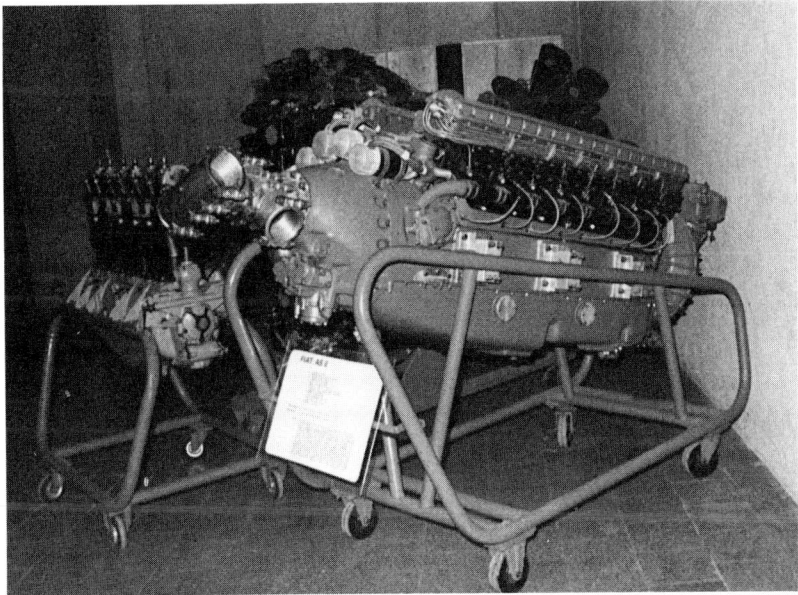

Fiat A.S.8 aero engine in the Museo Storico, Vigna di Valle.

undercarriage consisted of a single central undercarriage leg, with two transverse struts at its bottom end. The wheels were mounted at the outboard ends, and folded back into the slim fuselage on retraction. Windtunnel measurements had indicated a potential maximum speed of 850km/h at sea level. After Italy entered the war, on 10 June 1940, work on the machine continued at half the pace, and after the armistice on 8 September 1943 the project was stopped altogether. Little is known of the fate of the aeroplane, which was almost finished. Only the Fiat

A.S.8 aircraft engine survived, and today it is displayed in the Italian Aviation Museum at Vigna di Valle.

For years the Japanese had been striving to catch up with the West's developments in aviation technology, to the almost complete ignorance of the Western nations. Eventually even the world speed record seemed to lie within their reach, and so, towards the end of 1938, the Japanese air ministry approved a plan for designing a Japanese record-breaker. The contract was awarded to a small team in the Aviation Research Institute of the University of Tokyo, under the direction of Shoruku Wada. By May 1941 a full-size mockup of the Ken-3 was complete; it was an all-metal low-wing monoplane of conventional construction with a liquid-cooled in-line engine. In 1937 the firm of Kawasaki had acquired a licence to build German Daimler-Benz aircraft engines, so the choice of a DB 601A was an

Kawasaki Ken-3 (Ki.78), 1942.

easy one. This engine included the innovatory MW-50 methanol-water injection system, which gave a power increase to 1,550hp for brief periods. Two cooling intakes on either side of the rear fuselage, in conjunction with a small 80hp turbine, served to regulate the heat flow. The wing was of semi-elliptical planform, and utilised a laminar-flow aerofoil and combined Fowler/split flaps. After Japan entered the war, in December 1941, the Japanese army air force took over the project, and Kawasaki continued work on the aircraft under the designation Ki.78, with the intention of developing a superior fighter aircraft.

Only one of the two planned prototypes was built, and it flew for the first time on 26 December 1942. Its flight characteristics, especially at low speed, turned out to be troublesome. Modifications were made, and the second phase of testing

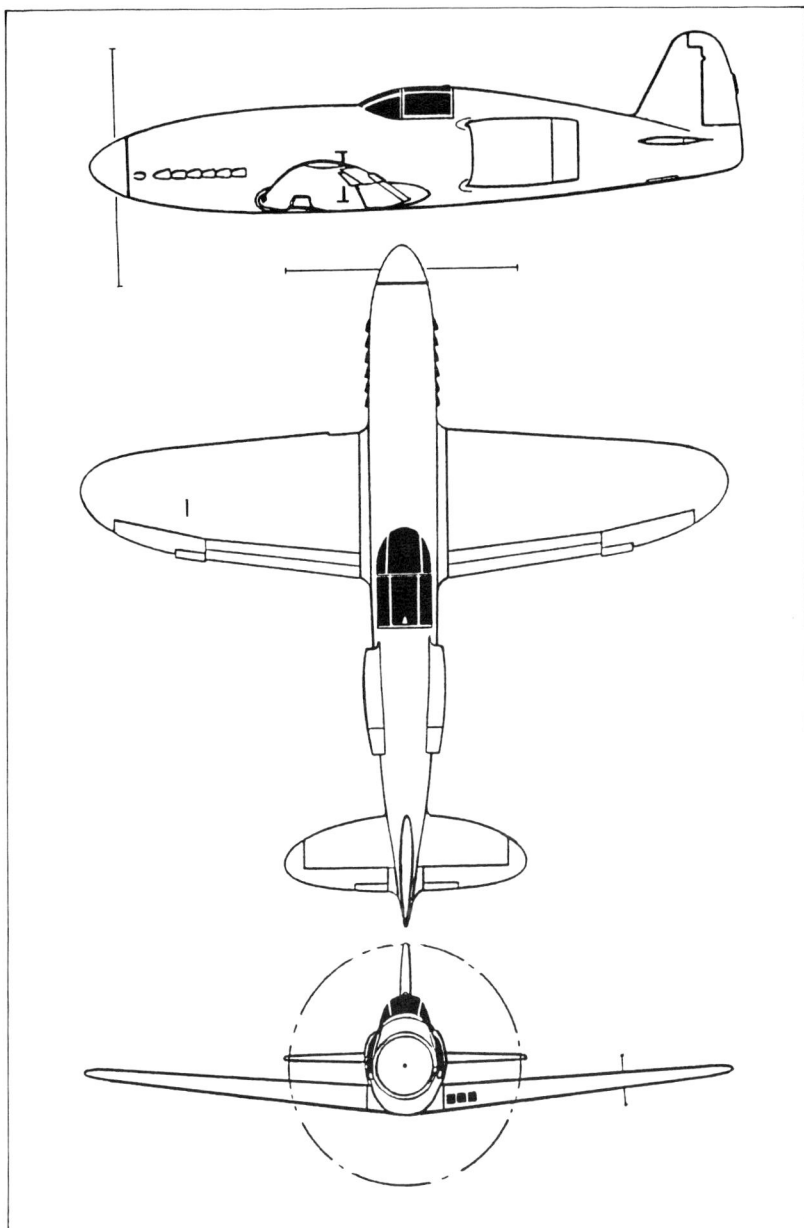

Kawasaki Ken-3 (Ki.78), 1942.

began in the summer of 1943. Test flights continued until 11 January 1944, and on the thirty-first and penultimate flight, on 27 December, a maximum speed of exactly 700km/h was recorded at an altitude of 3,500m, although 850km/h had been expected. The war eventually put a halt to the work.

In the USA the development of modern fighter aircraft had been neglected for all too long in favour of heavy bombers. It was not until 1937 that the US Army Air Corps had issued specification X-608 for a high-altitude fighter, to be powered by the new liquid-cooled, in-line Allison V-1710 engine, which was fitted with exhaust turbochargers to give power at high altitudes. Up to this point literally all American military aircraft had been fitted with bulky radial engines, and many of them retained them for the next ten years. The winning design in response to the specification came from the Californian Lockheed company, with its Model 22, a twin-engined single-seater with a short central nacelle and twin tail booms which were extensions of the engine nacelles. The machine had been designed by Hal Hibbard and Clarence 'Kelly' Johnson, and showed the influence of the Dutch Fokker G.1, which had been displayed at the 1936 Salon de l'Aeronautique in Paris. The turbochargers and the lateral 'cooling intakes' were installed in the twin booms, as in the Japanese Ki. 78. The design was allotted the USAAC number P-38. The competing designs from Bell and Curtiss were both single-engined, and featured mechanical superchargers. They were allotted the designations P-39 and P-40.

For a long period it was assumed that the XP-39, fitted with an Allison V-1710 turbocharged mid-fuselage engine, had achieved the noteworthy speed of 628km/h on one of its very first flights in April 1938, flying at an altitude of 6,100m, but more recently it has been claimed that the real date was April 1939, which is much more likely. In any case, the P-39 Airacobra, which was built in large numbers but lacked the turbocharger, turned out to be disappointingly slow. The first flight of the Lockheed XP-38, the first prototype, was carried out by the USAAC Project Officer, Maj Ben Kelsey, on 27 January 1939. So spectacular was its performance that, on the sixth flight, it was decided to make an attempt on the transcontinental

Lockheed XP-38, 1939.

speed record held by Howard Hughes. On 11 February 1939 Kelsey took just 7 hours 43 minutes to fly from California to New York, including two refuelling stops in Texas and Ohio, and recorded a top speed of 676km/h for a while, albeit with the assistance of a tailwind. The fact that the pilot was over-tired was probably the reason why he misjudged the landing, touching down on a golf course 600m short of Mitchel Field, New York, and completely wrecking the valuable machine. In spite of this setback, and in spite of serious delays, the Lockheed P-38 Lightning was destined to become one of the most powerful and successful US aircraft. Shortly afterwards Lockheed began planning an even faster successor, the XP-49. The Douglas Aircraft Company also planned an ultra-high-speed fighter aircraft, the XP-48 high-altitude fighter. However, the projected performance was considered over-optimistic, and the project was halted at the drawing-board stage. To expect 845km/h from only 525hp did, indeed, seem a little far-fetched.

APPROACHING THE OUTER LIMITS

1941 to the Present: Up to 800km/h and beyond

It goes without saying that the criteria for an effective single-seat fighter are more exacting than those for a pure racing or record-breaking aircraft. Specially designed machines with inadequate stability, powered by expensive, highly tuned engines with a useful life of half an hour, are no use for military purposes. For this reason it is not surprising that production aircraft with full military equipment could not approach the speeds attained by exotic, specially prepared examples. At the beginning of the Second World War the fastest production aircraft, the German Messerschmitt Bf 109E and the British Supermarine Spitfire I, were capable of 560 to 580km/h. A good five years later the final variants of the same single-seat fighters, the Bf 109K and the Spitfire 21, had achieved maximum speeds of 720 to 730km/h. In both cases these speeds were reached at altitudes of 5,000 to 6,000m.

Of course, ultra-high-speed military aircraft continued to take shape on the drawing boards of all nations. Most of these projects were for single-seat fighters. The calculated maximum speeds — some would call them optimistic guesses —

A model of the Heinkel He 176 V1 rocket aircraft of 1939.

assumed that new high-power engines would be available. These powerplants, if they progressed beyond the project stage, often turned out to be less powerful and/or less reliable than had originally been assumed. It was also becoming clear that further increases in speed would be increasingly difficult to achieve owing to the steep rise in the drag curve, and the problems of compressibility, which had previously been virtually unknown. In the early 1930s a few scientists had foreseen this kind of problem, and a handful of stalwart outsiders began experimenting and investigating the possibilities of jet propulsion for aircraft. In spite of the

Heinkel He 178 V1 jet aeroplane of 1939.

pessimistic views of many industry experts and aviation ministry officials, success eventually came. In June 1939 the first real rocket aircraft took to the air, followed in August 1939 by the first jet aircraft, propelled by a jet turbine. Both the He 176 (liquid rocket) and the He 178 (jet turbine) were built by Heinkel, but there was a long way to go before either of the engines could be considered for use in production aircraft. Machines powered by piston engines prevailed, and they continued to form the focus of development work.

Among the numerous designs for new, ultra-fast piston-engined aircraft were several which boasted extremely unorthodox configurations, most of which had again originated on German drawing boards. It was one of these unconventional machines which finally, in the spring of 1944, equalled the 755km/h in level flight previously achieved five years earlier by the Me 209; this was the twin-engined Dornier Do 335 V1.

The first design based on Dornier's 1937 patent was the DoP 59 high-speed bomber of 1937, but this came to naught due to lack of interest on the part of the RLM. To test and demonstrate the feasibility of the tail drive system, Dornier commissioned the Schempp-Hirth glider company at Göppingen to build the experimental Gö 9 aircraft. This had the planform of a Do 17, but was reduced to 40 per cent of its size, and featured a retractable nosewheel, a cruciform tail and a four-bladed pusher propeller in the tail, driven via an extension shaft by an 80hp Hirth HM 60 engine located immediately aft of the pilot's seat. Test flights of this

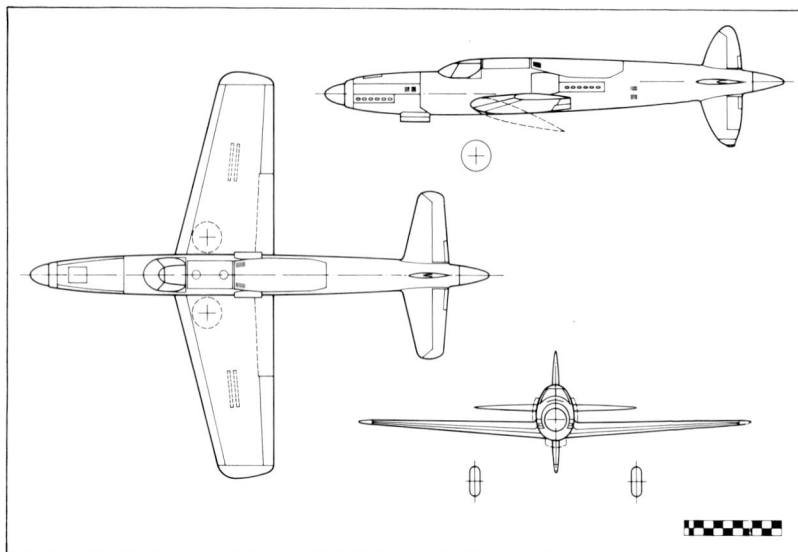

Dornier Do P59, 1937.

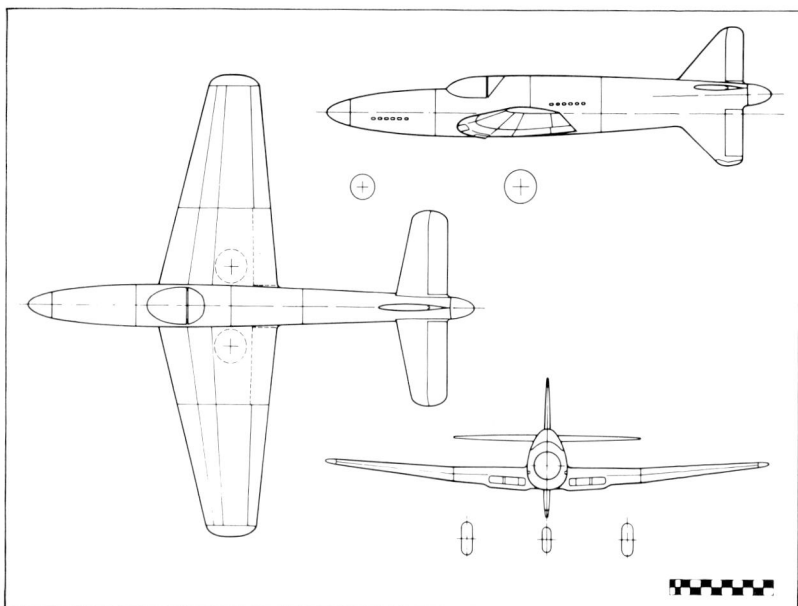

Dornier Do P231, 1939.

Dornier Do 335, 1943.

single-seater started in February 1940 and proved successful, with the result that Dornier developed it into the DoP 231 project. Originally planned as a fast bomber, the design was converted into a heavy multi-purpose fighter over the winter of 1942/43 at the instructions of the RLM. The result was the Do 335. The first flight of the Do 335 V1 was made by the former world record pilot Hans Dieterle on 26 October 1943. Flight testing then continued at the Rechlin testing centre, where the single-seat fighter, unofficially christened the 'Ameisenbär' (ant-eater), proved to be extraordinarily fast. At an altitude of 7,500m it reached a peak speed of over 750km/h. Other test aircraft reached even higher speeds.

Apart from its unusual appearance, the Do 335 was conventional in construction, having an all-metal monocoque fuselage and stressed-skin wings. The two water-cooled twelve-cylinder DB 603 engines produced 1,750hp for take-off. The front engine was fitted with an annular radiator and the rear one with a tunnel radiator having an air inlet on the underside of the fuselage and outlets on both sides below the tailplane. The Do 335 even featured a compressed-air ejector seat. In an emergency the tail propeller and lower fin could also be jettisoned. According to British reports, ejecting the canopy was not without risk to the pilot. Although about three dozen examples of the Do 335 were built and tested, including a few two-seaters, the aircraft saw virtually no service. The last remaining example was stored for a long time in the USA, but a few years ago it was brought back to Germany, where it underwent complete renovation, and was eventually placed on display in the Deutsches Museum in Munich.

By this time intensive work was under way in Germany on numerous jet aircraft projects, but there were also plans for many highly refined piston-engined propeller-driven machines which, at least on paper, were designed for high speeds. At Dornier much effort had been invested in the further development of the Do 335. The two main projects were the DoP 247 and DoP 252, both fighter aircraft with swept wings, and both devoid of the nose propeller. In the DoP 247

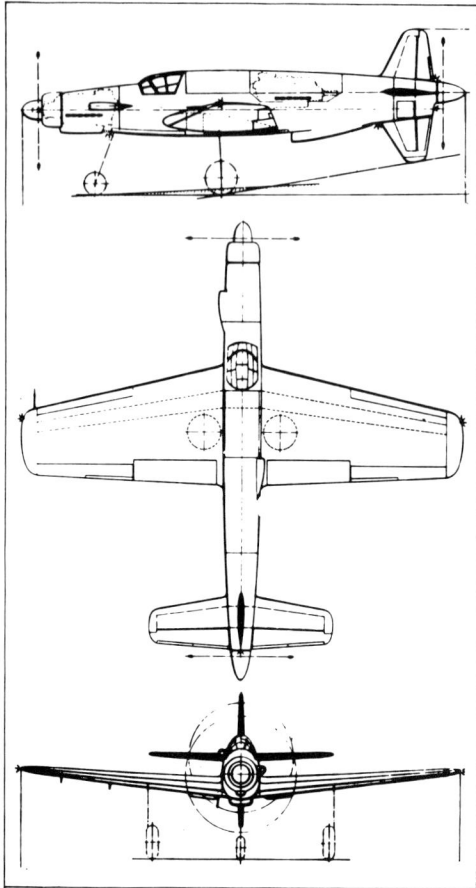

Dornier Do 335 V1, 1943.

single-seat fighter a Jumo 213T drove a tail-mounted propeller of conventional design, while the considerably larger and heavier DoP 252, a three-seat fighter, was powered by two Jumo 213J engines arranged in tandem and driving two contra-rotating 'sickle' propellers in the tail. Several different variants of each design were planned, and calculated maximum speeds were in the range of 835 to 900km/h.

Shortly before the end of the war, Heinkel decided to return to the development of the fast but ill-fated He 100 single-seat fighter. The Heinkel P.1076 project, dating from the spring of 1945, bore a strong family resemblance to the prewar design, although the all-up weight was now double that of the earlier aircraft. The

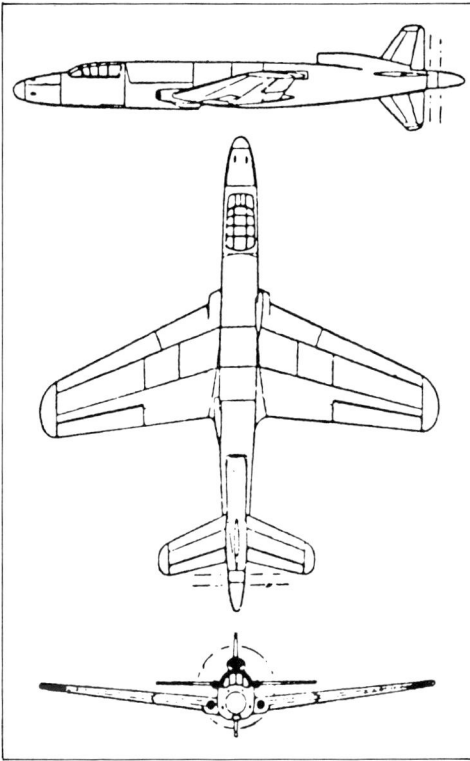

Dornier P.252, 1945.

low-set, trapezoid wing had slight forward sweep. Once again a low-drag condensation cooling system was adopted, although in this case the area of the wings, tail and fuselage utilised for cooling was 2.3 times greater than on the He 100. Heinkel originally planned to install a DB 603U engine, which, with the help of MW-50 injection (a mixture of water and methanol), was expected to produce a take-off power of 1,800hp, but later the Jumo 213E, the DB 603LM and the DB 603N were also considered. For take-off, the 603N was rated at 3,000hp. Although the pusher airscrew arrangement was considered benevolently by the RLM, a comparative evaluation of aircraft designs showed that this arrangement produced a much heavier machine. For this reason the P.1076 was to be fitted with contra-rotating, three-bladed tractor propellers. Depending on the engine finally selected, the expected maximum speed was in the region 825 to 880km/h, albeit at great altitude.

Of course, Messerschmitt, Heinkel's competitor, was making great efforts to convert the record-breaking Me 209 into a successful high-speed single-seat

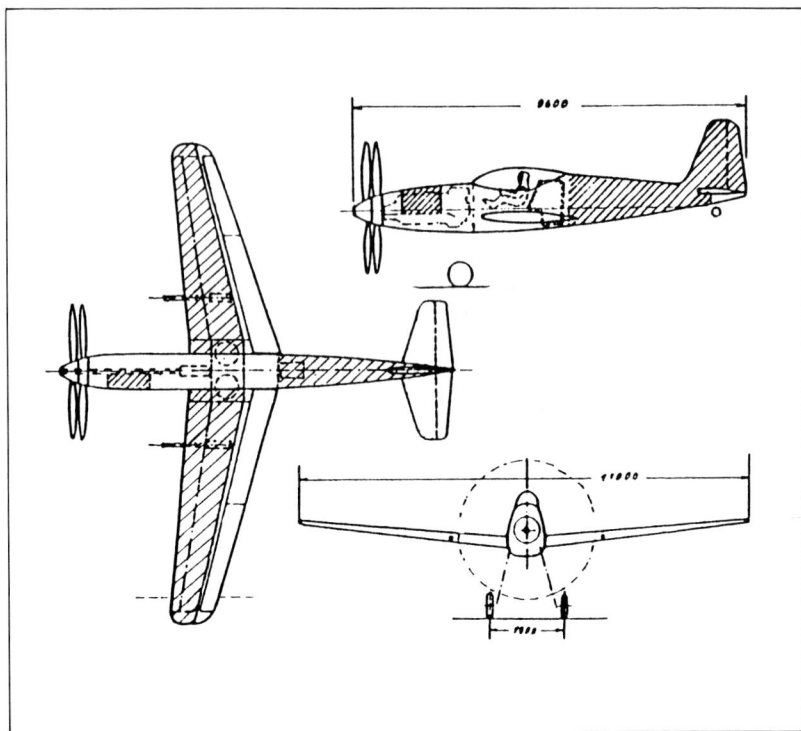

Heinkel P.1076, 1945.

fighter. However, the direct derivatives, the Me 209 V4, V5 and V6, turned out to be entirely unsuitable for this purpose, and a new Me 309 was designed with the aim of fulfilling these hopes. Once again the four experimental versions of the new single-seat fighter, which was fitted with a tricycle undercarriage, failed to produce the expected improvement in performance, with the result that series production of the Me 309A, planned for 1943, was abandoned, and the company concentrated fully on the promising Me 262 jet fighter.

Focke-Wulf and Arado were also working on several designs for aircraft powered by jet and propeller turbines, as well as projected fighters with conventional piston engines, some of them with contra-rotating pusher propellers. Planned developments of the As 413, BMW 801, DB 603 and Jumo 222 aero engines were all considered as possible powerplants, and once again the estimated maximum speeds were in the region of 840km/h at altitudes of nine to eleven kilometres.

In 1941/42 Henschel had designed a canard single-seat fighter with the project number P.75. The idea behind this layout was to position the 2,200hp DB 610

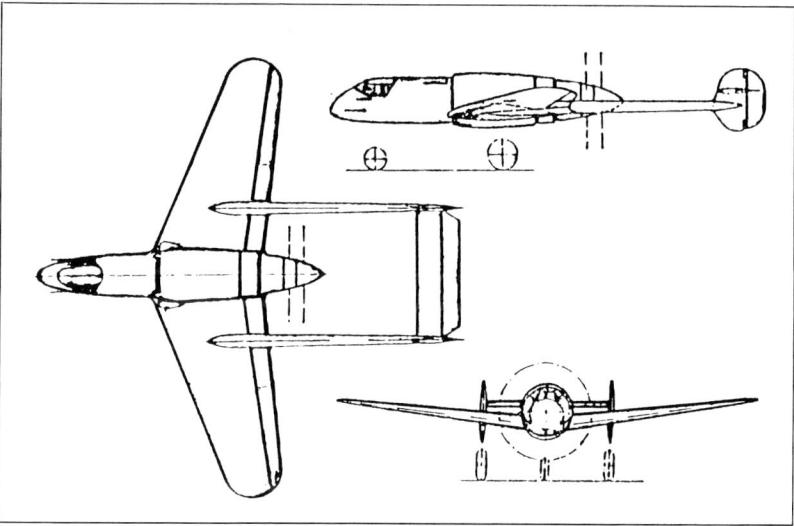

Focke-Wulf project, 1943.

double engine as close as possible to the aircraft's centre of gravity, as this would then permit the use of contra-rotating pusher propellers. The anticipated top speed was 790km/h at an altitude of seven kilometres. Various designs for high-speed propeller-driven aeroplanes were also developed at Blohm und Voss, where Dr Richard Vogt was chief designer in the aircraft division. Vogt was inclined to seek out unconventional solutions to problems — (the asymmetrical BV 141 is an example), and the P.170 fighter-bomber of 1942 was no exception. It was to be powered by three BMW 801E radial engines fitted with standard tractor propellers. The central engine was located in the usual position in the nose of the central fuselage, which also included the rear-mounted cockpit and the tailplane. The two outboard engines were to be mounted at the tips of the rectangular wing in long, extended pods, at the tail end of which were mounted the twin fins and rudders. The calculated maximum speed was around 820km/h at eight kilometres altitude. In contrast to the P.170, the P.205 project was relatively conventional in appearance, apart from its great wingspan. This was a preparatory study for the BV 155 high-altitude fighter, which was built later. Messerschmitt was responsible for its basic layout, but eventually it proved necessary to redesign it completely. In 1943 the P.207 project was developed. This was another single-seat fighter with a rear-mounted propeller. The last piston-engined fighter from the design office of Blohm und Voss was the P.208 project. This was a tailless single-seater with a direct-drive pusher propeller (no extension shaft) mounted in the short central fuselage. The sweptback wings had bullet fairings extending aft at the tips, carrying the tail surfaces. To test this concept a small experimental aircraft with a

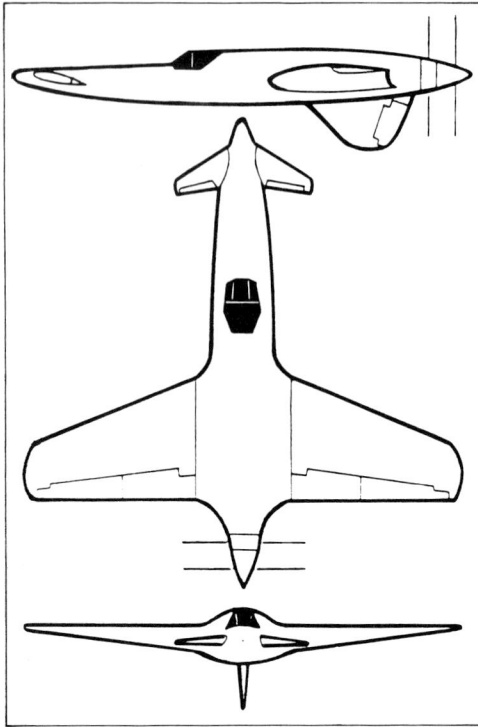

Henschel P.75, 1942.

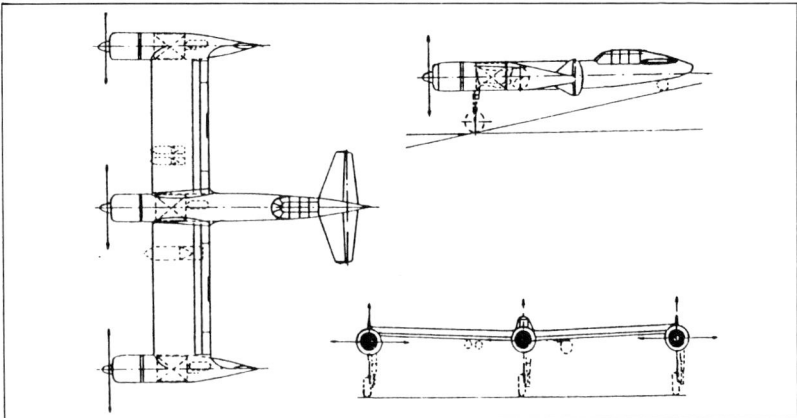

Blohm und Voss P.170, 1942.

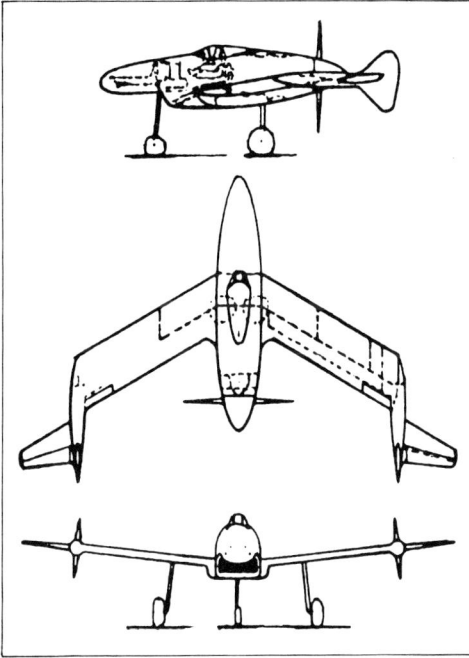

Blohm und Voss P.208, 1944.

pusher propeller and twin tailbooms, the Škoda-Kauba V-6, was converted to the new layout, renamed the ŠK SL 6, and test-flown successfully in 1944. Incidentally, the unusual name of Škoda-Kauba was used at this time by the well-known Czech aircraft company Avia. The company was based in Prague, and was a subsidiary of the Škoda company, which for a while operated under the leadership of the Austrian engineer Otto Kauba. His ŠK V-5, a single-seat fighter design intended as a competitor to Tank's Ta-152 (a development of the Fw 190), unfortunately came to nothing, just like the futuristic Blohm und Voss Project 208, which, like the other designs, was expected to have a top speed of around 800km/h.

A feature common to all of these projects was that their calculated performances were based on the optimistic power ratings claimed for aircraft engines which had not even been developed. In fact, the few examples of these high-power engines which were built failed to produce anything like the predicted power output in the short time available for testing. This problem was exacerbated by the fact that interest was rapidly swinging from piston engines to jet engines.

Blohm und Voss by no means had a monopoly on unusual ideas. In Britain Miles Aircraft also showed a highly imaginative approach. In 1941 the company

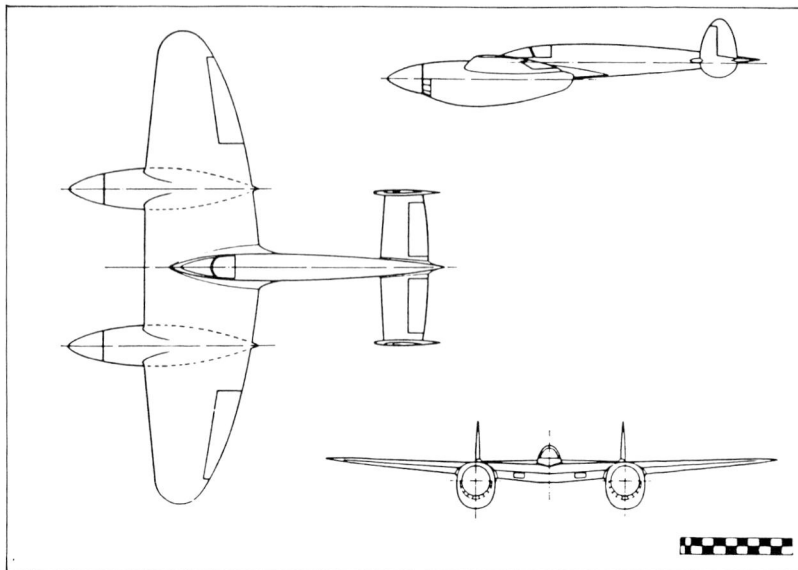

Miles M.22, 1941.

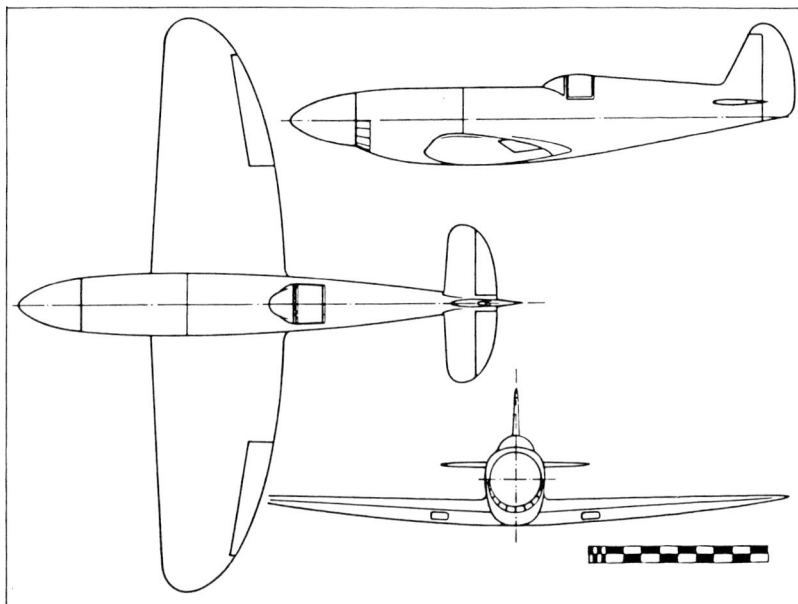

Miles M.23, 1941.

presented to the Ministry of Aircraft Production plans for two high-speed single-seat fighters, both of which, with the exception of their metal wing spars, were to be built entirely of wood, and were to be fitted with the new twelve-cylinder Rolls-Royce Griffon engine, a development of the proven Merlin. Miles estimated the maximum speed of the single-engined M.23 at 760km/h, and of the twin-engined M.22 at 811km/h at an altitude of 4,600m. One feature of the M.22 had been seen before on certain high-speed aircraft; the pilot sat deep in the fuselage, but could raise his seat by 30cm for take-off and landing. At the same time the cabin roof also rose to serve as a windshield. The Ministry declined to grant a contract to build the machine, probably because the predicted high speeds were considered over-optimistic, especially in view of the very thick wing — 18 to 20 per cent of the chord. However, another twin-engined single-seat fighter built largely of wood became the first British propeller-driven aircraft to reach this speed in level flight, although this did not happen until August 1944, three years later. The first prototype of the de Havilland D.H.103 Hornet, a development of the same manufacturer's successful Mosquito, was fitted with two 2,100hp Rolls-Royce Merlin engines, and recorded a level-flight speed of 782km/h at an altitude of 7,000m.

De Havilland D.H.103 Hornet, 1944.

In the late 1930s the British had also started developing more powerful aircraft engines; the liquid-cooled twenty-four-cylinder Napier Sabre and Rolls-Royce Vulture, and the air-cooled eighteen-cylinder Bristol Centaurus radial engine. At Hawker Aircraft, home of the famed Hurricane single-seat fighter, chief designer Sydney Camm produced various prototypes to be powered by these engines — the Tornado, the Typhoon, the Tempest and, finally, the Fury. The Rolls-Royce Vulture proved to be a complete failure and was abandoned, taking with it into oblivion the Hawker Tornado, for which it had been intended. The Hawker

Typhoon, fitted with the Napier Sabre, was developed into a successful ground-attack aircraft, once initial engine problems and weak points in the airframe had been eliminated. A thinner wing was then designed, and its adoption led to the next type in the series, the Hawker Tempest, powered first by the Napier Sabre and later by the Bristol Centaurus. The Tempest's high speed made it suitable for combatting the German Fieseler Fi 103, or V1, missile (the notorious 'reprisal weapon') which came into service in June 1944. A smaller and lighter variant of the Tempest appeared in the autumn of 1944. This was the Fury, prototypes of which flew with Centaurus, Sabre and Griffon engines for comparative testing. The second prototype (LA610) eventually reached a speed of

Hawker Fury with the Napier Sabre engine, 1946.

780km/h at an altitude of 5.6 kilometres. The Fury was originally fitted with a Griffon 85 and three-bladed contra-rotating propellers, then later with a Sabre VII and a single four-bladed propeller. It continued in series production as the Sea Fury after the end of the Second World War, now fitted with the Bristol Centaurus and a five-bladed propeller, and the type remained in service with the naval air arms of various nations, as a carrier-based fighter-bomber, before it, too, was superseded by jet fighters.

Several years earlier the Airspeed company had designed a single-seat fighter, the AS.56, of very similar appearance, but the design did not leave the drawing board, and its calculated top speed of 792km/h remained a speculative figure.

In contrast to its competitor, the Hawker Hurricane, the elegant Supermarine Spitfire had by no means exhausted its development potential, and over the years no fewer than forty-eight variants were built. At first the Rolls-Royce Merlin was retained, in more and more powerful forms, but the Merlin was eventually supplanted by the even more powerful Rolls-Royce Griffon. Even so, the Spitfire's maximum speed was no more than around 720km/h at best; to obtain higher performance there was no alternative to a completely new design. As aircraft speeds approached the speed of sound (defined as Mach 1, after the Austrian scientist Ernst Mach, and varying according to air density and temperature), compression shock waves affected the control surfaces, and in many cases rendered them ineffective when the airflow separated from the wing. The only means of regaining control was for the pilot to dive into strata of denser air, although this inevitably involved a drop in speed. New and much thinner wings, with modified aerofoils, were designed in an attempt to postpone the onset of turbulence and airflow separation. These were the so-called laminar wing sections, whose maximum thickness was moved back to between fifty and sixty per cent of the chord, compared with the thirty per cent chord position of maximum thickness in conventional aerofoils. Experimental flights using specially prepared aircraft appeared to justify these measures. Soon, however, it became apparent that even tiny irregularities and uneven patches on the wing surfaces would result in turbulence. The wings had to be mirror-smooth and absolutely true to aerofoil contours, the permissible tolerances being just 0.5mm on the top surface of the wing and 0.2mm on the underside. Surfaces of this quality could not be maintained in everyday flying, and for this reason the only change which had a measurable effect on attainable flight speeds was thinning the wing section; the laminar aerofoil had little influence. The German aircraft designer Kurt Tank once remarked that a single fleck on the polished leading edge of an aircraft ruined the entire laminar effect, and he was proved right.

In 1944 Supermarine produced the Spiteful, designed under the direction of Joseph Smith. The Spiteful featured a specially calculated thin laminar wing with straight leading and trailing edges, in contrast to the classic elliptical wing of the Spitfire. The Rolls-Royce Griffon drove either one five-bladed or two contra-rotating three-bladed Rotol propellers. For the reasons mentioned earlier, the measured increase in speed was disappointing. Nevertheless, impressive values

Supermarine 371 Spiteful F.Mk.XIV, 1947.

were recorded during testing of the small number of machines constructed. A Spiteful XIV reached a speed of 780km/h on one occasion, and in 1947 the sole example of the Spiteful XVI was measured at 795km/h in level flight at an altitude of almost nine kilometres, although the Griffon 101 responded immediately by losing power. However, by this time aircraft development as a whole had shifted towards the jet turbine, and the Spiteful, together with its carrier-based version, the Seafang, was abandoned after thirty-six had been built. The complex laminar wing, created at great expense, was not wasted. It was used on the first Supermarine jet fighter, the carrier-based Attacker.

By this time much higher speeds had been achieved during test flights of high-speed single-seat fighters, but only in dives. Because of its excellent aerodynamics, the Spitfire proved to be particularly well suited to this form of testing. In 1944, for example, Sqn Ldr A F Martindale of the RAF started a dive from an altitude of twelve kilometres and reached a measured speed of 975km/h, at which point the propeller and reduction gearbox departed to fly on alone. Even so, from his altitude of eight kilometres he was able to glide the thirty kilometres to the Royal Aircraft Establishment's aerodrome at Farnborough, where he carried out a smooth touch-down.

Republic XP-72 'Ultrabolt', 1944.

In view of the compressibility problems mentioned earlier, it was a singularly impressive feat for a powerful American single-seat fighter to achieve 772km/h in February 1944. This speed was recorded on a test flight literally at sea level, and a clear wake was visible on the water as the aircraft passed. The Republic XP-72 'Ultrabolt' was a development of the well-known P-47 Thunderbolt fitted with an even more powerful engine. The Pratt & Whitney R-4360 was a twenty-eight-cylinder four-row radial engine rated initially at 3,000hp. The intention was to uprate the unit to 3,500hp and eventually to 4,000hp. The XP-72 was a product of the Republic design team under the direction of Alexander Kartveli. The predicted top speed of production machines was 811km/h, with a figure of 870km/h

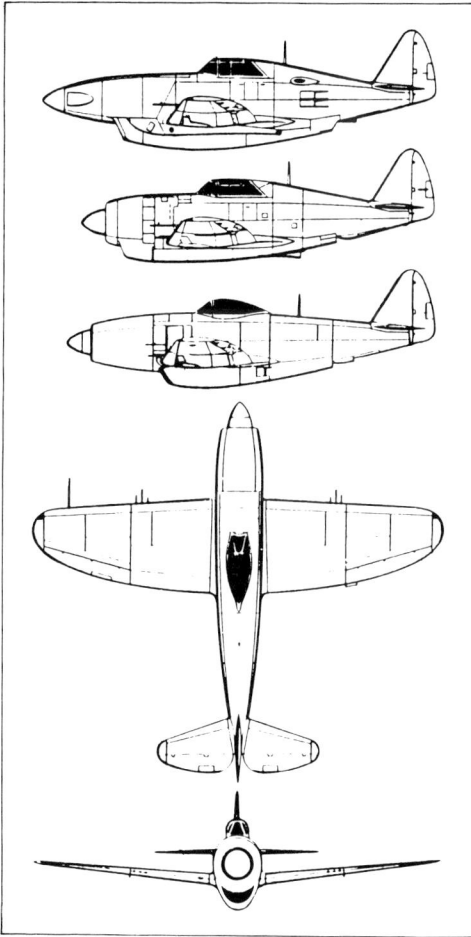

Thunderbolt comparisons: XP-47H, XP-47J and XP-72.

quoted at an altitude of just on eight kilometres. Amazingly, the S3 wing section, created in 1932/33 by the company founder Alexander de Seversky, in collaboration with the aerodynamicist Mike Gregor, proved to be suitable for this speed range.

As in the case of the Spiteful, the two prototypes of the XP-72 could be fitted with either a single four-bladed propeller or two contra-rotating three-bladed propellers (of 4.09m diameter). The version planned for series production, the P-72A, never saw the light of day. However, an indication that the predicted speeds were not simply based on guesswork was the fact that a different Thunder-

Republic XP-47J Thunderbolt 'Superman', 1944.

bolt variant was timed at 813km/h on 5 August 1944. This version, the XP-47J, had been built in 1943. Nicknamed 'Superman', it was flown by Republic pilot Mike Richie. Shortly after this the machine reached 816km/h at the same altitude. A third member of the Thunderbolt family, the XP-47H, fitted with a sixteen-cylinder liquid-cooled Chrysler engine, was also designed for high speed, but engine problems limited its maximum to 666km/h instead of the expected 790km/h. None of these prototypes went into production, but a further development was produced on a limited scale. The version in question was the P-47M, an indirect development of the XP-47J, of which 130 examples were built. It was fitted with supplementary dive brakes, and was capable of 760km/h. The production machines were shipped to Europe with the intention of using them to counter the V1, which generally flew at 650km/h.

The P-51 Mustang single-seat fighter was made by the California-based North American Aircraft Company. It had been designed and built in 1940 with the

North American XP-51G Mustang, 1944.

approval of the British, in place of the licence-built version of the Curtiss P-40 Warhawk which had been intended originally. It was initially powered by the water-cooled twelve-cylinder Allison V-1710 engine, a unit which only produced useful power at low altitudes, but this was replaced by the Rolls-Royce Merlin in 1942. With this powerplant the P-51 turned out to be an excellent long-range fighter. The Merlin was subsequently manufactured under licence by the American Packard company under the designation V-1650. Experience gained with the type in Europe was exploited in 1944, when several prototypes were built featuring greater aerodynamic refinement, with the aim of achieving even better performance with the same power output. One of these machines, the XP-51F, reached a speed of 750km/h at 8.8 kilometres, while the production version developed from it, the P-51H, did even better; 783km/h at 7.6 kilometres. However, it was the XP-51G which proved to be the fastest of all Mustangs, even though only two were built. The best speed achieved with this version was 797km/h at an altitude of eight kilometres.

Republic had managed to beat the 500mph barrier (more than 805km/h) with its specially prepared Thunderbolt. North American then made an attempt to better its competitor's achievement. For two solid weeks one man toiled at polishing one of the two XP-51Gs to a high gloss, in an effort to improve even further the efficiency of the laminar-flow wings. However, the recorded speed was only just on 800km/h, (497mph), and the Republic XP-47J remained the fastest propeller-driven aeroplane. Of course, other firms had projects under way for which even higher speeds were claimed, but most of them remained on paper. In November 1939 an official invitation to design an unorthodox single-seat fighter provided a stimulus for such developments. The document was Circular Proposal R-40C, and it resulted in three designs: the Vultee XP-54, with twin tailbooms; the canard Curtiss XP-55; and the tailless Northrop XP-56. All three were fitted with pusher propellers, and were designed to accommodate the new Pratt & Whitney X-1800 engine, which was also under development at that time. Of this unusual trio, the greatest claims were made for the XP-54, including a predicted top speed of 820km/h. However, the X-1800 engine was soon abandoned, and the aircraft had to be converted to accept other powerplants. They proved to be too difficult to fly, and considerably slower than their manufacturers had hoped, and in the end the whole project was abandoned.

The Japanese aviation industry had also been active in the development of high-speed projects. In the autumn of 1939 Kawasaki began to plan a heavy single-seat fighter — possibly inspired by the Heinkel He 119 — to be powered by the Kawasaki Ha.201 double engine, which consisted of two Ha.40 twelve-cylinder units; the Japanese version of the German DB 601. Contra-rotating tractor propellers were fitted, the rear one being of fixed pitch and the forward one variable. The prototype Ki.64 first flew in December 1943, fitted with an experimental engine rated at 2,350hp. The war prevented completion of the planned 2,800hp engine and an improved variable-pitch propeller, which it was hoped would push the machine up to a speed of around 800km/h. A similar fate befell the

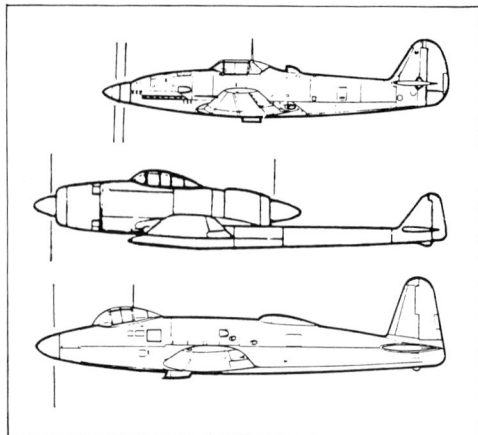

Size comparison of Japanese machines: Ki.64-KAI, Ki.94-I and R2Y-2.

R2Y-2 high-speed reconnaissance aircraft made by the Yokosuka Naval Arsenal. Only one prototype flew, and that with a less powerful engine. In 1943 the Tachikawa company produced the twin-boom Ki.94-I design for a high-altitude fighter, to be powered by two 2,200hp Ha.211 radial engines in the front and rear of the short central fuselage. Its predicted speed was 780km/h at ten kilometres, but it was never built. The fastest Japanese propeller-driven fighter was the Kyushu J7W1 Shinden, a canard design which did not take to the air until August 1945, in the final days of the war. It seems unlikely that the Shinden ever attained its predicted top speed of 750km/h at nine kilometres.

The French aviation industry, which after June 1940 was under the partial control of the German occupation authorities, and after November 1942 under their complete control, was to a very great extent affiliated to the German aviation industry until the country was liberated in 1944/45. Under the circumstances the industry was required to build German aircraft types. However, a large number of more or less independent new designs were developed, both for German companies and on the manufacturers' own initiative, although only a few were actually built.

Some of the companies which produced new designs of high-speed piston-engined aircraft — some of them of extremely unorthodox — in the war years and the immediate post-war period, were as follows: the Arsenal de l'Aéronautique (VG 60, VB 10 and 15), the Société Matra (R 100 and 110), the SNCA du Centre (NC 160 and 200), the SNCA du Sud-Est (SE 580 and 582), and the SNCA du Sud-Ouest (SO 8000). Only two of these designs were actually built, and then only in small numbers. The VB 10 was a heavy fighter-bomber fitted with one 1,500hp Hispano-Suiza 12 Z forward of the cockpit and a second aft of it, driving two contra-rotating propellers in the nose. It proved to be too slow (only 610km/h instead of the expected 720km/h) and unreliable. After three of the six test aircraft had crashed, construction was halted on the remaining forty-four production aircraft which had been ordered. When, in May 1948, the new state of Israel expressed a desire to purchase thirty of these machines, production was not resumed.

The SO 8000 Narval, intended for operation from aircraft carriers, fared no better. The Narval was a single-engined long-range fighter with twin tailbooms and contra-rotating pusher propellers, in the style of earlier Focke-Wulf projects. The two prototypes which were built exhibited unpleasant flying characteristics, and also failed to reach the promised top speed of 730km/h. Series production did not even start. Even so, the French State reimbursed seventy-five per cent of the expenses of SNCA du Sud-Ouest; a total of 476 million Francs.

The Soviet Union's fastest piston-engined aircraft of the Second World War came from the drawing boards of Aleksandr Yakovlev and Artem Mikoyan, although here again we are speaking of individual, highly tuned machines. An

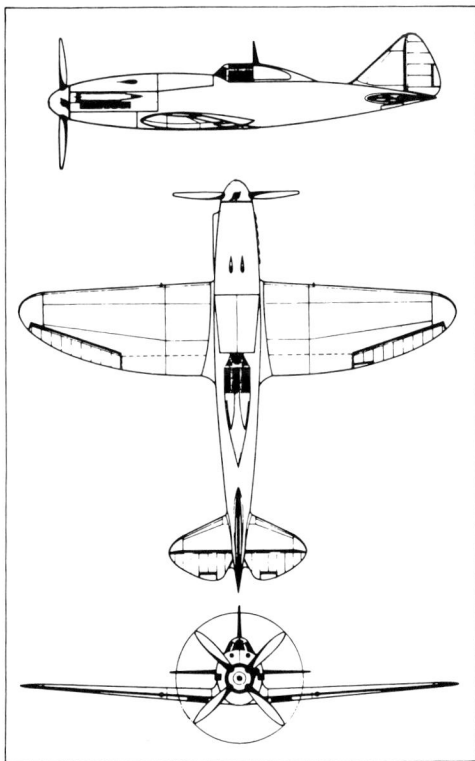

Reggiane 2006b, 1944.

experimental single-seat Yak-3 fighter, fitted with a Klimov VK-108 twelve-cylinder engine rated at 1,800hp, in place of the standard 1,250hp VK-105 unit, reached 745km/h at six kilometres in December 1944, while the prototype of the Mikoyan I.225 fighter attained 726km/h at an altitude of ten kilometres in March 1945.

Potentially the fastest Italian fighter of that period, with an estimated speed of 770km/h, was the Caproni-Reggiane Re.2006b, a direct descendant of the excellent Re.2005 Sagittario with a 1,850hp DB 603 engine in place of the DB 601, and radiators in the wing leading edges instead of under the centre section. The aerodynamically efficient Re.2005 had already been dived to speeds approaching 1,000km/h during testing. The prototype Re.2006b was completed in February 1944, but it never took off – the leader of the local partisans had threatened to blow the machine up if an attempt was made to fly it. In April 1945 the Istituto d'Aeronautica del Politecnico di Milano (Milan Polytechnic Institute of Aeronautics) asked that it be allowed to exhibit the aircraft, which was then in storage. The American occupation authorities agreed in principle, but insisted on certain mea-

Windtunnel model of the Reggiane 2006C, 1945.

sures being carried out beforehand. The engine, instruments, armament and undercarriage were to be removed, and the fuselage and wings were to be sawn into pieces. The company president, Count Caproni, had been certain that this high-performance fighter was an ideal candidate for series production and export once hostilities were at an end, and had entrusted his head designer, Roberto Longhi, with the task of developing two racing versions, designated the Re.2006C (C for Corsa, or race). These shorter-span versions were targeted at the Bendix and Thompson trophies. The Bendix variant was designed to be capable of flying non-stop from Los Angeles to New York at an altitude of eight kilometres and at an average speed of 800km/h, and to this end the whole of the wing was designed as a fuel tank. The Thompson Trophy version was to be fitted with a condensation cooling system, with cooling surfaces on fuselage and wings, and was expected to be capable of 850km/h at very low altitude. Even the pilot had been chosen; he was to be Riccardo Vaccari, a successful fighter pilot. The Bendix and Thompson races did indeed take place, but without the two Reggiane racers. Like the export Re.2006, they were never built.

In early September 1946 the American National Air Races were resumed after an enforced break of seven years. The site was the traditional one; Cleveland, Ohio. The previous races had been held in early September 1939, coinciding with the start of the Second World War. This time the stars were de-militarised propeller-driven single-seat fighters. With the war over, the US armed forces had no more use for them, and in any case they now had jet fighters, so the machines were sold off at low prices. In consequence, the first post-war air races in the USA saw the appearance of dozens of ex-fighters, many of them brightly painted and some of them 'improved' by means of extremely risky modifications. The most popular types were the Lockheed P-38 Lightning, Bell P-39 Airacobra, North American P-51 Mustang, Bell P-63 Kingcobra and Vought F4U Corsair. The first post-war winner of the Thompson Trophy was Alvin 'Tex' Johnston, flying his

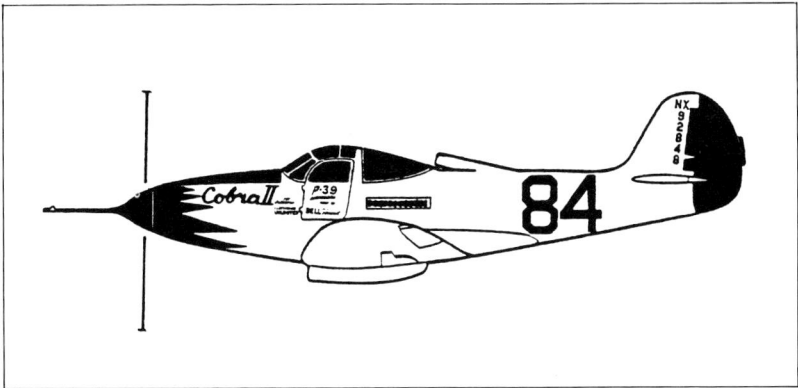

Tex Johnston's Bell P-39Q-10E Cobra II *1946.*

tuned P-39 *Cobra II*. His average speed was almost 602km/h, and his fastest lap was timed at 658km/h. His aircraft had cost little more than $1,000 to buy, but Johnston's prize money was more than $15,000. It seems likely that Johnston considered undertaking an attack on the world speed record set by the Me 209, but he could not raise enough money for the attempt. A few months after the end of the war, in November of the previous year, the absolute world speed record had been pushed up to 976km/h by a specially prepared British Gloster Meteor jet fighter, and it was destined never to be regained by a propeller-driven, piston-engined aircraft. For this type of machine the only prospects were the appropriate class record, and no great official or public enthusiasm could now be expected — just the enthusiasm of a small number of private pilots, male and female.

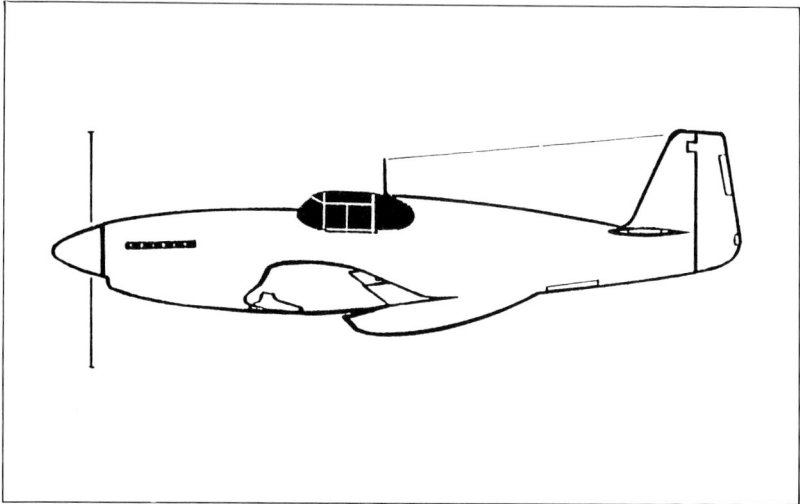

Jaqueline Cochran's P-51C-10 Mustang, 1947.

Of the latter, the best known and most successful was Jacqueline Cochran, who before the war had competed energetically against her male colleagues and had only just missed overall victory in the Bendix race of 1946. Her machine was a completely reworked early model Mustang, a P-51C, with which she also intended to chase records. First she took on the 100km closed-circuit record, which allowed her to fly at greater altitude. She had a measured 50km course laid out from her Californian upland ranch to the small town of Hemet, a course which had to be flown twice, including one steep turn. On 10 December 1947 she completed the course at an average speed of 755.668km/h, exactly 0.53km/h faster than Fritz Wendel eight years before, flying his Me 209. Wendel, however, had set his world record at very low altitude, and his speed had been the average of four successive flights over the prescribed three-kilometre course, which posed far greater problems. Jackie Cochran in turn discovered the truth of this to her regret, when, one week later, she made an attempt on the speed record in accordance with the standard regulations. This time she flew at a different site in California, over the Coachilla Valley, at a much lower altitude. Here the best she could do was 663km/h, insufficient to break the world record, but good enough for the US piston-engined record, which had been held by Howard Hughes since 1935.

Mrs Cochran subsequently turned her attention to the Bendix races again, but the aerobatic pilot Betty Skelton took up the record challenge. Six months later, in July 1948, she made several record attempts over the three-kilometre course flying a modified P-51D, but had to abandon the project after recurring engine problems.

Converted A-36A Mustang Beguine, *1949.*

There was a third female racing pilot who harboured record ambitions. Dot Lemon chose an A-36A Mustang (a fighter-bomber variant) which was named *Beguine*, and had been modified at great expense. The wings were shortened, the starboard panel by 15cm more than the port one, and the clumsy underfuselage radiator was removed and replaced by tunnel radiators on both wingtips. In June 1949 the pilot Ken Cooley had recorded an average speed of 808km/h at an air show in Texas, completing four passes over a one-mile course, but Dot Lemon's planned record attempt never took place. During the previous year the pilot Don Nolan had made an attack on the record, flying the *Cobra II* which had won the Thompson Trophy in 1946, but, in spite of reaching a claimed top speed of 758km/h, he failed to break the record.

The annual Cleveland Air Races involved considerable risk to the competing pilots and also to residents of the region, as the course passed over populated areas. In the 1947 Thompson Trophy races, three of the thirteen participating machines survived emergency landings, four were damaged or crashed on landing, and one

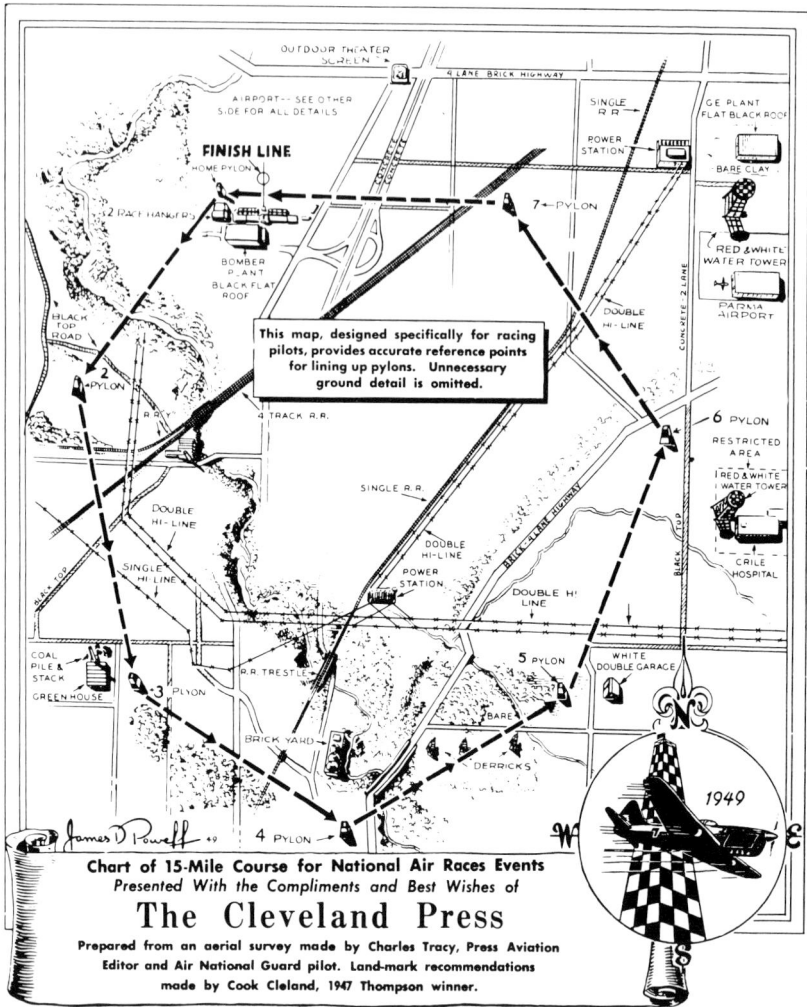

Cleveland race course, 1949.

pilot lost his life. In 1948 seven of the ten competitors dropped out, although in this case without further accident or damage. The 1949 event saw ten 'tuned-up' single-seat fighters on the starting line: one Kingcobra, three Corsairs and six Mustangs, among them the highly modified *Beguine*. For this event the Mustang was flown by the successful long-distance pilot William Odom, who evidently had his sights set on the short-distance records. Not long after take-off Odom misjudged a pylon turn in *Beguine* and crashed into a house, killing both himself and a young woman and her baby. The race was completed, but Cleveland never again allowed such risky activities to be held there.

Although the US Air Force (it had by now become an independent force) and the Navy now focussed their attention on jet-propelled aircraft, a handful of potentially fast propeller-driven aircraft remained to be tested. The elegant, four-engined Republic XF-12 Rainbow, for example, attained a speed of 800km/h, albeit at great altitude. The Rainbow was a long-range reconnaissance aeroplane, but only two were built. The Vought XF5U-1, nicknamed the 'flying pancake', was a completely new type of Navy fighter which was intended to have a top speed of more than 800km/h, but the prototype of this short-take-off machine never flew. It was scrapped some time later. In its 'civilian' form, under the designation Gulfhawk IV, an example of the Grumman F8F-1 Bearcat Navy fighter also showed a surprising turn of speed. Alford J Williams, a former record-breaking pilot of the 1920s who was now manager of an oil company, claimed to have reached 805km/h in it at a moderate altitude.

The FAI, with its headquarters in Paris, was still the international regulatory authority for world record flights, and about this time it established a new, alternative course for world record attempts. The traditional course was over a distance of three kilometres, flown four times in sequence at low altitude. The new regulation provided for a course fifteen to twenty-five kilometres long, to be flown at any altitude twice — once in each direction. In April 1951 Jacqueline Cochran set up a sixteen-kilometre course in the vicinity of her ranch. Another pilot had crashed her first Mustang, but she had acquired another, a short-range reconnaissance variant, the F-6C, which was otherwise identical to the P-51B. The machine underwent major modifications, and was christened *Thunderbird*. On 9 April 1951 Jackie Cochran flew the course six times, and the two fastest runs were averaged.

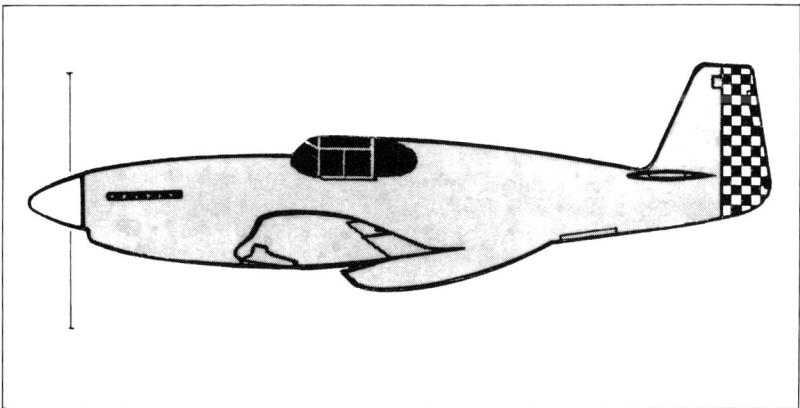

Jaqueline Cochran's F-6C Thunderbird, *1951.*

Cook Cleland's modified Goodyear F2G-1, 1949.

The official figure was 747.3km/h. Fritz Wendel's 755km/h record remained intact.

By this time the Cleveland Air Races had been stopped once and for all, and in consequence some of the former racing pilots now showed a renewed interest in the world record for piston-engined aircraft. Among them was Cook Cleland, who had won the ill-fated 1949 race and owned an F2G-1 which showed great promise. This was a licence-built variant of the Vought Corsair, which had been built in small numbers by Goodyear towards the end of the war. It was powered by a Pratt & Whitney R-4360, a 3,500hp twenty-eight-cylinder radial engine, which was now producing an estimated 4,100hp. The characteristic inverted-gull wing had been cropped, and the wingtips fitted with endplates in an effort to reduce drag. Once again the enterprise foundered; no serious attack on the record was ever made. However, another Cleveland veteran, Anson Johnson, the surprise winner in 1948, did make several official record attempts. He flew a P-51D Mustang to which he had made major modifications, including the removal of the belly-mounted radiator and the installation of a replacement system in the wing leading edges. He made his first attack on the three-kilometre record in June 1952, in the vicinity of Key Biscayne, Florida. Despite the fact that he claimed to have reached a speed of 820km/h, the best average speed he could manage after a series of passes was just over 690km/h. That was the end of his efforts.

By this time — the early 1950s — the focus of interest had shifted from the 'old-timers' to the so-called midget racers: tiny privately-designed racing machines with air-cooled three-litre in-line engines built by Continental. They proved to be surprisingly fast, although they were not quite as exciting as the Unlimited Racer

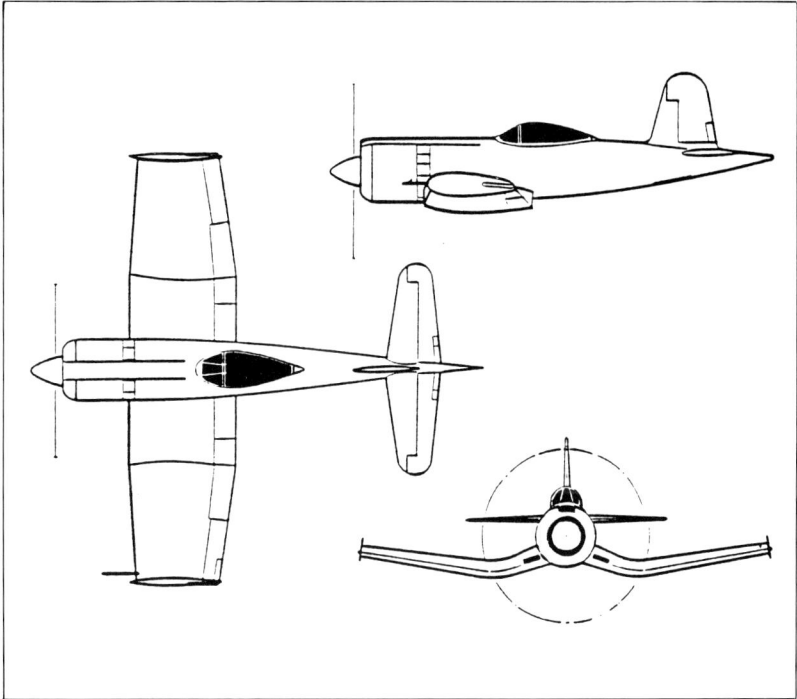

Modified F2G-1, 1949.

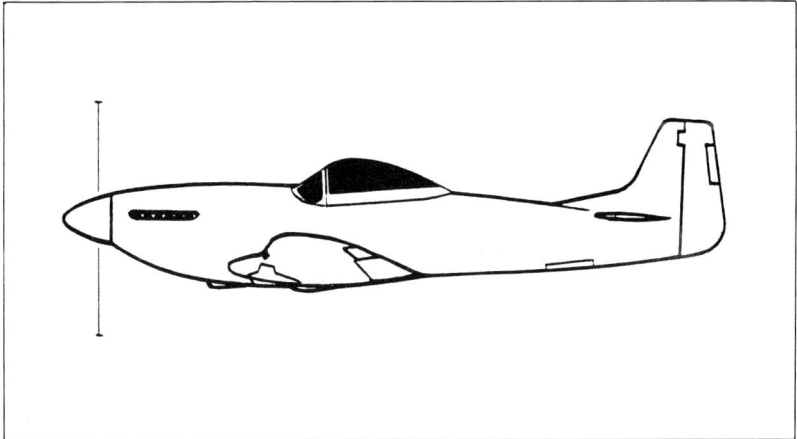

Anson Johnson's P-51D-20 Mustang, 1952.

category — converted single-seat fighters with no limit on engine capacity, whose V-12, in-line or multiple radial engines varied in capacity between 27 litres (Rolls-Royce Merlin) and more than 71 litres (Pratt & Whitney Wasp Major) and had correspondingly massive power outputs.

Eventually, in 1964, the Cleveland races were resumed at the initiative of Bill Stead, a wealthy rancher and private pilot. The event was renamed, and, of course, relocated to Reno, Nevada. More stringent safety regulations were imposed, and the new racing conditions, together with the largely unoccupied terrain, were intended to keep the consequences of any accident within reasonable bounds and limit them to the participating pilots, who, after all, were fully conscious of the risks. For the Unlimiteds there was a cross-country race, which replaced the earlier Bendix race, and a closed-course race, the successor to the Thompson Trophy event. Eight Mustangs entered for the first race, and five Mustangs and three Bearcats for the second, among them the F8F-2 belonging to the Lockheed works pilot Darryl Greenamyer, which had been fitted with a smaller canopy.

Greenamyer had decided, in consultation with a small group of friends and colleagues, including the airframe specialist Bruce Boland, to convert the F8F-2 into a competitive racer, and, if at all possible, into a record-breaker. The machine was a US Navy carrier-based single-seat fighter which had been built in 1949. In the aircraft's first event Greenamyer won a preliminary round, but decided against landing on the temporary Sky Ranch Airport strip and was promptly disqualified for breach of regulations. After its first, promising exploit the machine was subjected to an even more fundamental weight-reducing course. The wings had originally incorporated an outboard weak-link section, designed to break away in order to avoid overloading the inboard wing spars. They were now shortened by 1.07m on each side at the weak-link area, and the newly-developed Hoerner wingtips were installed. The slotted flaps on the underside of the wing were removed and the joint lines filled and smoothed. The standard canopy was replaced by a minuscule Plexiglas moulding. All of the oil cooler and carburettor openings were covered over, and a condensation cooling system was installed. To save weight, all of the electrical and hydraulic systems were removed and replaced by a 15V dry battery and a nitrogen container pressurised to 130 bar, the contents of which were just sufficient to retract the undercarriage once. The tail end of the fuselage was fitted with a streamlined extension. Finally, the power output of the engine was raised stage by stage. The standard propeller was removed and replaced by a 4.10m-diameter unit from a Douglas AD-1 Skyraider dive-bomber, with the large spinner from a P-51H finishing off the job. As the diameter of the new propeller was 28cm greater than that of the standard unit, the modified Bearcat had to be taken off and landed in strict three-point style. As expected, the aircraft was victorious at Reno in 1965. Six months later, at the Los Angeles Air Races in late May 1966, three pilots announced their intention of making an official attack on the world speed record for piston-engined aircraft: Darryl Greenamyer with his Bearcat, Tommy Taylor with a Hawker Fury, and Chuck Lyford with his specially prepared Mustang. Neither Lyford nor Taylor appeared at the start line, and even

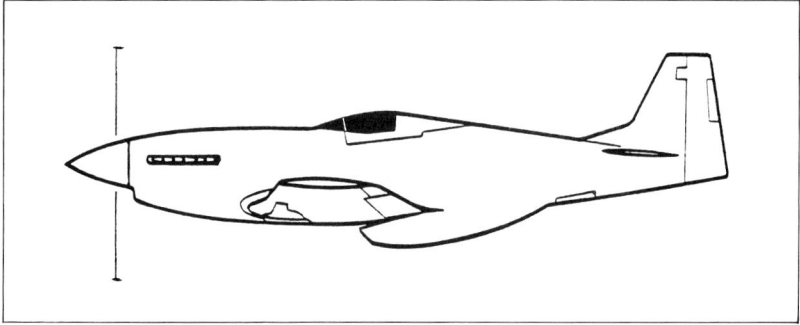

Charles Lyford's P-51D-25 Bardahl Special, *1972.*

Greenamyer had problems. On his two test runs over the three-kilometre course he was forced to concede that reducing the height of the Bearcat's fin by a good half a metre had made the aircraft virtually uncontrollable, and he landed as quickly as possible. There was no question of a record, but the pilot and aircraft proved to be a winning combination, and were victorious in the 1966, 1967 and 1968 races — albeit with a larger fin.

In 1968 Greenamyer planned a concerted record attempt in collaboration with another successful racing pilot, Michael Carroll, to be carried out at Edwards Air Force Base in California, the US Air Force Flight Test Centre, in the autumn. Carroll had acquired the Bell P-39Q *Cobra II* which had won in 1946, and had fundamentally modified it. The wings were shortened, the landing flaps filled in,

Mike Carroll's Bell P-39Q-10E Cobra III, *1968.*

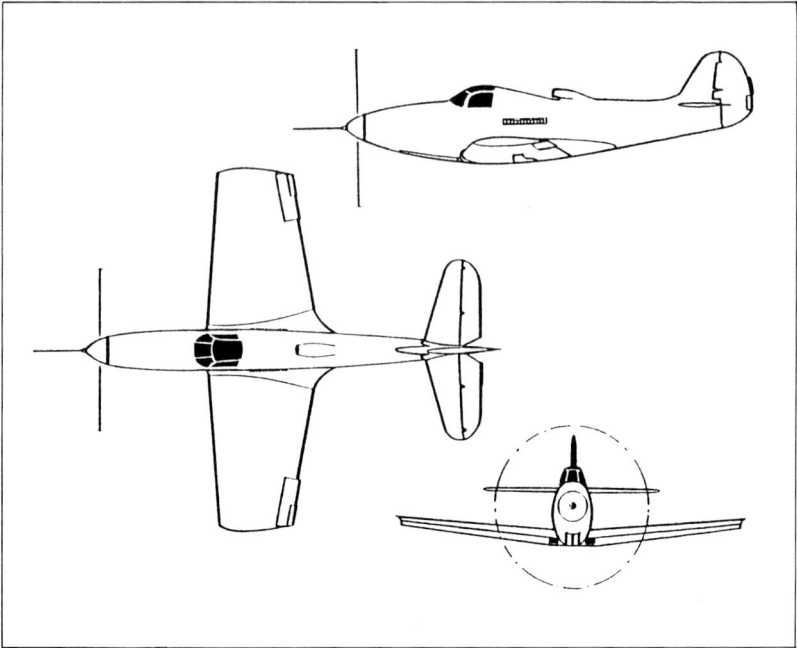

Mike Carroll's Cobra III, *1968.*

air intakes removed, and a new Allison twelve-cylinder engine, tuned to produce 2,900hp by engine specialist Dave Zeuschel, was installed. A speed of over 800km/h was expected of the snow-white *Cobra III*, but once again the dreams failed to come true. On the first flight, on 10 August, the machine became unstable shortly after take-off and crashed. Carroll baled out, but was apparently struck by the tail and sustained fatal injuries. Nevertheless, in late August 1968 Greenamyer undertook test flights of his Bearcat in preparation for the planned record attempt, and recorded an excellent maximum speed of 801km/h after several runs. Then one cylinder failed. Once again he was forced to abandon his attempt. In September he won again at Reno, the fourth time in succession, using a borrowed engine. Subsequently he enlarged the Bearcat's fin, and made further modifications to the engine, increasing its power to around 3,350hp. Internal pressure in the undercarriage wheel wells had forced them open by about 1cm, so small air outlet slots were cut in them. *Conquest I* was the new name given to the white aircraft, and in late summer 1969 Greenamyer set off for Edwards AFB again.

On the morning of 16 August 1969 Greenamyer swept over the three-kilometre course four times. In spite of a drop in oil pressure towards the end of the flight,

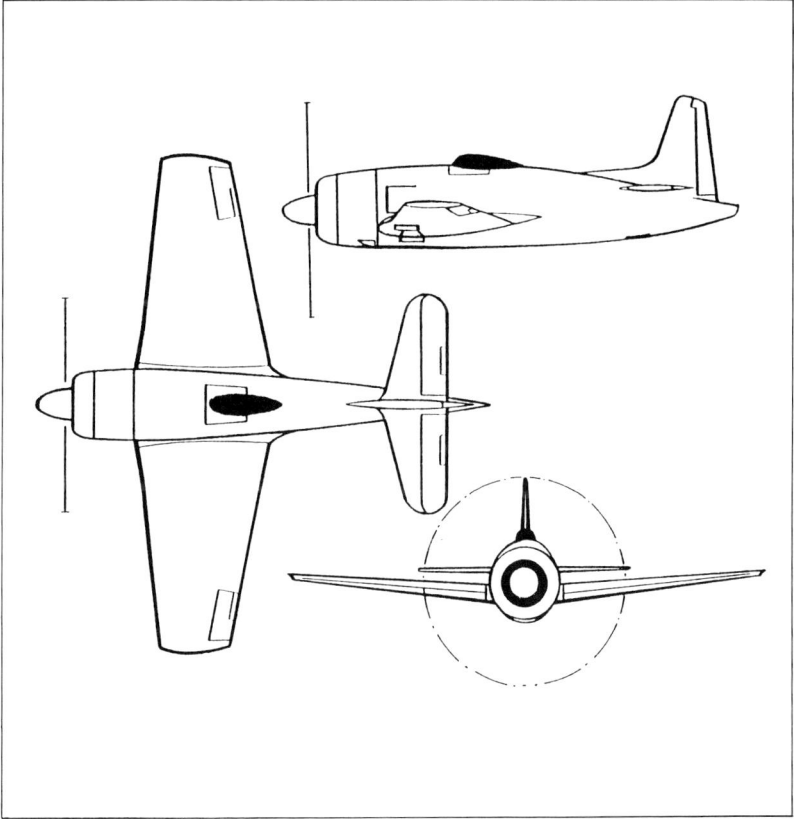

Darryl Greenamyer's converted Grumman F8F-2 Conquest I.

his average speed was 769.5km/h. He had finally succeeded. Yet Greenamyer was confident that he could squeeze a bit more speed out of the aircraft. In the afternoon he repeated his four passes. The fastest was over 820km/h, and the slowest, into wind, more than 730km/h. His new average speed was 776.449km/h — Fritz Wendel's record had finally been broken after exactly thirty years. The temperature inside the cockpit of *Conquest I* had been more than 90 °C during the record flights. The closely-cowled and highly supercharged engine developed such heat that Greenamyer could not touch the control levers without thick gloves, and he had strapped an ice bag to his chest so that he could cool his fingers now and then. His feet were protected from the heat by thick fur boots.

It was several years before there was any serious challenge to the new record. In the early 1970s Charles Lyford had completely rebuilt his fast P-51D Mustang,

Conquest I, *1969.*

Darryl Greenamyer makes his record flight in Conquest I.

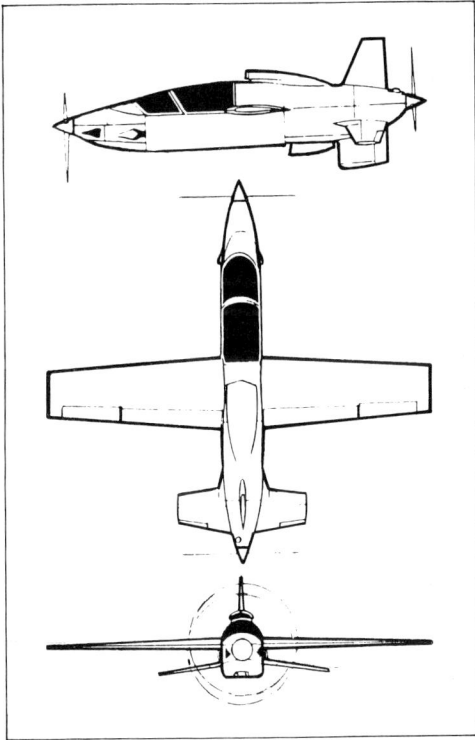

Aero Design DG-1, 1977.

Bardahl Special, for a planned attempt on the record, but he had abandoned the project again. David Garber, a commercial pilot and spare-time sports racing pilot, had more ambitious ideas. In late 1974 he began the construction in Florida of a twin-engined machine of his own design, the DG-1, which he intended to fly in circuit races and in record attempts. The machine was broadly similar in layout to a Do 335, reduced to about 45 per cent of the size, and featured a tractor propeller in the nose and a pusher propeller in the tail. The tiny single-seater was constructed using steel tubing, graphite-reinforced plastic and plywood, and power was supplied by two supercharged Mazda RX-3 Wankel engines rated at 330hp each. Using special Record wings Garber hoped to achieve more than 800km/h with his design. The aircraft was shown to the public when it was almost complete, and was due to carry out its first flight in spring 1977, but nothing has been heard of it since then.

Every year dozens of Mustangs battled hard and long for the top positions at Reno and at various other far-flung locations in the United States. Among them was a certain P-51D which had first turned up for the Reno races in 1964. It raced for several years in a relatively unmodified condition, but later it was slimmed down, utilising the conventional methods, and eventually reappeared with shorter wings, a more powerful Merlin engine, and a new propeller with a pointed spinner. The rejuvenated machine was now christened *Miss R J*. At Reno in 1969 it was just beaten by Greenamyer's *Conquest 1*, but only after its engine had lost power. Further modifications were made to the cockpit, but its racing exploits in succeeding years ended in a regular stream of wrecked engines. In 1971 the machine turned up again at Reno, this time with a new owner and sporting the name *Roto Finish*, but retaining its civil registration, N7715C. It did not do particularly well, and its owner carried out further modifications. This time the special treatment met with success, achieving an impressive victory over its chief opponent, *Conquest 1*. In the autumn of 1973 the Mustang again changed hands, then again in February 1974. The new owner, a wealthy rancher and businessman named Ed Browning, christened the bright-red Mustang *Red Baron*, and entrusted it to the talented young pilot Roy 'Mac' McClain. Unfortunately the engine gave up the ghost at Reno early in the race.

It was decided that the over-tuned Merlin needed to be replaced, this time by a larger Rolls-Royce Griffon, a ploy which had proved successful with the Spitfire. After a long search two Griffons were located in an English scrapyard. They were from different production series, but were complete with their contra-rotating

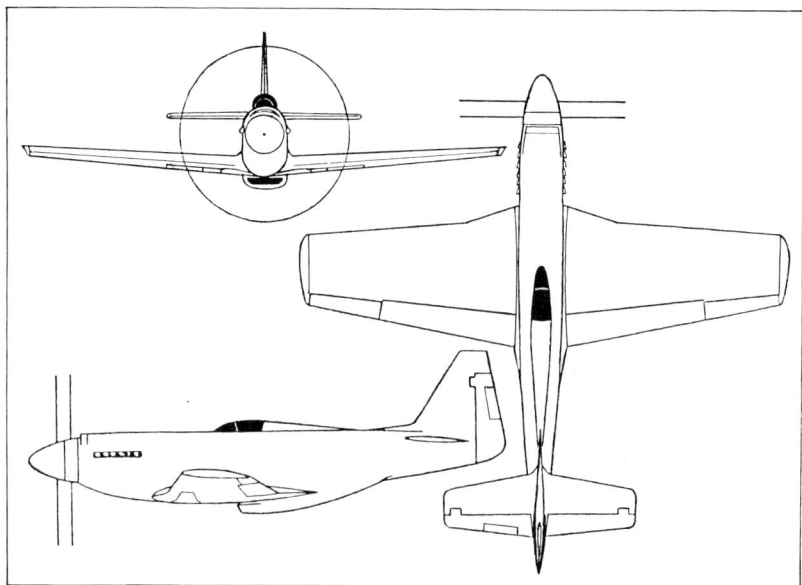

North American P-51D-25/RB-51 Red Baron, *1979.*

propellers. The *Red Baron* team, which included the designer Bruce Boland and the engine expert Dave Zeuschel, got down to the work of installing the new engine, which was larger and about 250kg heavier, into the old Mustang airframe. It was not a simple task, but the Griffon 54, originally produced for the Avro Shackleton long-range reconnaissance aircraft, proved to be extremely reliable, and produced between 3,400 and 4,000hp, depending on the composition of the fuel. The Mustang, now designated the RB-51, first flew in the summer of 1975. A series of supplementary modifications proved necessary, including the installation of additive injector systems and a considerably larger fin, but the aeroplane then proved to be virtually unbeatable. In the late 1970s pilots exploited the machine's enormous superiority to record a string of impressive victories in the hands of various pilots, among them Darryl Greenamyer. After Greenamyer had retired from the *Red Baron* team, the young pilot Steve Hinton took his place at the controls. Eventually the series of racing successes convinced the owner that it was

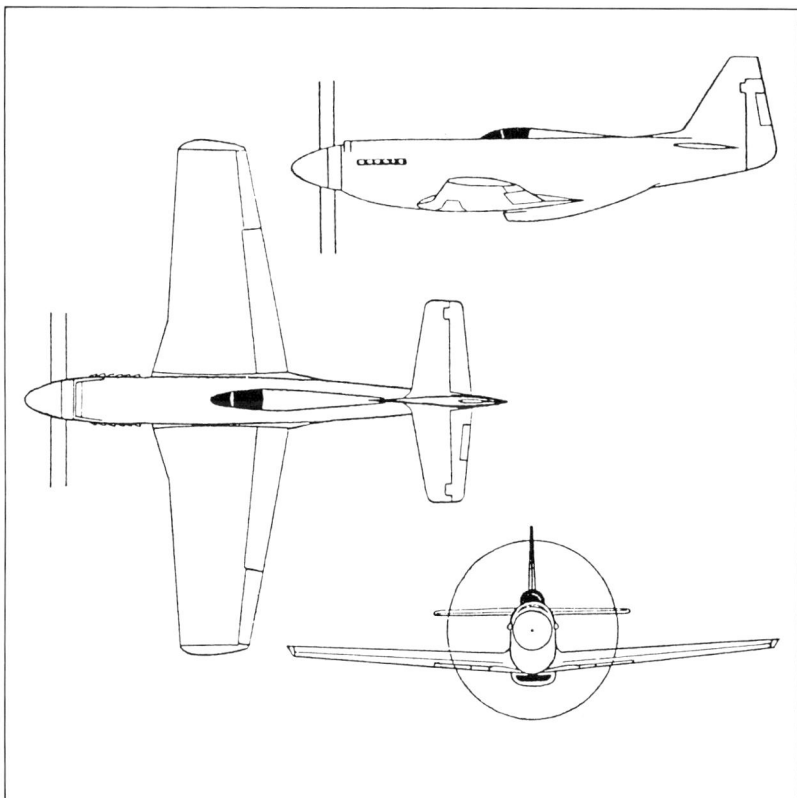

RB-51 Red Baron, *1979.*

time for an attempt at the world speed record for propeller-driven aircraft, still held by *Conquest 1*. In July 1976 McClain had been timed at 810km/h close to ground level, and now the decision was made to prepare for an official record attempt. In August 1979 the team assembled at the Tonopah Mud Flats in Nevada. Steve Hinton was selected to be the pilot for the record attempt. On 10 August, after a number of test flights, the first attempt was made, but engine problems thwarted the effort. For good or ill the decision was made to install the second Griffon there and then, overnight. During test flying on the following day another tiny leak showed up in the engine, but it proved possible to seal it satisfactorily. Finally, on 12 August, Hinton took off again for another record attempt. It was early in the morning, because air turbulence was expected later.

RB-51 Red Baron, *1979.*

Apart from a tailwheel door which failed to close, there were no particular difficulties. The measuring equipment recorded a satisfying record average speed of 787km/h, but the team decided to try again on the following day — the 500mph (804.5km/h) frontier was beckoning. Poor weather and a burned-out sparking plug delayed them, but on the morning of 14 August 1979 things at last went well on all four runs, the fastest of them being clocked at about 808km/h. The new, officially notified record now stood at 803.092km/h. Although this was just short of 500mph, it was the first time that the 800km/h limit had been exceeded officially by an aircraft powered by a piston engine and propeller.

The *Red Baron* was destined to survive this triumph by just one month. At the end of an exciting Reno competition with two other Mustangs named *Jeannie* and *Sumthin' Else*, a piston in the RB-51's engine disintegrated on the final straight.

The six stationary propeller blades had the same effect as a giant airbrake, and the machine stalled, crashed on to a stone-covered hillside, and was written off. Steve Hinton survived, but suffered severe injuries.

That was the end of the road for the outstanding RB-51, but it was by no means the end of the struggle for the piston-engined aircraft speed record. Both *Jeannie* and *Sumthin' Else* had turned out to be serious aspirants, and hints about record attempts were made from time to time. Both P-51D-based aircraft were constantly modified and improved by their owners, with maximum performance always in mind, and thus it was that the 1980 and 1981 Reno races once again saw exciting duels between the two machines, with the other participants generally left well behind. In 1982, however, another contender turned up at Reno and staked its claim, winning the race literally in the last second. This was *Dago Red*, a Mustang modification based on the lines of *Jeannie*. As was the case with several other successful racing aircraft, the high-speed experts Bruce Boland and Pete Law were vital members of the team. Instead of the *Jeannie's* Merlin, highly tuned by Dave Zeuschel, the red, yellow and white *Dago Red* was fitted with a licence-built version of the same unit made by Packard and prepared by engine specialist Mike Nixon. The young pilot Ron Hevle 'came, saw and conquered', to the surprise of all the participants. But that was not enough for the owner, Frank Taylor. In the summer of 1983 he prepared to fulfil the dream that he had harboured for so long,

Dago Red *and* Dreadnought *at the 1983 Reno races.*

Dago Red, *1983*.

and took his team to California's Mojave Desert to attack the speed record for propeller-driven aircraft. Complex calculations had indicated a slightly higher chance of success over the 15/25-kilometre course allowed by the regulations, in preference to the three-kilometre course, which had to be flown at ground level, not least because hot-air turbulence was less of a problem at high altitude. The result confirmed the computer prognosis: 832.12km/h was the surprisingly high average value from the two passes which were flown on 30 July 1983.

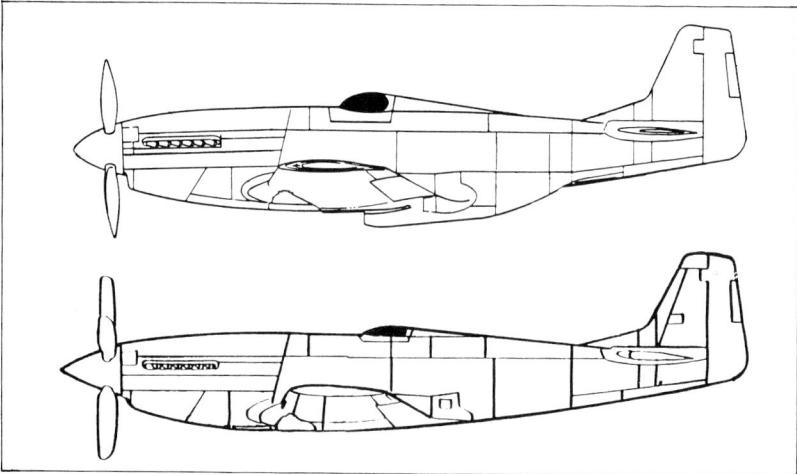

Comparison of Dago Red *and* Stiletto.

Stiletto, *a former P-51D-25 Mustang.*

Although the *Dago Red* team's achievement was extremely impressive, it goes without saying that this is not the end of the story. Other teams are still striving for the record, both in the USA and in other countries. Although the majority of the record hopefuls are based on single-seat fighters from the 1940s, modified to a more or less drastic extent, there have also been reports of a number of interesting new designs, some of them downright peculiar, and most of them, unfortunately, unlikely ever to see the light of day. In the spring of 1989 the latter category was joined by a group of British enthusiasts from Skysport Engineering in Bedford-shire, who announced their intention to resurrect the 1940 Heston Type 5 Racer for an attack on the world speed record. Alas, the project came to nothing, as did a plan proposed by their compatriot, Patrick Luscombe. He wanted to exploit the supposed record potential of the Hawker Sea Fury F.B.11 single-seat fighter. For the record attempt he intended fitting the aircraft with a more powerful version of the Bristol Centaurus eighteen-cylinder two-row radial engine.

One German designer also had ideas for future record aircraft. In the early 1970s Luigi Colani published the first of his designs, the C-309, its designation harking back to Messerschmitt history. Like virtually all the projects emanating from this style-conscious designer, this was highly unusual. It was a tiny aircraft, only 4m long, with nose and tail propellers in the style of the Do 335. Two NSU Wankel engines, each producing 180hp, were to provide the power, while the pilot lay prone in the fuselage between the engines. The wing was sharply swept back, and featured an extreme degree of anhedral. The nosewheel and auxiliary wheels were retractable, while the tailwheel at the point of the ventral fin could be covered by flaps. Some years later Colani presented a substantially revised version of his design in the form of a full-size mockup, this time in collaboration with some Japanese companies. The fuselage had grown much longer, and now featured a pronounced 'Coke-bottle' shape in accordance with the area rule established by the NASA aerodynamicist Richard Whitcomb, in an attempt to improve the airflow when flying close to the speed of sound. The two propellers were fitted with five blades, again sickle-shaped, and swept forward, against the direction of flight.

Once again the pilot lay prone between two Wankel engines, this time made by Mazda and producing 320hp each. The span of the diminutive wing, which had winglets at its tips, was only 2.64m.

The maximum speed of this design, the C-309 Bohu, had been calculated at 892km/h, in spite of the fixed undercarriage legs, which doubled as supplementary stabilising surfaces. In 1985 a further Colani study, the Pontresina, was shown

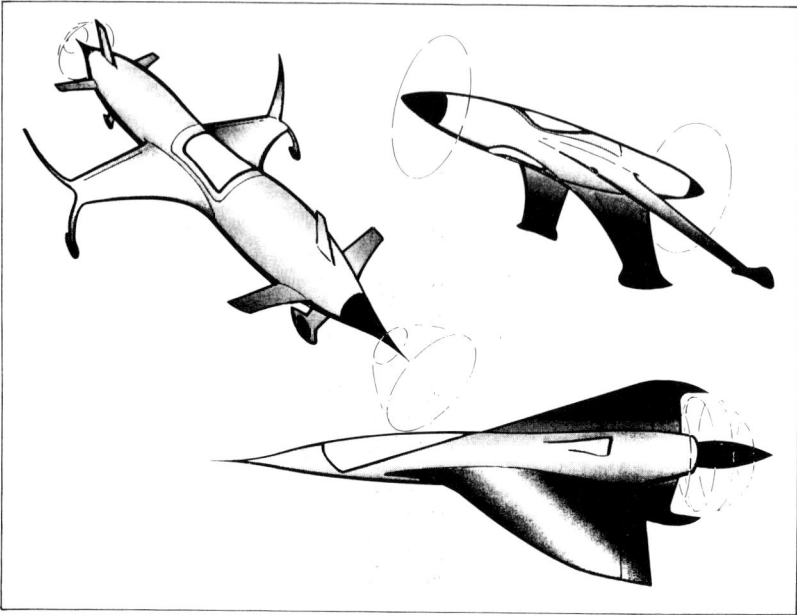

Three designs by Luigi Colani: the C-309, Bohu and Pontresina.

full-size. This was a racy little single-seater with delta wings, to be manufactured using composite materials, and again featured two airscrews with sickle-form blades, this time arranged as contra-rotating pusher propellers in the tail. Two Mazda turbo-Wankel engines were expected to propel the tiny projectile at an astonishing 940km/h.

All the other record aspirants were and are to be found in the USA, not least for financial reasons. Here, too, various versions of the Hawker Sea Fury have been making their mark. This venerable British carrier-based single-seat fighter has now become a highly desirable aeroplane. Approximately 920 were built between 1944 and 1951, and of those about forty are still in existence worldwide, most of them no longer in airworthy condition, as is the case with most surviving piston-engined aircraft of the period. The most successful and famous of them to date is a two-seat Sea Fury Mk 20 named *Dreadnought*, which has been fitted with a twenty-eight-cylinder Pratt & Whitney R-4360 Wasp Major radial engine producing around 50 per cent more power than the 2,540hp eighteen-cylinder Bristol Centaurus radial engine which was its original powerplant. Because of its unusual shape, this engine is also known by the nickname 'Corncob'. The transplant was bold but worthwhile, for in 1983 the *Dreadnought* showed a clean pair of heels to the assembled Mustang fleet, winning the Unlimited race by a substantial margin. In 1984 the race went badly for the team, and in 1985 the aeroplane suffered the imposition of a few penalty seconds when the pilot cut the last pylon. The winner on this occasion was another radial-engined racer, a reincarnated Vought-Goodyear Corsair, also fitted with an R-4360, and flown by Steve Hinton, who had by now recovered from his injuries. In 1986 *Dreadnought* again kept its nose in front. It was followed by a similarly modified, brilliant red Sea Fury named *Furias*.

In the succeeding years of 1987, 1988 and 1989 *Dreadnought* appeared to be destined to be permanent runner-up: first behind a tuned Mustang named *Strega*, ahead of *Dago Red*, but on the next two occasions chasing another representative of the radial-engine faction, a similarly highly tuned Grumman F8F-2 named *Rare Bear*. Lyle Shelton, a former Navy and later TWA pilot, acquired this aircraft as scrap in 1968, and devoted his own time to making it airworthy and competitive. He shortened the wings slightly, and in place of the Pratt & Whitney R-2800, which was missing, he installed a Wright R-3350 — another eighteen-cylinder double-row radial engine — which had come from a Douglas Skyraider. The four-bladed propeller, complete with spinner, came from a Douglas DC-7.

In the following year, 1969, Shelton entered the machine at Reno, and took fifth place at the first attempt, despite the fact that he had been so rushed that the machine, christened *Able Cat*, was still finished in primer. There had been no time to apply the final paint finish. In the following years the Bearcat was steadily improved, and bore a succession of names: *Phoenix I*, *Phast Phoenix*, *US Thrift 7¼% Special*, *Omni Special*, *Spirit of 77*, and, since 1980, *Rare Bear*. It has achieved a number of outstanding successes, including an international time-to-climb record on 6 February 1972, from zero to 3,000m altitude in exactly 91.9 seconds; and overall victory at Reno in 1973, 1974 and 1975. However, it also suffered a series of misfortunes, including a spectacular belly landing in 1976. It was a good twelve years before Lyle Shelton and *Rare Bear* were successful again. Overall victory at Reno finally fell to the pair again in 1988. In the race *Rare Bear's* fastest circuit was timed at a breathtaking 763.830km/h, which included eight pylon turns over the 14,841m circuit.

Encouraged by this success, the Rare Bear Racing Team moved to Las Vegas, New Mexico, in August 1989, for an attempt on the piston-engined-aircraft world speed record, at first over the three-kilometre, low-altitude course. After completing a number of test flights the team removed the usual four-bladed propeller and installed a specially manufactured three-bladed unit. This promised even higher speeds, but required further exhaustive test flights. As the Reno Air Races were due to take place a few weeks later, the decision was taken to spare the aircraft the extra testing, and the proven four-bladed propeller was re-fitted for the actual record attempt. The first official attempt on the morning of 20 August had to be abandoned when a minor leak developed in the cooling system. After the fault had been repaired, Shelton took off again, shortly after midday. After four passes, two in each direction, the result was announced: 830.045km/h — enough for the three-kilometre record, but still 2km/h under the fifteen-kilometre record set by Frank Taylor. Shelton immediately decided to make a further record attempt on the following morning. Once again cooling problems thwarted him, and he was forced to land after the third of the requisite four runs, although he had achieved a sensational 871km/h on one pass. At about 1530hrs the aircraft was ready again, and this time everything went smoothly. Shelton set a new record average speed of 850.263km/h: more than enough to beat the previous best mark, set by Frank Taylor's *Dago Red*, by the minimum margin of one per cent.

If further proof of the performance of this 'winning combination' was required, the 1989 Reno result provided it. Shelton won again, this time with a long lead over his most powerful rival, Rick Brickert, flying the amazing *Dreadnought*. Shelton intends to try again in 1990, and he is confident of pushing the three-kilometre record even higher — there is even talk of 925km/h. This is even more amazing when the greater frontal area of the large-volume (71.5-litre swept capacity) radial engine, compared with that of the V-12 in-line engine (Merlin 27 litres, Griffon 36.7 litres), is considered. In fact, a tuned Merlin produces the same level of power, albeit at the high rotational speed of around 3,800rpm and at supercharging pressures of 4-5 atmospheres, factors which militate against durability. In every race several of these expensive (£50,000) racing engines, producing around 4,000hp, lose power and suffer damage.

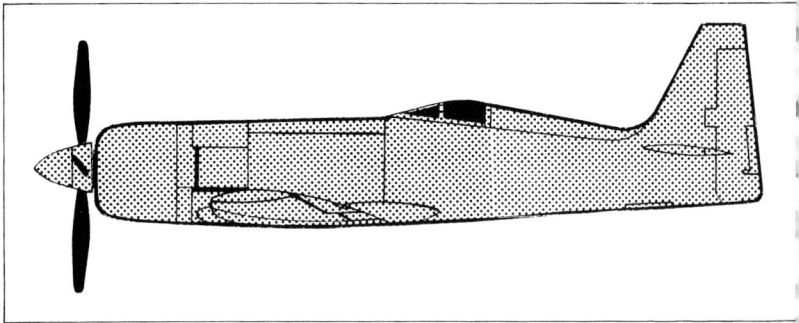

Levolor Sea Fury Blind Man's Bluff, *1987.*

The greater durability of the large radial engines compensates to some extent for their relatively large frontal area. This may also have been one reason why the American racing enthusiast Eric Lorentzen decided to use another Sea Fury for his racing machine — and possibly for record attempts, too. In 1987 he produced *Blind Man's Bluff*, a much modified Sea Fury Mk 20 which had originally been a two-seater. It was now powered by a Wright R-3350, enclosed in a cowling from a Douglas Invader. Alcohol was originally intended as the fuel, but difficulties arose, and the decision was made to use standard fuel for the Reno races. However, it seems that the machine did not fulfil the expectations vested in it. The planned record flight did not take place, and shortly after this the aircraft changed hands.

Many of the Rolls-Royce-powered Mustang conversions bear no more than a remote similarity to the original. For example, the *Stiletto*, the 1984 winner at Reno, had had the wings cropped short, the clumsy tunnel radiator removed, and air intake slots cut in the wing leading edge.

Two Mustang variants did stay somewhat closer to the shape of the original aeroplane, apart from much shorter wings and mini-canopies. These are the *Strega*, the Reno victor in 1987, and *Precious Metal*, powered by a Rolls-Royce Griffon with contra-rotating three-bladed propellers. But the sleek silver *Precious Metal* was dogged by misfortune. At the 1988 Reno Air Races the engine failed in flight, and it was seriously damaged in the resultant belly landing in the desert. The aircraft was painstakingly rebuilt, and in May 1989 its owner, Don Whittington, made an attempt on the world record, but once again his effort came to grief, ending with engine damage and a subsequent belly landing. Again the promising machine was repaired, but early in 1990 Whittington ran out of fuel and was forced to ditch. The aircraft was severely damaged, but the pilot escaped with his life.

Another Mustang-based racer, the *Vendetta*, which first appeared in 1988, exhibited the most extensive modifications yet. It was fitted with the wings and tailplane of a Learjet 23 business jet. Engine problems prevented this interesting aircraft from competing in the Reno Air Races, where it was entered under the official name of 'North American-Dilly 1001 Vendetta', but unofficially as 'Learfang' or 'Learstang'. Unfortunately this machine sustained severe damage in June 1989, as the result of an emergency landing after engine problems, before it had had a chance to show its considerable potential.

Although the American racing and record scene is still dominated by former single-seat fighters whose basic airframes are more than forty years old, there has been a slow but steady trend towards completely new aircraft, which now have to be considered as serious competition. The first of them was the Tsunami, a sort of

Tsunami, 1986.

mini-Mustang. Designed and built by designer Bruce Boland and his team for the aircraft engine specialist and racing fan John Sandberg (JRS Enterprises), this small all-metal racer is powered by a Packard-built Rolls-Royce Merlin producing 3,300hp or more, but its frontal area is only 65 per cent that of a full-size Mustang. Although it is of advanced conception, it is largely based on standard materials and proven components from other machines, in an effort to keep the risks as low as possible. For example, its four-bladed propeller came from a North American T-28 Trojan two-seat trainer, the undercarriage from a Piper Aerostar, the main wheels from a Learjet, and the tailwheel from a P-51H Mustang. The team encountered an unexpected problem when it came to procuring the rivets, screws and nuts required. At the time, the Boeing company was just starting series production of their 757 and 767 models, and had swept the entire market clean.

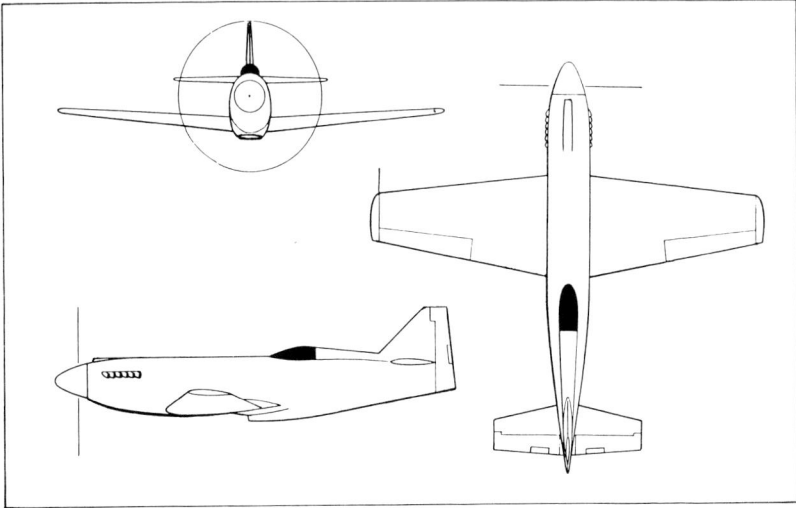

Tsunami.

Nevertheless, the first flight took place on 17 August 1986, and the new aeroplane was adjusted and trimmed over the following months. Its first competitive appearance, in the Reno races of September 1987, was promising, although it ended prematurely with an overheated engine, one damaged undercarriage leg, a bent propeller and some minor skin damage. When the necessary repairs were carried out a number of improvements were made, including the installation of a dynamic carburettor air inlet in place of the former NACA 'flush intake', an enlarged tunnel radiator on the underside of the fuselage and a more angular fin, with a larger aerodynamic balance on the rudder. An attempt on the world record had been slated for July 1988, but the extensive modifications forced a postponement. At Reno, two months later, the Tsunami was flown by Steve Hinton, who had recovered once more from his injuries. The machine held its own extremely well, but again suffered from problems with the cooling system, which necessitated further time-consuming adjustments.

A new record attempt was planned for early September 1989, at Wendover, Nevada, but while preparations were being made for the record flights the devastating news broke of *Rare Bear's* successful attack on the record. This meant that the minimum one per cent margin required an average speed of at least 859km/h. Late in the afternoon of 5 September 1989 everything was ready, and John Sandberg took off for his record effort. But after two fast passes he had to break off the flight. Severe turbulence had unsettled both pilot and aeroplane. At noon on the following day he took off again. One fast pass, two, then the aircraft suddenly started to belch smoke — engine damage looked likely. After a smooth landing the reason became evident: the piston rings on the left bank had failed, and they had to be changed. This was a great disappointment, but, after all, the highly-tuned Merlin was being asked to cope with prodigious demands. The octane rating of the aircraft fuel had been raised from 145 to 160 with a Boron additive, and finally raised to 200 with supplementary alcohol-water injection. Overnight the engine was readied again. The renewed attempt was made on the afternoon of 7 September. First a few gentle test circuits were flown to warm up. Everything was in order, but the landing was none too smooth, and first the port undercarriage leg gave way, followed by the starboard leg, resulting in a belly landing. An hydraulic control valve had failed. But the Tsunami team does not intend to give up; after all, the computer has predicted a top speed of 885km/h. The team also intends to install a pair of floats later, to allow the aircraft to attack the existing world speed record for seaplanes of 709km/h, set by the Italian Macchi-Castoldi MC.72 in 1934. After all, the name Tsunami is the Japanese for 'Killer Wave'.

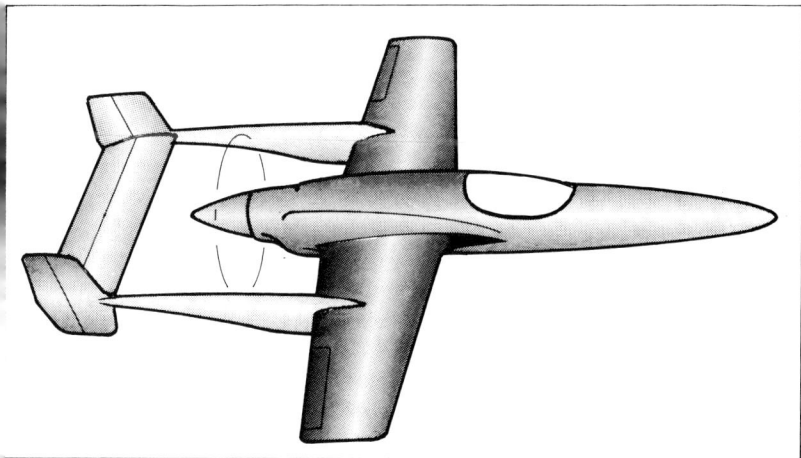

Schapel S-175 Finesse, 1983.

The Tsunami is by no means the only new American design intended for record attempts; a number of others are in preparation. For example, Rodney Schapel, who lives in Reno, Nevada, and works for the Lockheed company, made a name for himself back in the 1950s and 1960s by designing low-drag bodies for high-speed and world record cars, including the jet-powered *Spirit of America*. In the very early 1980s he published designs for agricultural, civil and military aircraft, among them the S-1275 Finesse, a racing and record aircraft to be built using composite materials. This mid-wing machine, with a central fuselage and twin tailbooms, was intended to be powered by a modified Chrysler Stake II car engine rated at 1,400hp, driving a pusher propeller. However, this interesting design, which is reminiscent of the German Focke-Wulf projects of the 1940s, now appears to have been shelved.

Burt Rutan's Pond Racer under construction, 1990.

Another twin-boom aeroplane has progressed beyond the drawing board. This is the Pond Racer, a product of the unique talent of Burt Rutan, designer of the world-encircling Voyager of 1986. Two Nissan six-cylinder turbo-charged engines burning methanol fuel, and each producing 1,000hp at 8,000rpm, provide the power for this unusual small aircraft, which is built entirely of composite materials: epoxy impregnated carbon-fibre sandwich laminate with balsa core material. The wings feature slight forward sweep. In racing events the Pond Racer is to be flown by its owner, Bob Pond, but for record attempts — speeds around 900km/h are expected — Burt's brother, Dick Rutan, will take the controls. It was Dick who co-piloted the Voyager with Jeana Yeager in the round-the-world flight. The sleek single-seater is intended to fly for the first time in 1990.

The latest and most ambitious machine to join the group of record challengers is the Mach Buster I built by Californian Bill Montagne. This is a two-seat shoulder-wing monoplane, slightly reminiscent of the Northrop T-38 Talon, but powered by a 2,130hp V-8 engine in the fuselage, driving a sickle-shaped four-bladed

Rutan's Pond Racer as it might appear at a future Reno meeting.

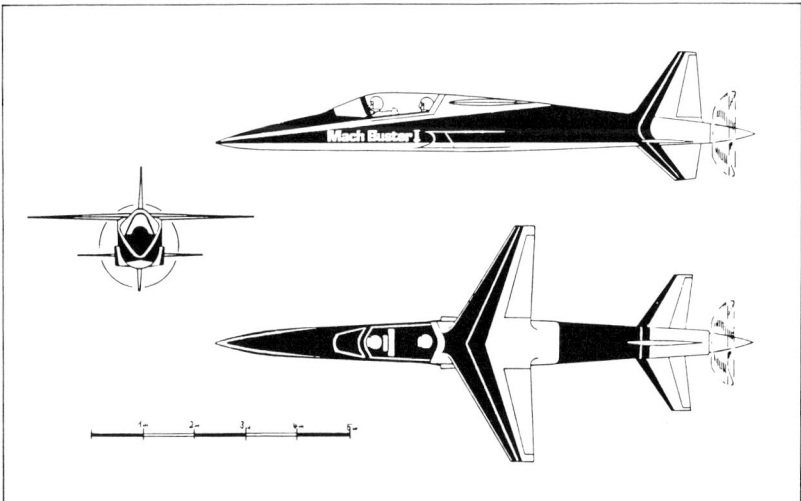

Bill Montagne's Mach Buster I, 1988.

pusher propeller located aft of the cruciform tail. The half-finished machine was shown to the public at Oshkosh in 1987, but the claims made for this amateur design invite a measure of scepticism. Its aim is to break the sound barrier, a target long considered unattainable by propeller-driven aircraft. It seems likely to remain unattainable.

CHRONOLOGICAL DATA

A Date
B Location
C Pilot / nationality
D Aeroplane (registration)
E Reference number, technical data list
F Maximum speed, theoretical, in km/h at ( ) km altitude
G Maximum speed, achieved,   in km/h at ( ) km altitude
H Average speed, officially measured, in km/h
I Time, officially measured, in seconds
K Distance, officially measured, in km (in m where indicated)

TECHNICAL DATA

1 Reference number
2 Aeroplane / Designer(s)
3 Year
4 Engine(s), number, designation / maximum power in hp,
   type, number of cylinders/ number of propeller blades
   type: H, I = in-line, R = radial, RC = rotary piston engine (Wankel),
   Rot = rotary, V, W, X
5 Wing span, in m
6 Overall length, in m
7 Wing area, in m^2
8 Wing aspect ratio
9 Wing leading edge sweep angle(s), in degrees
10 Take-off weight, in kg
11 Power loading, in kg/DIN hp
12 Wing loading at t/o weight, in kg/m^2
13 Configuration:

HW high wing	1,2,3F 1,2,3 fin(s)	2,3W	2,3 wheels fixed
MW mid wing	TF ` T-type fin	(2,3W)	2,3 wheels retr.
LW low wing	+F cross-type fin	1S	1 skid
2W biplane	YF Y-type fin		

CONVERSION TABLE

1 kilometre (km) = 0.62137 statute miles   1kg (kg) = 2.2046lb
1 statute mile = 1.609344km   1lb = 0.4536kg
1 metre = 3.28ft   1 DIN hp = 0.986hp
1 foot = 0.3048m   1hp = 1.014 DINhp
1 square metre (m^2) = 10.764 sq ft
1 square foot = 0.0929m^2

A	B	C	D	E	F	G	H	I	K
17.12.1903	Kill Devil Hills, NC, USA	Wilbur Wright USA	Wright Flyer I	868		50		59.0	800m
9.11.1904	Dayton Ohio, USA	Wilbur Wright USA	Wright Flyer II	869		52		304.0	4420m
29. 9.1905 4.10.1905	Dayton Ohio, USA	Orville Wright USA	Wright Flyer III	870		58 60		1,195.0 1,997.0	19.3 33.4
5.10.1905	Dayton Ohio, USA	Wilbur Wright USA	Wright Flyer III	870		61		2,283.0	39.0
12.11.1906	Bagatelle F	Alberto Santos-Dumont F	Santos-Dumont 14bis (mod) (14bis)	246			**41.292**	7.2 21.2	82.6m 220m
26.10.1907 9.11.1907	Issy-les-Moulineaux F	Henry Farman F	Voisin-Farman I	256		67	**52.768** 50.1	52.6 74.0	771m 1113m
14. 5.1908	Kill Devil Hills, NC, USA	Orville Wright Wilbur Wright USA	Wright Flyer IIImod	871		65		220.0 449.0	4,000m 8,000m
12. 9.1908	Fort Myer Wash DC, USA	Orville Wright USA	Wright A	872		65		4,460.0	80.0
30.10.1908	Reims F	Henry Farman F	Voisin-Farman I(bis)	256		81		1,200.0	27.0
20. 5.1909	Pau F	Paul Tissandier F	Wright A (France)	872		65	**54.795** 55.645	3,720.0	57.5
7.1909	Fort Myer Wash DC, USA	Orville Wright USA	Wright A mod (Signal Corps)	873		72			
22. 8.1909	Reims F	Paul Tissandier F	Wright A (France)	872			63.187	1,709.2	30.0
22. 8.1909	Reims F	Eugène Lefebvre F	Wright A (France)	872			66.8		

Date	Place	Pilot	Aircraft						
23. 8.1909	Reims F	Glenn H Curtiss USA	Curtiss-Herring Reims Machine	806	96	78	**69.822**	515.6	10.0
24. 8.1909	Reims F	Louis Blériot F	Blériot XII (23)	209			**74.318**	484.4	10.0
8.1909	Reims F	Eugène Lefebvre F	Wright A (France)	872	84				
28. 8.1909	Reims F	Glenn H Curtiss USA	Curtiss-Herring Reims Machine	806			75.742	950.6	20.0
28. 8.1909	Reims F	Louis Blériot F	Blériot XII (23)	209			**76.956**	467.8	10.0
1.1910	Hammondsport NY, USA	Glenn H Curtiss USA	Curtiss-Herring Reims Machine	806	88				
23. 4.1910	Nice F	Hubert Latham F	Antoinette VII (5)	201			**77.562**	336.8	7,242m
10. 7.1910	Reims F	Léon Morane F	Blériot XI(mod) (53)	207			**106.509**	169.0	5.0
9.1910	— F	Hubert Latham F	Antoinette VII (5)	201		110			
1.10.1910						112			
10.1910	Long Island NY, USA	Orville Wright USA	Wright R Baby Grand	874	120	113			
29.10.1910	Long Island NY, USA	Alfred Leblanc F	Blériot XIbis	208		114	**109.756**	164.78	5.0
12. 4.1911	Pau F	Alfred Leblanc F	Blériot XIbis	208			**111.801**	161.0	5.0
5.1911	Châlons F	Edouard de Niéport F	Nieuport IIN	232			116.5		
11. 5.1911							**119.760**	3006.0	100.0
12. 6.1911	Etampes F	Alfred Leblanc F	Blériot XXIII	210			**125.000**	144.0	5.0

A	B	C	D	E	F	G	H	I	K
16. 6.1911	Châlons F	Edouard de Niéport F	Nieuport IIG Astra	233			130.058	138.4	5.0
21. 6.1911	Châlons F	Edouard de Niéport F	Nieuport IIG	234		150	133.136	270.4	10.0
							145.51		20.0
13. 1.1912	Pau F	Jules Védrines F	Deperdussin Course	220			145.161	124.0	5.0
22. 2.1912	Pau F	Jules Védrines F	Deperdussin Course	221			161.290	223.2	10.0
29. 2.1912							162.455	221.6	10.0
1. 3.1912							166.821	215.8	10.0
2. 3.1912							167.910	214.4	10.0
13. 7.1912	Reims F	Jules Védrines F	Deperdussin Monocoque Gordon Bennett	222		179	170.777	210.8	10.0
9. 9.1912	Chicago Ill, USA	Jules Védrines F	Deperdussin Monocoque Gordon Bennett	222			174.100 (173.098)	415.95	20.0
9.1912	Chicago Ill, USA	Glenn L Martin USA	Burgess Cup Defender (did not fly)	805	180				
17. 6.1913	Reims F	Maurice Prévost F	Deperdussin Monocoque Gordon Bennett (F–1)	223	220		179.820	200.2	10.0
27. 9.1913	Reims F	Emile Védrines F	Ponnier Gordon Bennett (F–5)	245	220		184.805	1,948.0	100.0
27. 9.1913	Reims F	Maurice Prévost F	Deperdussin Monocoque Gordon Bennett (F–1)	223	220		191.898	187.6	10.0
29. 9.1913	Reims F	Eugène Gilbert F	Deperdussin Monocoque Gordon Bennett (F–2)	225	220		199.335	180.6	10.0
29. 9.1913	Reims F	Emile Védrines F	Ponnier Gordon Bennett (F–5)	245	230	230	200.893	179.2	10.0

Date	Place	Pilot	Aircraft						
29. 9.1913	Reims F	Maurice Prévost F	Deperdussin Monocoque Gordon Bennett (F–1)	224	220		**203.850**	176.6	10.0
1. 4.1914	Reims F	Emile Védrines F	Ponnier Gordon Bennett	245	230		203.4	177.0	10.0
6.1914	Farnborough UK	Norman Spratt UK	Royal Aircraft Factory S.E.4 (628)	717	230	217			
1918	— F	— F	SPAD S.XVII	249		240			
26. 4.1918	Langley Field Virginia, USA	Gianfelice–Gino I	Ansaldo S.V.A.5 Primo	401		238	233.35	3,600.0	
4.1918	— UK	Harry Hawker UK	Sopwith 7F.1 Snipe (B9967)	718		251			
19. 8.1918	— USA	Roland Rohlfs USA	Curtiss 502/18–T–1 Wasp (A–3325)	807		263			
10.1918	Dessau D	Hellmuth von Krohn D	Junkers J9/I (DI)	335		240			
28. 5.1919	Turin I	Francesco Brack–Papa I	Fiat B.R. (9001)	403		270			
26. 6.1919 / 9.1919	— UK	Harry Hawker UK	Sopwith 107 Schneider (G–EAKI)	719		273	261.629		
2. 9.1919 / 25. 9.1919 / 3.10.1919	Paris F	Sadi Lecointe F	Spad-Herbemont S.20bis 1	250	265	290	249.307	2,888.0	200.0
15.10.1919	Paris F	Sadi Lecointe F	Spad-Herbemont S.20bis 2	251		323?	247.720	2,767.0	190.4
20.10.1919	Paris F	Sadi Lecointe F	Spad-Herbemont S.20bis 3	252		266	252.000	2,720.0	190.4

A	B	C	D	E	F	G	H	I	K
22.10.1919	Paris F	Bernard de Romanet F	Nieuport 29V	235			268.631	2,551.0	190.4
20.11.1919	Montecello I	— I	Savoia MVT	408			274	3,600.0	
16.12.1919	Paris F	Sadi Lecointe F	Nieuport 29V	235		365?	307.225		1.0
3. 1.1920	Paris F	Sadi Lecointe F	Nieuport 29V (6)	235			266.314	2,573.0	190.4
1. 2.1920	Villacoublay F	Sadi Lecointe F	Nieuport 29V (6)	235			274		1.0
7. 2.1920							275.862	13.05	1.0
28. 2.1920	Villacoublay F	Jean Casale F	Spad-Herbemont S.20bis 4	253		288	283.464	12.70	1.0
3. 3.1920	Mirafiori/Turin I	Francesco Brack–Papa I	Fiat ARF	404		273	276.888	8,100.0	623.0
4. 3.1920							279.923		
3. 5.1920									
2. 8.1920	— USA	Rudolph W Schroeder USA	Engineering Division VCP–R	816	325	306			
25. 9.1920	Villesauvage F	Howard M Rinehart USA	Dayton-Wright RB (2)	814	306		265		100.0
9.10.1920	Buc F	Bernard de Romanet F	Spad-Herbemont S.20bis 6	254		320	292.683	12.30	1.0
9.10.1920	Buc F	Sadi Lecointe F	Nieuport 29V(bis) (10)	236			293.877	12.25	1.0
10.10.1920							296.643	12.10	1.0
20.10.1920	Villacoublay F	Sadi Lecointe F	Nieuport 29V(bis) (10)	236			302.529	11.90	1.0
4.11.1920	Buc F	Bernard de Romanet F	Spad-Herbemont S.20bis 6	255		321	309.013	11.65	1.0

Date	Location	Pilot	Aircraft						
27.11.1920	Mitchel Field NY, USA	Corliss C Moseley USA	Engineering Division VCP–R	816			299.5		1.0
12.12.1920	Villacoublay F	Sadi Lecointe F	Nieuport 29V(bis)	236		321	**313.043**	11.50	1.0
6.1921	Orly F	Bernard de Romanet F	de Monge 5.1	219		240			
7.1921	— UK	Denis G Westgarth-Heslam	Avro 539B/1 Lion (G–EAXM)	703					
23. 9.1921	Villesauvage F	Bernard de Romanet F	de Monge 5.1	219					
25. 9.1921	Villesauvage F	Sadi Lecointe F	Nieuport-Delage Sesquiplan (6)	237		393	339		1.0
26. 9.1921							**330.275**	10.90	1.0
28. 9.1921	Etampes F	Maurice Rost F	Hanriot HD.22 (did not fly)	230	360				
21.10.1921	Curtiss Field NY, USA	Bert Acosta USA	Curtiss 22 Cox Racer (Cactus Kitten)	808	344	310			
3.11.1921	Omaha Nebraska, USA	Bert Acosta USA	Curtiss 23 CR (A–6081)	809			284.45		247.2
22.11.1921	Curtiss Field NY, USA	Bert Acosta USA	Curtiss 23 CR (A–6081)	809		318	297.5		1.0
19.12.1921	Martlesham Heath, UK	James H James UK	GAC Gloster Mars I/ Bamel (G–EAXZ)	707		341	316.4		1.0
30. 4.1922	Curtiss Field NY, USA	Bert Acosta USA	Curtiss 22 Cox Racer (Cactus Kitten)	808	344	335			
7.1922	Bristol UK	Cyril F Uwins UK	Bristol 72 Racer (G–EBDR)	704	354				
26. 8.1922	Mirafiori/Turin I	Francesco Brack–Papa I	Fiat R.700	405		349	335.664	10.725	1.0

A	B	C	D	E	F	G	H	I	K
9.1922	— F	Sadi Lecointe F	Nieuport-Delage Ni-D 41 Course	240	400				
10. 9.1922	Villesauvage F	Sadi Lecointe F	Nieuport-Delage Sesquiplan (*Eugène Gilbert*)(5)	238		358			
21. 9.1922						346	**341.232**	10.55	1.0
24. 9.1922	Villesauvage F	Georges Felix Madon F	Simplex-Arnoux	247	380				
9.1922	(Project) F	Charles Nungesser F	Landwerlin-Berreur	231	450				
9.1922	Curtiss Field NY, USA	Lester D Maitland USA	Curtiss 23 R-6 (AS.68563)	810		359	339.6		1.0
2.10.1922	Curtiss Field NY, USA	Russell Maughan USA	Curtiss 23 R-6 (AS.68564)	810		376	353.1		1.0
3.10.1922	Villesauvage F	James H James UK	GAC Gloster I/Mars I Bamel (G-EAXZ)	707		346	338.824	10.625	1.0
4.10.1922						367	341.232	10.55	1.0
8.10.1922	Curtiss Field NY, USA	Russell Maughan USA	Curtiss 23 R-6 (AS.68564)	810		360	354.680	10.15	1.0
11.10.1922	Selfridge Field Michigan, USA	Lawson H Sanderson USA	Navy Wright NW-1 Mystery (A-6544)	833	354	336			
16.10.1922	Selfridge Field Michigan, USA	Russell Maughan USA	Curtiss 23 R-6 (AS.68564)	810		400	373.72		
18.10.1922	Selfridge Field Michigan, USA	William Mitchell USA	Curtiss 23 R-6 (AS.68563/68564)	810		381	345.158	10.43	1.0
31.12.1922	Istres F	Sadi Lecointe F	Nieuport-Delage Sesquiplan (*Eugène Gilbert*)	239		389	**358.923**	10.03	1.0
							347.826	10.35	1.0
2. 1.1923	Istres	Sadi Lecointe	Nieuport-Delage	239			348		

Date	Place	Pilot	Aircraft					
15. 2.1923	F	F	Sesquiplan (Eugène Gilbert)		391	**375.000**	9.60	1.0
26. 3.1923	Wright Field Ohio, USA	Russell Maughan USA	Curtiss 23 R–6 (AS.68564)	811	377	376.372	9.565	1.0
29. 3.1923	Wright Field Ohio, USA		Curtiss 23 R–6 (AS.68563)	811	435	**380.751**	9.455	1.0
29. 3.1923	Wright Field Ohio, USA	Lester D Maitland USA		811	453	386.174	9.32	1.0
10. 9.1923	Mitchel Field NY, USA	Lawson H Sanderson USA	Wright F2W–1 (TX) (A–6743)	875	383			2 St M
13. 9.1923	Mitchel Field NY, USA	Harold J Brow USA	Curtiss 32 R2C–1 (A–6691)	812	410	392.92		2 St M
16. 9.1923	Mitchel Field NY, USA	Lawson H Sanderson USA	Wright F2W–1 (TX) (A–6743)	875		398.63		2 St M
16. 9.1923	Mitchel Field USA	Alford J Williams USA	Curtiss 32 R2C–1 (A–6692)	812		410		2 St M
17. 9.1923					428	398		2 St M
1.10.1923	St Louis Mo., USA	Alex Pearson USA	Verville-Sperry R–3 (48)	860	375			
3.10.1923	St Louis Mo., USA	Alford J Williams USA	Curtiss 32 R2C–1 (A–6692)	812		392.23		
6.10.1923	St Louis Mo., USA					392.38	917.48	100.0
2.11.1923	Curtiss Field NY, USA	Harold J Brow USA	Curtiss 32 R2C–1 (A–6691)	812		414.314		3.0
2.11.1923	Curtiss Field NY, USA	Alford J Williams USA	Curtiss 32 R2C–1 (A–6692)	812		416.193		3.0
2.11.1923	Curtiss Field NY, USA	Harold J Brow USA	Curtiss 32 R2C–1 (A–6691)	812		**417.590**		3.0
4.11.1923	Curtiss Field NY, USA	Alford J Williams USA	Curtiss 32 R2C–1 (A–6692)	812	435	423.529	25.50	3.0
4.11.1923	Curtiss Field NY, USA	Harold J Brow USA	Curtiss 32 R2C–1 (A–6691)	812	443	427.300	25.275	3.0
4.11.1923	Curtiss Field NY, USA	Alford J Williams USA	Curtiss 32 R2C–1 (A–6692)	812	432	**428.397**	25.175	3.0

A	B	C	D	E	F	G	H	I	K
1923	— CS	— CS	Letov Š-8 Osmička (4)	101		360	342		3.0
5.1924	Istres F	Florentin Bonnet F	Bernard (SIMB) V.1	202	420				
12. 6.1924 7. 7.1924	Istres F	Sadi Lecointe F	Nieuport-Delage Ni–D 42S (3)	241	450				
8.11.1924	Istres F	Florentin Bonnet F	Bernard (SIMB) V.2	203	450	439	389.892	27.70	3.0
11.12.1924	Istres F	Florentin Bonnet F	Bernard (SIMB) V.2	204	470	454	**448.133**	24.10	3.0
1924	(Project) USA	— USA	Verville–Sperry	861					
11. 6.1925	Cranwell UK	Larry L Carter UK	Gloster II Bluebird (J7505)	708		400			3.0
8.1925	Istres F	Fernand Lasne F	Nieuport-Delage Ni–D 42S	241	450				
11. 9.1925	Curtiss Field NY, USA	James H Doolittle USA	Curtiss 42 R3C–1 (A–6978)	813		480			
18. 9.1925	Curtiss Field NY, USA	Alford J Williams USA	Curtiss 42 R3C–1 (A–6978)	813		486	459		3.0
1925	(Project) F	— F	Bernard (SIMB) V.3	205	500				
6.11.1927	— USA	Alford J Williams USA	Kirkham-Williams Vespa (X–648)	828	519				
1. 9.1931	Cleveland	Lowell H Bayles	Granville Brothers	818		460	430		3.0

Date	Place	Pilot / Country	Aircraft					
7. 9.1931	Ohio, USA	USA	Gee Bee Z (NR77V)(4) (City of Springfield)			414		3.0
8. 9.1931	Cleveland Ohio, USA	James R Wedell USA	Wedell-Williams No 44 (NR278V) (44)	864		392		3.0
30.10.1931	Detroit Michigan, USA	Lowell H Bayles USA	Granville Brothers Gee Bee Z (NR77V)(4) (City of Springfield)	819		505		3.0
1.12.1931							435.674	3.0
5.12.1931						485		3.0
31. 8.1932	Cleveland Ohio, USA	James R Doolittle USA	Granville Brothers Gee Bee R-1 (NR2100) Super Sportster (11)	820		472		3.0
1. 9.1932						497	455	3.0
3. 9.1932							**473.820**	3.0
4. 9.1933	Cleveland Ohio, USA	James R Wedell USA	Wedell-Williams No 44 (NR278V)(44)	865		510	**490.080**	3.0
1933	Istres F	Jean Doumerc F	Bernard V.4 (did not fly)	206	540			
1933	Istres F	— F	Payen Pa.100 Flèche Volante	242	570			
3.1934	— USA	Roscoe Turner USA	Wedell-Williams No 44 (NR61Y) (57)	866	500		482	3.0
2. 9.1934	Cleveland Ohio, USA	John A Worthen USA	Wedell-Williams No 45 (NR62Y) (45)	867	500		486.6	3.0
2. 9.1934	Cleveland Ohio, USA	Douglas Davis USA	Wedell-Williams No 44 (NR278V) (44)	865	500	523	492.805	3.0
12.1934	Istres F	Raymond Delmotte F	Caudron C.460 (6907)	213				3.0
25.12.1934						552	**505.848**	3.0
1934	— USSR	USSR	Stal-8 (did not fly)	601	640 (3)			
1934	(Project) USA	— USA	Keith Rider Super-Speed Racer	854	748			

A	B	C	D	E	F	G	H	I	K
1934	(Project) USA	— USA	Stock High Speed Project	859	911				
6.1935	Martlesham Heath, GB	— UK	Bristol 142 *Britain First* (R–12)	705		494			
12. 9.1935 13. 9.1935	Santa Ana Cal., USA	Howard Hughes USA	Hughes Special 1B (H–1) (NR258Y)	827	587		555 **567.115**		3.0 3.0
1936	Istres F	Raymond Delmotte F	Caudron C.561 (7460)	214	580	550			
1936	(Project) UK	— UK	Airspeed A.S.31	701	724				
1936	— F	— F	Caudron C.711 Cyclone (did not fly)	215					
12.1936	Springfield Mo., USA	Frank Hawks USA	Hawks *Time Flies* (NR1313)	826	604	500			
19.12.1936	Istres F	Maryse Hilsz F	Caudron C.460 (6909)	213	600 (0)	600 (0)			
26.12.1936	Istres F	Raymond Delmotte F	Caudron C.712 Cyclone	216	677 (0)	495	475.175		3.0
29. 4.1937	Istres F	Raymond Delmotte F	Caudron C.712 Cyclone	217	677 (0)	630 (0)			
10.1937	Rechlin D	— D	Heinkel He 119 V2 (D-ASKR)	328	584 (4.5)				
11.11.1937	Augsburg D	Hermann Wurster D	Messerschmitt Bf 109 V13 (Bf 113) (D-IPKY)	336			**610.950**		3.0

Date	Location	Pilot	Aircraft						
11.1937 22.11.1937	Oranienburg D	Gerhard Nitschke D	Heinkel He 119 V4 (He 111U/He 606) (D-AUTE)	329		620 (4.5)	504.988 590		1,000.0
12.1937	(Project) D	— D	Dornier DoP 59	310	815 (0)				
2.1938	Marienehe D	Hans Dieterle D	Heinkel He 100 V1 (D-ISVR)	322	700	620 (5)			
3.1938	Rechlin D	— D	Heinkel He 100 V1/U1 (D-ISVR)	323	700	672 (5)			
5. 6.1938	Wustrow D	Ernst Udet D	Heinkel He 100 V2 (He 112 U) (D-IUOS)	324	710		**634.473**	567.4	100.0
9.1938	Warnemünde D	Gerhard Nitschke D	Heinkel He 100 V3/UR (D-IDGH)	325	717				
11.1938	Oranienburg D	— D	Heinkel He 100 V5 (He 100 B-01)	326		682 (5)			
1938	(Project) F	— F	Dewoitine D.530	226	625 (0)				
1938	(Project) F	— F	Payen Pa.350. CD Flèchair	243					
1938	(Project) F	— F	Payen Pa.430.CV Flèchair	244	800				
1938	(Project) UK	— UK	Supermarine 327	721	748 (7)				
1.1939	—	— D	Focke-Wulf Fw 187 V6 Falke (CJ+NY)	317		635 (0)			
11. 2.1939	Mitchel Field NY, USA	Ben S Kelsey USA	Lockheed 22 XP-38 (Lightning)(37457)	830	671	676			

A	B	C	D	E	F	G	H	I	K
3.1939	Eastleigh UK	Harry Purvis UK	Supermarine 323 High Speed Spitfire (N17)	720	684	657			
3.1939; 30. 3.1939	Oranienburg D	Hans Dieterle D	Heinkel He 100 V8/R (He 112 U/He 113) (HE+BE/42C+11)	327	770		**746.606** (746.681)	14.464	3.0; 3.0
4.1939	Wright Field Ohio, USA	James Taylor USA	Bell 11 XP-39 Airacobra (38326)	802		628 (6)			
26. 4.1939	Augsburg D	Fritz Wendel D	Messerschmitt Me 209 V1 (Me 109 R) (D-INJR)	337		782	**755.138**		3.0
7.1939	Augsburg D	Fritz Wendel D	Messerschmitt Me 209 V3 (D-IVFP) (did not fly)	337					3.0
7.1939	Augsburg D	Hans Dieterle D	Heinkel He 100 V8/R (did not fly)	327	765 (0)				3.0
22.11.1939	Toulouse F	Marcel Doret F	Dewoitine D.550-01	227		702			
1939	— F	— F	Caudron C.714R (did not fly)	218	795 (0)				
1.1940	— USSR	G Shiyanov USSR	TSAGI SK	602					
24. 2.1940	Toulouse F	Marcel Doret F	Dewoitine D.550-01	228		703 (6.6)			
12. 6.1940	Heston UK	G L G Richmond UK	Heston Type 5 Racer (G-AFOK)	713	775 (0)	677 (5)			
1940	— UK	— UK	Heston Type 5 Racer (G-AFQL) (not built)	714	820 (0)				

Date	Country	Pilot	Aircraft	No.	Max. speed
1940	— / I		C.M.A.S.A. CS.15 (did not fly)	402	850 (0)
1940	— / USA		Lockheed 522 XP-49 (did not fly)	831	805 (6)
1940	— / F	Maurice Arnoux	Bugatti 100P (did not fly)	211	830 (0)
1940	(Project) F / F		Bugatti 110P	212	720 (0)
1940	(Project) F / F		Dewoitine D.550	229	770 (0)
1940	(Project) USA / USA		Douglas 312 XP-48	815	845 (11)
1941	— / USA		Vultee 70 XP-54 (did not fly)	863	820 (6.1)
1941	(Project) UK / UK		Miles M22	715	811 (4.6)
1941	(Project) UK / UK		Miles M23	716	760 (4.6)
1942	(Project) UK / UK		Airspeed A.S.56	702	792 (7)
1942	(Project) D / D		Blohm und Voss P.170	302	820 (8)
1942	(Project) D / D		Henschel P.75	334	790 (7)
27.12.1943	— / J		Kawasaki Ki.78 (Ken-3)	502	850 700 (3.5)
1943	(Project) J / J		Tachikawa Ki.94-I	503	780 (10)

A	B	C	D	E	F	G	H	I	K
1943	(Project) D	— D	Arado E 530	301	770				
1943	(Project) D	— D	Blohm und Voss P.205	303	790 (16)				
1943	(Project) D	— D	Dornier DoP 231/2	311	855 (9)				
1943	(Project) D	— D	Messerschmitt Me 309 A-1	338	775				
2.1944	Bethpage NY, USA	Carl Bellinger USA	Republic XP-72 (Ultrabolt) (4336599)	851		772 (0)			
1944	Oberpfaffen-hofen, D	— D	Dornier Do 335 V1(M1) (Ameisenbär) (CP+UA)	311	800	752 (7.4)			
7.1944	Rechlin D	Heinrich Beauvais D	Dornier Do 335 V9(M9) Pfeil (CP+UI)	312		760			
5. 8.1944 8.1944	Bethpage NY, USA	Mike Richie USA	Republic XP-47J Thunderbolt (*Superman*) (4346952)	850		813 816 (10)			
8.1944	Burbank Cal., USA	Ed Virgin USA	North American NA–105A XP–51G Mustang (4343336)	837		800 (6.9)			
8.1944	— UK	G H Pike UK	de Havilland D.H.103 Hornet (RR915)	706		782 (7)			
1944	— I	— I	Reggiane Re 2006 b (MM.540)(did not fly)	406	770 (8)				
1944	(Project) USA	— USA	Republic P–72A	852	870 (7.6)				
1944	(Project) D	— D	Blohm und Voss P.208.01	304	835 (10)				

Date			Aircraft	No.	Speed
1944	(Project) D	— D	Blohm und Voss P.208.02	305	895 (10)
1944	(Project) D	— D	Focke–Wulf P.222.001	318	805 (11)
1944	(Project) D	— D	Focke–Wulf P.222.018	319	815 (9.3)
1944	(Project) D	— D	Focke–Wulf P.310.025	320	840 (10)
1944	(Project) D	— D	Focke–Wulf P.603.001	321	793 (11)
2.1945	— USA	— USA	North American NA–126 P–51H–5 Mustang	847	784 (7.6)
1945	— D	— D	Dornier Do 335 M19 Pfeil (Do 335 B–3) (did not fly)	312	790 (10)
1945	(Project) D	— D	Bohm und Voss P.208.03	306	794 (10)
1945	(Project) D	— D	Dornier DoP 247/6	314	835 (0)
1945	(Project) D	— D	Dornier DoP 252/1	315	900 (11)
1945	(Project) D	— D	Dornier DoP 252/3	316	900 (7)
1945	(Project) D	— D	Heinkel P.1076 A	330	860 (11)
1945	(Project) D	— D	Heinkel P.1076 B	331	865
1945	(Project) D	— D	Heinkel P.1076 LM	332	880

A	B	C	D	E	F	G	H	I	K
1945	(Project) D	— D	Heinkel P.1076 N	333	880 (10)				
1945	(Project) D	— D	Skoda–Kauba Sk V–5	339	770				
6.1945	— USA	— USA	North American NA–124 P–51M–1 Mustang (4511743)	841		790			
9.1945	— USA	— USA	Republic XP-47H Thunderbolt (4223297)	849	790	666			
1945	UK	UK	Supermarine 371 Spiteful F.XIV (RB515)	722		780			
1945	(Project) J	— J	Kawasaki Ki.64–KAI	501	800				
1945	(Project) J	— J	Yokosuka Y–40 R2Y–2 Keiun	504	796 (8)				
1945	(Project) I	Riccardo Vaccari I	Reggiane Re 2006 C	407	850 (0)				
1945	(Project) F	— F	SNCA du Centre NC 160	248	815 (10)				
1946	— UK	— UK	Hawker P.1026 Fury (F.2/43) (LA610)	709		780 (5.6)			
6.1947	— USA	Alford J Williams USA	Grumman G–58A F8F–1 Bearcat (Gulfhawk IV) (NL3025)	821		805 (5.8)			
1947	Boscombe Down UK	— UK	Supermarine 371 Spiteful F.XVI (RB518)	723		795 (8.7)			

Date	Location	Pilot	Aircraft					
10.12.1947	Indio Cal., USA	Jacqueline Cochran USA	North American NA–103 P–51C–10 Mustang (NX28388)(13)	835			755.668	100.0
17.12.1947	Coachilla Valley, Cal., USA						633.54	3.0
1947		— USA	Chance Vought VS–315 XF5U–1 Skimmer (33958) (did not fly)	862	811 (8.8)			
1948	Niagara Falls NY, USA	Don Nolan USA	Bell 26E P–39Q–10E Airacobra (*Cobra II*) (N92848)(11)	803	800 (0)	758 (0)		
1948		— USA	Republic XF–12 Rainbow (4491003)	853		800 (14)		
6.1949	Texas, USA	Ken Cooley USA	North American NA–97 A–36A Mustang (*Beguine*) (N4845N)	834	800 (0)		808	1 st. m
4. 7.1949	La Porte Texas, USA	Dot Lemon USA	North American NA–97 A–36A Mustang (*Beguine*) (N4845N) (did not fly)	834	800 (0)			3.0
6. 9.1949	Cleveland Ohio, USA	William P Odom USA	North American NA–97 A–36A Mustang (*Beguine*) (N4845N) (7)	834	800 (0)			
6. 9.1949	Cleveland Ohio, USA	Cook Cleland USA	Goodyear F2G–1 Corsair (N5590N) (94)	817	800 (0)			
9. 4.1951	Indio Cal., USA	Jacqueline Cochran USA	North American NA–103 F–6C Mustang (N5528N) (*Thunderbird*) (90)	836			747.339	15.0

A	B	C	D	E	F	G	H	I	K
5. 6.1952	Key Biscayne Florida, USA	Anson Johnson USA	North American NA-122 P-51D-20 Mustang (N13Y) (45)	839	800	805			3.0
6. 6.1952					(0)	820			3.0
8. 6.1952						715	690.248		3.0
2.1953	Key Biscayne Florida, USA	Anson Johnson USA	North American NA-122 P-51D-20 Mustang (N13Y) (did not fly)	839	800 (0)				3.0
2.1954	Boca Raton Florida, USA	Anson Johnson USA	North American NA-122 P-51D-20 Mustang (N13Y) (did not fly)	839	800 (0)				3.0
28. 5.1966	Lancaster Cal., USA	Darryl C Greenamyer USA	Grumman G-58B F8F-2 Bearcat (N1111L)	822	800 (0)	724			3.0
31. 5.1966	Lancaster Cal., USA	Thomas Taylor USA	Hawker Sea Fury FB.11 (N260X) (33) (did not fly)	710	800 (0)				3.0
31. 5.1966	Lancaster Cal., USA	Charles Lyford USA	North American NA-124 P-51D-25 Mustang (8) (Challenger) (N2869D) (did not fly)	842	800 (0)				3.0
8.1966	— Texas, USA	Michael D Carroll USA	Hawker Sea Fury FB.11 (Miss Merced)(N878M)(87)	711		837			
8.1968	Edwards AFB Cal., USA	Michael D Carroll USA	Bell 26E P-39Q-10E Airacobra (Cobra III) (N9284) (did not fly)	804	800 (0)				3.0
24. 8.1968	Edwards AFB Cal., USA	Darryl C Greenamyer USA	Grumman G-58B F8F-2 Bearcat (N1111L) (1)	823	800 (0)	744	733		3.0
25. 8.1968						801			3.0
8. 9.1968									
16. 8.1969	Edwards AFB Cal., USA	Darryl C Greenamyer USA	Grumman G-58B F8F-2 Bearcat (Conquest I)	824			769.50		3.0
						831	776.440		3.0

Date	Place	Pilot / Nat.	Aircraft	No.	km/h	Record km/h	Course
1972	— USA	Charles Lyford USA	North American NA-124 P-51D-25 Mustang (*Bardahl Special*) (N2869D)(8)(did not fly)	843	800 (0)		
1975	(Project) D	— D	Colani C-309	307	800 (0)		
4. 7.1976	— USA	Roy McClain USA	North American NA-124 P-51D-25 Mustang (RB-51 *Red Baron*) (N7715C) (5)	844	810 (0)		
1977	(Project) D/J	— D/J	Colani C-309 Bohu	308	892 (0)		
9. 8.1979	Tonopah Nevada, USA	Steve Hinton USA	North American NA-124 P-51D-25 Mustang (RB-51 *Red Baron*) (N7715C) (5)	845	768		3.0
12. 8.1979						787.372	3.0
14. 8.1979					817	**803.152**	3.0
1981	— USA	Roy McClain USA	North American NA-109 P-51D-15 Mustang (*Jeannie*)(N79111) (69) (did not fly)	838	810 (0)		
1981	— USA	David Garber USA	Aero Design DG-1	801	820		
30. 7.1983	Mojave Cal., USA	Frank Taylor USA	North American NA-124 P-51D-25 Mustang (*Dago Red*)(N5410V) (4)	846	850	**832.120**	15.0
1983	— USA	— USA	Sanders Sea Fury T.20 (*Dreadnought*) (NX20SF) (8) (did not fly)	856	850		

A	B	C	D	E	F	G	H	I	K
1985	(Project) USA	— USA	Schapel S–1275 Finesse	858	850				
1985	(Project) D/CH	— D/CH	Colani Pontresina	309	940				
1987	— USA	Steve Hinton USA	Sandberg Tsunami (N39JR) (18)	855	845	853			
1988	— UK	Patrick Luscombe UK	Hawker Sea Fury FB.11 (WJ288) (did not fly)	712	850				
1988	— USA	Eric Lorentzen USA	Levolor Sea Fury T.20 (*Blind Man's Bluff*) (N85SF) (88) (did not fly)	829					
1988	— USA	— USA	North American/Dilley 1001 (*Learfang/Vendetta*) (NX91KD)(91)(did not fly)	848	858 (1.7)				
5.1989	— USA	Don Whittington USA	North American NA–122 P–51D–20 Mustang (*Precious Metal*) (5483V) (09)	840					
20. 8.1989	Las Vegas New Mexico, USA	Lyle Shelton USA	Grumman G–58B F8F–2 Bearcat (*Rare Bear*) (N777L) (7)	825	885		830.045		3.0
21. 8.1989					(0)	871 (0)	**850.263**		3.0
5. 9.1989	Wendover Utah, USA	John R Sandberg USA	Sandberg Tsunami (NX39JR) (18)	855	885	837			3.0
6. 9.1989					(0)	(0)			3.0
7. 9.1989									3.0
1990	— USA	John R Sandberg USA	Sandberg Tsunami (NX39JR) (18)	855	885 (0)				3.0

1990	— USA	Lyle Shelton USA	Grumman G–58B F8F–2 Bearcat (*Rare Bear*) (N777L) (7)	825	925 (0)	3.0
1990	Tonopah Nevada, USA	Richard Rutan USA	Scaled Composites 21 Pond Racer PR–01	857	885 (0)	3.0
1990	— USA	Skip Holm USA	Mach Buster I	832	1200 (9.1)	

1	2	3	4	5	6	7	8	9	10	11	12	13
Czechoslovakia (CS)												
101	Letov Š–8 Osmička Alois Šmolik	1923	1 × Napier Lion 450 W12/P2	11.40	8.30	16.50	7.9	0°	1230	2.7	75	HW/1F/2W
France (F)												
201	Antoinette VII Léon Levavasseur	1910	1 × Antoinette/ Levavasseur V8/P2	12.80	11.30	34.00	4.8	5°	590	10.7	17	HW/+/1S2W
202	Bernard (SIMB) V.1 Jean Hubert S Georges Bruner	1924	1 × Lorraine-Dietrich 12Ew (14) 540 W12/P2	8.75	6.50	12.08	6.3	4°	1050	2.3	87	HW/1F/2W
203	Bernard (SIMB) V.2 Hubert Bruner	1924	1 × Hispano-Suiza 50 (12Gb) 620 W12/P2	9.90	6.80	11.60	8.4	2°	1183	1.9	102	MW/1F/2W
204	Bernard (SIMB) V.2 Hubert, Bruner	1924	1 × Hispano-Suiza 50 (12Gb) 620 W12/P2	9.05	6.80	10.80	7.6	2°	1172	1.9	109	MW/1F/2W
205	Bernard (SIMB) V.3 Hubert, Bruner (Project)	1925	1 × Lorraine-Dietrich W12/P2									MW/1F/(2W')
206	Bernard V.4 S Georges Bruner Roger Robert	1933	1 × Hispano-Suiza 18-R 1,680 W18/P2	8.65	7.45	11.00	6.8	4°	1900	1.1	173	LW/1F/2W
207	Blériot XI (mod) Louis Blériot Raymond Saulnier	1910	1 × Gnome Gamma 80 Rot 7/P2	8.90	7.65	15.00	5.3	0°	300	3.7	20	HW/1F/2W
208	Blériot XIbis Blériot, Saulnier	1910	1 × Gnome Double Oméga 100 Rot 14/P2	7.90	8.10	12.00	5.3	0°	340	3.4	28	HW/1F/2W

No.	Name / Designer	Year	Engine										
209	Blériot XII Blériot, Saulnier	1909	1 × ENV F 60 V8/P2	10.00	8.00	21.40	4.7	0°	575	9.6	27	HW/1F/2W
210	Blériot XXIII Blériot, Saulnier	1911	1 × Gnome Double Oméga 100 Rot14/P2	8.94	7.52	9.00	8.9	0°	300	3.0	33	HW/1F/2W
211	Bugatti 100P Ettore Bugatti Louis P de Monge	1940	2 × Bugatti T50 B1 2 × 450 18/P2×2	8.24	7.75	11.40	6.0	−3°	1700	1.9	149	LW/YF/(2W)
212	Bugatti 110P Bugatti, de Monge (Project)	1940	2 × Bugatti T50 B1 2 × 450 18/P2×2	6.70	7.75	8.20	5.5	−3°	2000	2.2	244	LW/YF/(2W)
213	Caudron C.460 Marcel Riffard Georges Otfinovsky	1934	1 × Renault 4.56 370 I6/P2	6.75	7.12	6.90	6.6	7°	775	2.1	112	LW/1F/2W
214	Caudron C.561 Riffard, Otfinovsky Maurice Devlieger	1936	1 × Renault 4.46 500 V12/P2	6.75	7.52	6.90	6.6	7°	998	2.0	145	LW/1F/(2W)
215	Caudron C.711 Cyclone Riffard, Otfinovsky Devlieger (Project)	1936	1 × Renault 4.46 500 V12/P3	8.97	8.53	12.50	6.4	10°	1300	2.6	104	LW/1F/(2W)
216	Caudron C.712 Cyclone Riffard, Otfinovsky Devlieger	1936	1 × Renault 6.13 450 V12/P3	6.75	8.62	6.90	6.6	7°	1175	2.6	170	LW/1F/(2W)
217	Caudron C.712 Cyclone Riffard, Otfinovsky Devlieger	1937	1 × Renault 6.13 730 V12/P3	6.75	8.62	6.90	6.6	7°	1225	1.7	178	LW/1F/(2W)
218	Caudron C.714R (C.712R) Riffard, Otfinovsky Devlieger	1939	1 × Renault 12 R Spécial 900 V12/P3	6.75	8.68	6.90	6.6	7°	1225	1.7	178	LW/1F/(2W)

1	2	3	4	5	6	7	8	9	10	11	12	13
France (F)												
219	de Monge 5.1 Louis P de Monge	1921	1 × Hispano-Suiza 42 (8Fe) 320 V8/P2	8.00	7.00	20.00 15.00	4.3	10° 10°	900	2.8	45	HW/1F/2W
220	Deperdussin Course Louis Béchereau Frits Koolhoven	1912	1 × Gnome Double Oméga 100 Rot14/P2	7.00	6.25	10.00	4.9	0°	370	3.7	37	MW/1F/2W
221	Deperdussin Course Béchereau, Koolhoven	1912	1 × Gnome Double Gamma 140 Rot14/P2	7.00	6.25	10.00	4.9	0°	400	2.9	40	MW/1F/2W
222	Deperdussin Monocoque Gordon Bennett Louis Béchereau André Herbemont	1912	1 × Gnome Double Gamma 140 Rot14/P2	7.00	6.25	11.50	4.3	0°	500	3.6	43	MW/1F/2W
223	Deperdussin Monocoque Gordon Bennett Béchereau, Herbemont	1913	1 × Gnome Double Lambda 160 Rot14/P2	7.15	6.20	9.86	5.2	0°	650	4.1	66	MW/1F/2W
224	Deperdussin Monocoque Gordon Bennett Béchereau, Herbemont	1913	1 × Gnome Double Lambda 160 Rot14/P2	6.60	6.20	9.00	4.9	0°	640	4.0	71	MW/1F/2W
225	Deperdussin Monocoque Gordon Bennett Béchereau, Herbemont	1913	1 × Le Rhône 18E 160 Rot18/P2	6.60	6.20	9.00	4.9	0°	680	4.2	76	MW/1F/2W

No.	Aircraft / Designer	Year	Engine										Code
226	Dewoitine D.530 Emile Dewoitine Robert Castello Jaques Henrat (Project)	1938	1 × Hispano-Suiza 12Y 1,800 V12/P3	8.20	8.75								LW/1F/((2W))
227	Dewoitine D.550-01 Dewoitine, Castello, Henrat	1939	1 × Hispano-Suiza 12 Y 51 1,000 V12/P3	8.20	8.02	10.79	6.2	4°	1814	1.8	188		LW/1F/(2W)
228	Dewoitine D.550-01 Dewoitine, Castello, Henrat	1940	1 × Hispano-Suiza 12Z (89) 1,320 V12/P3	8.20	8.22	10.79	6.2	4°	1950	1.5	181		LW/1F/(2W)
229	Dewoitine D.550 Dewoitine, Castello, Henrat (Project)	1940	1 × Hispano-Suiza 12Z 1,800 V12/P3	8.20	8.22	10.79	6.2	4°					LW/1F/(2W)
230	Hanriot HD.22 M R Pouit	1921	1 × Hispano-Suiza 42 (8Fe) 320 V8/P2	6.38	5.71	7.50	5.4	0°	830	2.6	111		HW/1F/(2W)
231	Landwerlin-Berreur (Project) Georges-Maria Landwerlin Georges André Berreur	1922	1 × Fiat A.14 700 V12/P2	13.26	6.00	22.20	7.9	−22°	1720	2.5	77		HW/1F/2W
232	Nieuport IIN Edouard de Niéport M Pagny	1911	1 × Nieuport-Darracq 28 O2/P2	8.40	7.50	14.00	5.0	0°	290	10.4	21		MW/1F/1S2W
233	Nieuport IIG Astra Niéport, Pagny	1911	1 × Gnome Gamma 70 Rot7/P2	8.40	7.50	14.00	5.0	0°	310	4.4	22		MW/1F/1S2W
234	Nieuport IIG Niéport, Pagny	1911	1 × Gnome Monosoupape A 80 R7/P2	8.40	7.50	14.00	5.0	0°	320	4.0	23		MW/1F/1S2W
235	Nieuport 29V Gustave Delage	1919	1 × Hispano-Suiza 42 (8Fb) 280 V8/P2	6.05	6.23	13.20		0°	834	3.0	63		2W/1F/2W

1	2	3	4	5	6	7	8	9	10	11	12	13
France (F)												
236	Nieuport 29V(bis) Delage	1920	1 × Hispano-Suiza 42 (8Fe) 320 V8/P2	6.00	6.20	12.30		0°	936	3.0	76	2W/1F/2W
237	Nieuport-Delage Sesquiplan Delage	1921	1 × Hispano-Suiza 42 (8Fe) 320 V8/P2	8.00	6.10	11.00	6.4	0°	980	3.1	89	HW/1F/2W
238	Nieuport-Delage Sesquiplan Delage	1922	1 × Hispano-Suiza 42 (8F) 363 V8/P2	8.00	6.10	11.00	6.4	0°	935	2.6	85	HW/1F/2W
239	Nieuport-Delage Sesquiplan (*Eugène Gilbert*) Delage, Albert Mary	1923	1 × Wright H-3 414 V8/P2	8.00	6.10	11.00	6.4	0°	1014	2.5	92	HW/1F/2W
240	Nieuport-Delage Ni-D 41 Course Delage, E Dieudonné	1922	1 × Wright H-3 414 V8/P2	8.20	7.08	12.70	5.3	0°	1016	2.5	80	HW/1F/2W
241	Nieuport-Delage Ni-D 42S Delage	1924	1 × Hispano-Suiza 51 (12Hb) 620 V12/P2	9.50	7.30	15.50	6.4	0°	1440	2.3	93	HW/1F/2W
242	Payen Pa.100 Flèche Volante Roland Payen	1933	1 × Gnome & Rhône 7 Kdr 380 R7/P2	4.15	5.75			$\frac{15°}{67}$	750	2.0		MW/1F/2W
243	Payen Pa.350.CD Flèchair Roland Payen Francois Baudot (Project)	1938	1 × Regnier 400 V12/P2×2	3.30	6.55	6.87		$\frac{33°}{78}$				MW/2F/(1W)
244	Payen Pa.430.CD Flèchair Payen, Baudot (Project)	1938	2 × Gnome & Rhône 14M 2 × 650 R14/P2×2	7.20	10.00	27.00		$\frac{4°}{67}$	2500	1.9	93	MW/1F/(2W)

No.	Aircraft / Designer	Year	Engine									
245	Ponnier Gordon Bennett / Alfred Pagny	1913	1 × Gnome Double Lambda 160 Rot14/P2	6.96	5.45	7.80	6.2	0°	590	3.7	76	MW/1F/2W
246	Santos-Dumont 14bis (mod) / Alberto Santos-Dumont	1907	1 × Antoinette/Levavassseur 50 V8/P2	11.46	9.60	50.00	5.2	0°	300	6.0	6	2W/2F/2W
247	Simplex-Arnoux / René Arnoux / I Carmier	1922	1 × Hispano-Suiza 42 (8F) 320 V8/P2	9.00	4.25	16.30	5.0	2°	880	2.7	54	HW/1F/2W
248	SNCA du Centre NC 160 / M Pillon (Project)	1945	2 × Hispano-Suiza 12Z 2 × 1,400 V12/P2×3	13.50	11.30				6500			
249	SPAD S.XVII / André Herbemont	1918	1 × Hispano-Suiza 42 (8Fb) 280 V8/P2	8.08	6.30	23.00		0°	900	3.2	39	2W/1F/2W
250	Spad-Herbemont S.20bis1 / Herbemont	1919	1 × Hispano-Suiza 42 (8Fb) 280 V8/P2	10.02	7.20	25.00		8°/0				2W/1F/2W
251	Spad-Herbemont S.20bis2 / Herbemont	1919	1 × Hispano-Suiza 42 (8Fb) 280 V8/P2	9.47	7.30	23.00		8°/0				2W/1F/2W
252	Spad-Herbemont S.20bis3 / Herbemont	1919	1 × Hispano-Suiza 42 (8Fb) 280 V8/P2	8.10	7.30	21.50		8°/0				2W/1F/2W
253	Spad-Herbemont S.20bis4 / Herbemont	1920	1 × Hispano-Suiza 42 (8Fb) 280 V8/P2	6.60	7.30	16.00		8°/0	1050	3.7	66	2W/1F/2W
254	Spad-Herbemont S.20bis6 / Herbemont	1920	1 × Hispano-Suiza 42 (8Fb) 300 V8/P2	6.48	7.50	15.20		8°/0	1050	3.5	69	2W/1F/2W

1	2	3	4	5	6	7	8	9	10	11	12	13
France (F)												
255	Spad-Herbemont S.20bis6 Herbemont	1920	1 × Hispano-Suiza 42 (8Fe) 320 V8/P2	6.48	7.50	15.20		5.0	8°/0	995	3.1	65	2W/1F/2W
256	Voisin-Farman I (Ibis) Gabriel and Charles Voisin Henry Farman	1907	1 × Antoinette/ Levavasseur 50 V8/P2	10.00	10.50	40.00		5.0	0°	530	10.6	14	2W/2F/2W
Germany (D)												
301	Arado E 530 Walter Blume (Project)	1943	2 × Daimler-Benz DB 603G 2 × 1,900 V12/P4	16.25	13.15				0°/4	10410	2.7		LW/2F/(2W)
302	Blohm & Voss P.170 Richard Vogt (Project)	1942	3 × BMW 801E 3 × 2,100 R18/P3	16.00	13.25	44.00			0°	13300	2.1	302	HW/2F/(3W)
303	Blohm & Voss P.205 Vogt (Project)	1943	1 × Daimler-Benz DB 603G 1 × Daimler-Benz DB 603G (Supercharger) 1,750 V12/P4	18.65	11.65	35.00	9.8		0°	6000	3.4	171	LW/1F/(3W)
304	Blohm und Voss P.208.01 Vogt (Project)	1944	1 × Jumo 222N 2,950 R24/P4	12.00	9.15	19.50	7.4		30°	5595	1.9	287	LW/2F/(3W)
305	Blohm und Voss P.208.02 Vogt (Project)	1944	1 × Argus As 413 4,000 H24/P4	12.10	8.85	19.00	7.7		30°	4670	1.2	246	LW/2F/(3W)
306	Blohm und Voss P.208.03 Vogt (Project)	1945	1 × Daimler-Benz DB 603L 2,100 V12/P4	12.08	9.20	19.00	7.7		30°	5050	2.4	266	LW/2F/(3W)
307	Colani C-309 Luigi Colani (Project)	1975	2 × NSU/Wankel Ro 80 mod 2 × 180 RC/P5	4.00	4.00					400	1.1		MW/1F/(4W)

No.	Aircraft / Designer	Year	Engine	Power / Type									
308	Colani C-509 Bonu / Colani (Project)	1977	2 × Mazda Wankel RX-3	2 × 320 RC/P5	2.04	0.52	2.02	2.7		800	1.2	503	MW/+F/(3W)
309	Colani Pontresina / Colani (Project)	1985	2 × Mazda/Wankel	2 × 1,400 RC/P2×5	4.80	8.00	7.40	3.1	40°	800	0.3	108	LW/+F/(3W)
310	Dornier DoP 59 / Claude H D Dornier (Project)	1937	2 × Daimler-Benz DB 601R	2 × 2,000 V12/P3/4	11.00	12.80	24.00	5.0	15°	4500	1.1	187	LW/+F/(2W)
311	Dornier DoP 231/2 / Gustav Wieland / H Herzog (Project)	1943	2 × Daimler-Benz DB 603G	1,900 V12/P4	13.20	13.25	35.00	5.0	15°	8200	2.2	234	LW/+F/(3W)
312	Dornier Do 335 V1(M1) (Ameisenbär) / Wieland, Herzog	1944	2 × Daimler-Benz DB 603AS	2 × 1,850 V12/P3	13.80	13.85	38.50	4.9	13°	8300	2.2	216	LW/+F/(3W)
313	Dornier Do 335 V9(M9) Pfeil / Wieland, Herzog	1944	2 × Daimler-Benz DB 603E	2 × 1,800 V12/P3	13.80	13.85	38.50	4.9	13°	9000	2.5	234	LW/+F/(3W)
314	Dornier DoP 247/6 / Wieland, Herzog (Project)	1945	1 × Jumo 213J	2,600 V12/P3	12.50	12.06	26.00	6.0	28°				LW/+F/(3W)
315	Dornier DoP 252/1 / Wieland, Herzog (Project)	1945	2 × Jumo 213J	2 × 2,600 V12/P2×3	16.40	15.20	43.00	6.3	37°	10500	2.0	244	LW/+F/(3W)
316	Dornier DoP 252/3 / Wieland, Herzog (Project)	1945	2 × Jumo 213J	2 × 2,600 V12/P2×3	15.80	17.10	43.20	5.8	24°	11150	2.1	258	LW/+F/(3W)
317	Focke-Wulf Fw 187 V6 Falke / Kurt W Tank, R Blaser	1939	2 × Daimler-Benz DB 600A	2 × 1,050 V12/P3	15.30	11.12	30.40	7.7	0°	5000	2.4	164	LW/1F/(2W)
318	Focke-Wulf P.222.001 / Tank (Project)	1944	1 × Jumo 222E/F	2,450 R24/P4	12.80	13.70	33.00	5.0		6730	2.7	204	MW/+F/(3W)
319	Focke-Wulf P.222.018 / Tank (Project)	1944	1 × Jumo 222E/F	2,900 R24/P4	12.60	13.70	32.00	5.0	37°	6680	2.3	209	MW/+F/(3W)
320	Focke-Wulf P.310.025 (Fw 205?) / Tank (Project)	1944	1 × Argus As 413	4,000 H24/P2×4	16.40	14.20	55.00	4.9	33°	9800	2.4	178	MW/+F/(3W)

1	2	3	4	5	6	7	8	9	10	11	12	13
Germany (D)												
321	Focke-Wulf P.603.001 Tank (Project)	1944	1 × Daimler-Benz DB 603N 2,800 V12/P2×4	11.00	11.70	26.00	4.7		6000	3.4	231	
322	Heinkel He 100 V1 (P.1035) Siegfried Günter Karl Schwärzler	1938	1 × Daimler-Benz DB 601Aa 1,100 V12/P3	9.42	8.17	14.40	6.2	0°	2158	2.0	150	LW/1F/(2W)
323	Heinkel He 100 V1/U1 Günter, Schwärzler	1938	1 × Daimler-Benz DB 601Aa 1,175 V12/P3	9.42	8.17	14.40	6.2	0°	2555	2.2	177	LW/1F/(2W)
324	Heinkel He 100 V2 (He 112 U) Günter, Schwärzler	1938	1 × Daimler-Benz DB 601 R.III 1,660 V12/P3	9.42	8.17	14.40	6.2	0°	2470	1.5	172	LW/1F/(2W)
325	Heinkel He 100 V3/UR Günter, Schwärzler	1938	1 × Daimler-Benz DB 601 R.IV 2,060 V12/P3	6.70	8.17	11.00	5.2	0°	2475	1.2	225	LW/1F/(2W)
326	Heinkel He 100 V5 (He 100B–01) Günter, Schwärzler	1938	1 × Daimler-Benz DB 601M 1,175 V12/P3	9.40	8.20	14.50	6.1	0°	2437	2.1	168	LW/1F/(2W)
327	Heinkel He 100 V8/R (He 112 U/He 113) Günter, Schwärzler	1939	1 × Daimler-Benz DB 601M 159/R.V 2,770 V12/P3	7.60	8.18	11.00	5.2	0°	2050	0.74	186	LW/1F/(2W)
328	Heinkel He 119 V2 Heinrich Hertel Siegfried Günter	1937	1 × Daimler-Benz DB 606A–1 2,350 VV24/P4	16.00	14.80	51.60	5.0	15°	8100	3.4	157	LW/1F/(2W)
329	Heinkel He 119 V4 (He 111 U/He 606) Hertel, Günter	1937	1 × Daimler-Benz DB 606A–2 2,350 VV24/P4	15.90	14.80	50.00	5.0	12°	7160	3.0	143	LW/1F/(2W)

No.	Aircraft / Designer	Year	Engine									
330	Heinkel P.1076 A Günter, Schwärzler (Project)	1945	1 × Daimler-Benz DB 603U 1,810 V12/P2×3	11.00	9.64	18.00	6.7	−6°	4400	2.4	244	LW/1F/(2W)
331	Heinkel P.1076 B Günter, Schwärzler (Project)	1945	1 × Jumo 213E 1,750 V12/P2×3	11.00	9.60	18.00	6.7	−6°	4480	2.6	249	LW/1F/(2W)
332	Heinkel P.1076 LM Günter, Schwärzler (Project)	1945	1 × Daimler-Benz DB 603 LM 2,100 V12/P2×3	11.00	9.60	18.00	6.7	−6°	4380	2.1	243	LW/1F/(2W)
333	Heinkel P.1076 N Günter, Schwärzler (Project)	1945	1 × Daimler-Benz DB 603 N 3,000 V12/P2×3	12.40	9.60	26.00	5.9	−6°	5230	1.7	201	LW/1F/(2W)
334	Henschel P.75 Heinrich Nicolaus (Project)	1942	1 × Daimler-Benz DB 610 2,200 VV24/P2×3	11.30	12.20			20°				MW/YF/(3W)
335	Junkers J 9/I (D I) Hugo Junkers	1918	1 × BMW IIIa 185 I6/P2	9.00	6.70	14.80	5.5	0°	835	4.5	56	LW/1F/2W
336	Messerschmitt Bf 109 V13 (Bf 113) Willy Messerschmitt Robert Lusser	1937	1 × Daimler-Benz DB 610 R.III 1,700 V12/P3	9.90	8.70	16.40	6.0	4°	1900	1.1	116	LW/1F/(2W)
337	Messerschmitt Me 209 V1 (V3) (Me 109 R) Willy Messerschmitt Walter Rethel	1939	1 × Daimler-Benz DB 601 R.V. (V10) 2,770 V12/P3	7.80	7.24	10.55	5.8	0°	2164	0.8	205	LW/1F/(2W)
338	Messerschmitt Me 309 A–1 Messerschmitt, Rethel (Project)	1943	1 × Daimler-Benz DB 603H 1,750 V12/P3	11.00	9.56	15.80	7.7	4°	3450	2.0	218	LW/1F/(3W)
339	Škoda–Kauba Sk V–5 Otto Kauba (Project)	1945	1 × Daimler-Benz DB 603 1,750 V12/P3	12.00	8.50			16°	4500	2.6		LW/1F/(2W)
Italy (I)												
401	Ansaldo S.V.A.5 Primo U Savoia, R Verduzio Celestino Rosatelli	1918	1 × S.P.A.6 A 213 I6/P2	9.10	8.10	26.92		0°	975	4.6	36	2W/1F/2W

1	2	3	4	5	6	7	8	9	10	11	12	13
Italy (I)												
402	CMASA CS.15 Manlio Stiavelli	1939	1 × Fiat A.S.8 2,250 V18/P2×3	9.00	8.91	10.23	7.9	4°	2270	1.0	222	MW/1F/(2W)
403	Fiat B.R. Celestino Rosatelli	1919	1 × Fiat A.14 836 V12/P2	15.80	10.47			0°	3200	3.8		2W/1F/2W
404	Fiat ARF Rosatelli	1920	1 × Fiat A.14 836 V12/P2	16.40				0°	4900	5.9		2W/1F/2W
405	Fiat R.700 Rosatelli	1922	1 × Fiat A.14 S 837 V12/P2	10.80	7.85	33.00	6.8	0°	2250	2.7	68	2W/1F/2W
406	Reggiane Re 2006 b Roberto Longhi	1944	1 × Daimler-Benz DB 603A 1,850 V12/P4	11.00	9.08	20.40	5.9	4°	3950	2.1	194	LW/1F/(2W)
407	Reggiane Re 2006 C Longhi (Project)	1945	1 × Daimler-Benz DB 603A 1,850 V12/P4	11.00	9.08	16.40	7.4	4°				LW/1F/(2W)
408	Savoia MVT Allessandro Marchetti	1919	1 × S.P.A.6 A 213 I6/P2	8.40	7.20	21.50		5°	890	4.2	41	2W/1F/2W
Japan (J)												
501	Kawasaki Ki.64–KAI Takeo Doi (Project)	1945	1 × Kawasaki Ha.201–KAI 2,800 V24/P2×2	13.50	11.03	28.00	6.5	5°	5100	1.8	182	LW/1F/(2W)
502	Kawasaki Ki.78 (Ken–3) Shoruku Wada, Isamu Imashi	1943	1 × Daimler–Benz DB 601A 1,550 V12/P3	8.00	8.10	11.00	5.8	4°	2300	1.5	209	LW/1F/(2W)
503	Tachikawa Ki.94–I (Project)	1943	2 × Mitsubishi Ha.211ru 2 × 2,200 R18-P4	15.00	13.05	37.00	6.1	8°	8800	2.0	238	LW/2F/(3W)
504	Yokosuka Y–40 R2Y–2 Keiun (Project)	1945	1 × Aichi Ha.70–01 3,400 V24/P6	14.00	13.05	34.00	5.8	9°	8100	2.4	238	LW/1F/(3W)

Union of Soviet Socialist Republics (USSR)

No.	Name / Designer	Year	Engine											
601	Stal–8 / Roberto L Bartini	1934	1 × Klimov M–100A 860 V12/P2	9.00	6.88	14.30	5.7	3°	1500	1.7	105	LW/1F/(1W)
602	TSAGI SK / Matus R Bisnovat	1940	1 × Klimov M–105 1,050 V12/P3	7.30	8.28	9.50	5.6	7°	2100	2.0	221	LW/1F/(2W)

United Kingdom (UK)

No.	Name / Designer	Year	Engine											
701	Airspeed A.S.31 (F.35/35) / Alfred H Tiltman (Project)	1936	1 × Rolls-Royce Merlin E 860 V12/P3	10.06	8.88	18.12	5.6	20°				MW/1F/(2W)
702	Airspeed A.S.56 / Arthur E Hagg (Project)	1942	1 × Napier Sabre IV 2,300 H24/P4	12.19	9.14	22.02	6.7	4°				LW/1F/(2W)
703	Avro 539B/1 / A Verdon Roe	1921	1 × Napier Lion II 538 W12/P2	7.77	5.54	18.58		0°				2W/1F/2W
704	Bristol 72 Racer / Wilfrid T Reid	1922	1 × Bristol Jupiter I 495 R9/P2	7.6	6.58			0°				MW/1F/(2W)
705	Bristol 142 Britain First / Frank Barnwell	1935	2 × Bristol Mercury VIS2 2 × 650 R9/P3	17.17	12.12	43.57	6.8	$\frac{1°}{3}$	4244	3.3	97	LW/1F/(2W)
706	de Havilland D.H.103 Hornet / Geoffrey de Havilland R E Bishop	1944	2 × Rolls-Royce Merlin 130/131 2 × 2,100 V12/P4	13.72	11.18	33.54	5.6	$\frac{0°}{4}$	7113	1.7	212	LW/1F/(2W)
707	Gloucestershire Mars I/Bamel / Henry P Folland	1921	1 × Napier Lion II 538 W12/P2	6.17	6.71	15.33		0°	1200	2.2	78	2W/1F/2W
708	Gloster II Bluebird / Folland	1925	1 × Napier Lion V 640 W12/P2	6.10	8.18	15.33		0°	1406	2.2	92	2W/1F/2W
709	Hawker P.1026 Fury (F.2/43) / Sydney Camm	1946	1 × Napier Sabre VII 3,100 H24/P4	11.70	10.56	26.43	5.2	0°	5500	1.8	208	LW/1F/(2W)

1	2	3	4	5	6	7	8	9	10	11	12	13
United Kingdom (UK)												
710	Hawker Sea Fury FB.11 Camm	1966	1 × Bristol Centaurus 18 2,540 R18/P5	11.70	10.57	26.01	5.3	0°				LW/1F/(2W)
711	Hawker Sea Fury FB.11 Camm (*Miss Merced*)	1966	1 × Bristol Centaurus 18 2,540 R18/P5	9.85	10.59	20.90	4.6	0°	4500	1.8	215	LW/1F/(2W)
712	Hawker Sea Fury FB.11 Camm	1988	1 × Bristol Centaurus 175 2,890 R18/P5	11.70	10.57	26.01	5.3	0°				LW/1F/(2W)
713	Heston Type 5 Racer Arthur E Hagg George Cornwall	1940	1 × Napier Sabre I 2,230 H24/P3	9.77	7.50	15.57	6.1	8°	3265	1.5	210	LW/1F/(2W)
714	Heston Type 5 Racer Hagg, Cornwall (Project)	1940	1 × Napier Sabre 2,485 H24/P3	9.77	7.50	15.57	6.1	8°				LW/1F/(2W)
715	Miles M22 Don L Brown (Project)	1941	2 × Rolls-Royce Griffon 1,620 V12/P3	11.89	10.06	30.19	4.7	$\frac{0°}{5}$	5900	1.8	195	MW/2F/(3W)
716	Miles M23 Brown (Project)	1941	1 × Rolls-Royce Griffon 2 × 1,620 V12/P3	9.45	8.74	17.19	5.2	3°	3357	2.1	195	LW/1F/(3W)
717	Royal Aircraft Factory S.E.4 Henry P Folland	1914	1 × Gnome Double Lambda 160 Rot14/P4	8.38	6.40	17.47		0°				2W/1F/2W
718	Sopwith 7F.1 Snipe TOM Sopwith Fred Sigrist	1918	1 × ABC Dragonfly 323 R9/P2	9.47	6.05	25.08		0°	916	2.8	37	2W/1F/2W
719	Sopwith 107 Schneider Sopwith Sigrist	1919	1 × Cosmos Jupiter 456 R9/P2	7.31	6.55	20.62		0°	1000	2.2	48	2W/1F/2W

No.		Year	Aircraft / Engine										Code
720	Supermarine 323 (35/35) High Speed Spitfire, Mitchell, Smith	1939	1 × Rolls-Royce Merlin IIIm, 2,190 V12/P4	10.26	9.12	21.74	4.8	0°				LW/1F/(2W)
721	Supermarine 327 (F.18/37), Reginald J Mitchell, Joseph Smith (Project)	1938	2 × Rolls-Royce Merlin, 2 × 1,257 V12/P3	12.19	10.21	27.22	5.5	7°	5130	2.0	188	MW/1F/(2W)
722	Supermarine 371 (F.1/43) Spiteful F.XIV, Joseph Smith	1945	1 × Rolls-Royce Griffon 69, 2,408 V12/P5	10.67	10.06	19.51	5.8	5°/7	4513	1.9	231	LW/1F/(2W)
723	Supermarine 371 (F.1/43) Spiteful F.XVI, Smith	1947	1 × Rolls-Royce Griffon 101, 2,408 V12/P5	10.67	10.06	19.51	5.8	5°/7	4513	1.9	231	LW/1F/(2W)

United States of America (USA)

No.		Year	Aircraft / Engine										Code
801	Aero Design DG-1, David Garber	1981	2 × Mazda/Wankel RX-3, 2 × 330 RC/P3	6.20	6.10	4.88	7.6	3°	1137	1.7	233	MW/+F/(3W)
802	Bell 11 XP-39 Airacobra, Robert L Woods, H M Poyer, O L Woodson	1939	1 × Allison V-1710-17, 1,165 V12/P3	10.92	8.74	18.58	6.4	3°	2517	2.2	135	LW/1F/(3W)
803	Bell 26E P-39Q-10E Airacobra (Cobra II), Woods, Poyer, Woodson	1948	1 × Allison V-1710-G-6, 2,890 V12/P4	10.36	9.19	19.80	5.4	3°	3850	1.2	181	LW/1F/(3W)
804	Bell 26E P-39Q-10E Airacobra (Cobra III), Woods, Poyer, Woodson	1968	1 × Allison V-1710-G-6, 2,890 V12/P4	7.98	9.19			3°				LW/1F/(3W)
805	Burgess Cup Defender, W Starling Burgess, Greely S Curtis	1912	1 × Gnome Double Lambda 160 Rot14/P2	8.92	7.47	11.89	6.7	0°	515	3.2	43	MW/2F/2S4W

United Kingdom (UK)

1	2	3	4	5	6	7	8	9	10	11	12	13
806	Curtiss–Herring Reims Machine / Glenn L Curtiss / Augustus Herring	1909	1 × Curtiss 52 V8/P2	10.16	9.20	20.90	7.3	0°	318	6.1	15	2W/1F/2W
807	Curtiss 502/18–T–1 Wasp / Charles B Kirkham	1918	1 × Curtiss K–12 V12/P2 / 400	9.75	7.11	26.70	10.7	4°	1382	3.4	52	3W/1F/2W
808	Curtiss 22 Cox Racer (Cactus Kitten) / William L Gilmore / H T Booth, A L Thurston	1921	1 × Curtiss C–12 433 V12/P2	6.10	5.87	16.68	6.7	0°	1091	2.5	65	3W/1F/2W
809	Curtiss 23 CR (L–17–3) / Gilmore, Booth, Thurston	1921	1 × Curtiss CD–12 427 V12/P2	6.91	6.41	15.61	6.1	0°	1003	2.3	64	2W/1F/2W
810	Curtiss 23 R–6 (L–19–1) / Gilmore, William Wait	1922	1 × Curtiss D–12 470 V12/P2	5.79	5.75	12.63	5.3	0°	962	2.0	76	2W/1F/2W
811	Curtiss 23 R–6 (L–19–1) / Gilmore, Wait	1923	1 × Curtiss D–12 510 V12/P2	5.79	5.75	12.63	5.3	0°	962	1.9	76	2W/1F/2W
812	Curtiss 32 R2C–1 (L–111–1) / Gilmore, Wait	1923	1 × Curtiss D–12A 514 V12/P2	6.71	6.01	13.74		0°	939	1.8	68	2W/1F/2W
813	Curtiss 42 R3C–1 (L–114–1) / Gilmore, Wait, T P Wright	1925	1 × Curtiss V.1400 608 V12/P2	6.71	6.13	13.38		0°	989	1.6	74	2W/1F/2W
814	Dayton–Wright RB / H H Rinehart / C H Grant, M C Baumann	1920	1 × Hall–Scott L–6A 253 I6/P2	6.45	6.91	9.54	4.4	0°	839	3.5	88	HW/1F/(2W)
815	Douglas 312 XP–48 (Project) / Edward H Heinemann	1940	1 × Ranger SGV–770 525 V12/P3	9.75	6.62	8.55	11.0	3°	1542	2.9	180	LW/1F/(2W)

No.	Aircraft / Designer	Year	Engine										
816	Engineering Division VCP–R / Alfred V Verville / V E Clark	1920	1 × Packard 1A–2025 / 608 V12/P2	8.58	7.37	21.23		3°	1450	2.4	68	2W/1F/2W
817	Goodyear F2G–1 Corsair / R B Beisel	1949	1 × Pratt & Whitney R–4360–4 / 4,560 R28/P4	10.11	10.97	25.45	4.0	0°/5	5253	1.1	206	LW/1F/(2W)
818	Granville Brothers Gee Bee Z / Robert L Hall	1931	1 × Pratt & Whitney R–985 / 542 R9 /P2	7.16	4.60	6.96	7.4	0°	1034	1.9	149	LW/1F/2W
819	Granville Brothers Gee Bee Z / Hall	1931	1 × Pratt & Whitney R–1344 / 760 R9/ P2	7.16	4.60	6.96	7.4	0°				LW/1F/2W
820	Granville Brothers Gee Bee R–1 Super Sportster / Howell Miller	1932	1 × Pratt & Whitney R–1344 / 810 R9/ P2	7.62	5.41	9.29	6.2	0°	1095	1.4	118	LW/1F/2W
821	Grumman G–58A F8F–1 Bearcat (Gulfhawk IV) / William T Schwendler	1947	1 × Pratt & Whitney R–2800–34W / 2,840 R18/P4	10.92	8.61	22.67	5.3	12°/5	3850	1.4	170	LW/1F//(2W)
822	Grumman G–58B F8F–2 Bearcat / Schwendler, Greenamyer	1966	1 × Pratt & Whitney R–2800–83A / 2,540 R18/P4	9.04	9.60		3.7	12°/5				LW/1F/(2W)
823	Grumman G–58B F8F–2 Bearcat / Schwendler, Greenamyer	1968	1 × Pratt & Whitney R–2800–83A / 2,540 R18/P4	8.69	9.60	20.62	3.7	12°/5				LW/1F/(2W)
824	Grumman G–58B F8F–2 Bearcat (Conquest I) / Schwendler, Greenamyer	1969	1 × Pratt & Whitney R–2800 CB–17 / 3,350 R18/P4	8.69	9.60	20.62	3.7	12°/5	3515	1.0	170	LW/1F/(2W)
825	Grumman G–58B F8F–2 Bearcat (Rare Bear) / Schwendler, Lyle Shelton	1989	1 × Wright R–3350–26WD / 3,850 R18/P4	9.45	9.35	22.67	3.9	12°/5				LW/1F/(2W)

1	2	3	4	5	6	7	8	9	10	11	12	13
United States of America (USA)												
826	Hawks *Time Flies* Howell Miller	1936	1 × Pratt & Whitney R–1830BG 1,166 R14/P3	9.25	7.16	14.86	5.8	3°	2724	2.3	183	LW/1F/(2W)
827	Hughes Special 1B (H–1) Richard W Palmer	1935	1 × Pratt & Whitney R–1535 (SA–1G) 910 R14/P2	7.59	8.23	12.82	4.5	9°	2491	2.7	194	LW/1F/(2W)
828	Kirkham-Williams Vespa Harry T Booth Arthur L Thurston	1927	1 × Packard X–2775 1,265 X24/P2	9.09	6.86	20.16		0°			2W/1F/2W	
829	Levolor Sea Fury (T. 20 mod) (*Blind Man's Bluff*) Sydney Camm Larry Burton	1988	1 × Wright R–3350–26WD 4,100 R18/P4	9.82		20.90	4.6	0°				LW/1F/(2W)
830	Lockheed 22 XP–38 (Lightning) Hal Hibbard Clarence L Johnson	1939	2 × Allison V–1710–11/15 2 × 1,165 V12/P3	15.85	11.53	30.42	8.3	5°	6508	2.8	214	MW/2F/(3W)
831	Lockheed 522 XP–49 Hibbard, Johnson M C Haddon Project	1940	2 × Pratt & Whitney X–1800 2 × 2,330 X24/P4	15.85	11.53	30.42	8.3	5°	9050	1.9	297	MW/2F/(3W)
832	Mach Buster I William Montagne	1990	1 × General Motors 2,130 V8/ P4	4.27	10.36	4.46	4.1	33°	1134	0.5	254	HW/+F/(3W)
833	Navy Wright NW–1 Mystery Jerome C Hunsaker	1922	1 × Wright T–2 660 V12/P2	9.30	7.32	16.72		0°	1360	2.1	81	2W/1F/2W

No.	Aircraft	Year	Engine								
834	North American NA–97 A–36A Mustang (*Beguine*) Raymond H Rice, Walter Beech L Waite, E Schmued, E H Horkey	1949	1 × Packard-Rolls-Royce V–1650 Merlin 3,450 V12/P4	11.35	9.83	21.65	5.9	$\frac{10°}{3}$	3660	1.1	169 LW/1F/(2W)
835	North American NA–103 P–51C–10 Mustang Rice, Waite, Schmued, Horkey	1947	1 × Packard-Rolls-Royce V–1650–7 Merlin 2,300 V12/P4	11.28	9.83	21.65	5.9	$\frac{10°}{3}$			LW/1F/(2W)
836	North American NA–103 F–6C Mustang (*Thunderbird*) Rice, Waite, Schmued, Horkey	1951	1 × Packard-Rolls-Royce V–1650–7 Merlin 2,300 V12/P4	11.28	9.83	21.65	5.9	$\frac{10°}{3}$			LW/1F/(2W)
837	North American NA–105A XP–51G Mustang Rice, Waite, Schmued, Horkey	1944	1 × Rolls-Royce Merlin 145 2,100 V12/P5	11.28	9.82	21.65	5.9	3°	4030	1.9	186 LW/1F/(2W)
838	North American NA–109 P–51D–15 Mustang (*Jeannie*) Rice, Waite, Schmued, Horkey	1981	1 × Packard-Rolls-Royce V–1650–9 Merlin 2,840 V12/P4	9.60	9.84			$\frac{15°}{3}$	3900	1.4	LW/1F/(2W)
839	North American NA–122 P–51D–20 Mustang Rice, Waite, Schmued, Horkey	1952	1 × Packard-Rolls-Royce V–1650–25 Merlin 2,300 V12/P4	10.06	9.68	20.90	4.8	$\frac{15°}{3}$	3660	1.6	175 LW/1F/(2W)
840	North American NA–122 P–51D–20 Mustang (*Precious Metal*) Rice, Waite, Schmued, Horkey Whittington Bros	1989	1 × Rolls-Royce Griffon 57A 3,600 V12/P2×3					$\frac{15°}{3}$			LW/1F/(2W)
841	North American NA–124 P–51M–1 Mustang Rice, Waite, Schmued, Horkey	1945	1 × Packard-Rolls-Royce V–1650–9A Merlin 2,250 V12/P4	11.28	10.16	21.65	5.9	3°	4300	1.9	199 LW/1F/(2W)

1	2	3	4	5	6	7	8	9	10	11	12	13
United States of America (USA)												
842	North American NA–124 P–51D–25 Mustang (*Challenger*) Rice, Waite, Schmued, Horkey Charles Lyford	1966	1 × Packard-Rolls-Royce V–1650–7 Merlin 3,600 V12/P4	9.32	9.83			$\frac{15°}{3}$				LW/1F/(2W)
843	North American NA–124 P–51D–25 Mustang (*Bardahl Special*) Rice, Waite, Schmued, Horkey Lyford	1972	1 × Rolls–Royce Griffon 3,500 V12/P4	9.32				$\frac{15°}{3}$				LW/1F/(2W)
844	North American NA–124 P–51D–25 Mustang (RB–51 *Red Baron*) Rice, Waite, Schmued, Horkey Bruce Boland, Pete Law	1976	1 × Rolls-Royce Griffon 57A 3,450 V12/P2×3	10.06	9.91	20.90	4.8	$\frac{15°}{3}$	4700	1.4	225	LW/1F/(2W)
845	North American NA–124 P–51D–25 Mustang (*Red Baron*) Rice, Waite, Schmued, Horkey Boland, Law	1979	1 × Rolls-Royce Griffon 57A 3,600 V12/P2×3	10.06	9.91	20.90	4.8	$\frac{15°}{3}$	4700	1.3	225	LW/1F/(2W)
846	North American NA–124 P–51D–25 Mustang (*Dago Red*) Rice, Waite, Schmued, Horkey Boland, Law	1983	1 × Packard-Rolls-Royce V–1650–9 Merlin 3,000 V12/P4		9.83			$\frac{15°}{3}$				LW/1F/(2W)
847	North American NA–126 P–51H–5 Mustang Rice, Waite, Schmued, Horkey	1945	1 × Packard-Rolls-Royce V–1650–9 Merlin 2,250 V12/P4	11.28	10.16	21.65	5.9	3°	4300	1.9	199	LW/1F/(2W)

848	North American/Dilley 1001 (*Learfang/Vendetta*) Thomas Kelley, John Dilley	1988 1 × Packard–Rolls-Royce V–1650 Merlin 622 3,000 V12/P4	9.50	9.83	21.50	4.2	17°	3350	1.1	156	LW/1F/(2W)
849	Republic XP–47H Thunderbolt Alexander Kartveli	1945 1 × Chrysler XIV–2220–1 2,330 V16/P4	12.44	11.68	27.87	5.6	3°	6355	2.7	228	LW/1F/(2W)
850	Republic XP–47J Thunderbolt (*Superman*) Kartveli	1944 1 × Pratt & Whitney R–2800–57(C) 2,840 R18/P4	12.50	10.13	27.87	5.6	3°	5643	2.0	202	LW/1F/(2W)
851	Republic XP–72 ('Ultrabolt') Kartveli	1944 1 × Pratt & Whitney R–4360–13 3,050 R28/P4	12.47	11.15	27.87	5.6	3°	6538	2.1	235	LW/1F/(2W)
852	Republic P–72A Kartveli (Project)	1944 1 × Pratt & Whitney R–4360–19 4,065 R28/P2×3	12.47	11.15	27.87	5.6	3°	6500	1.6	233	LW/1F/(2W)
853	Republic XF–12 Rainbow Kartveli	1948 4 × Pratt & Whitney R–4360–37 4 × 3,550 R28/P4	39.37	28.61	152.3	10.2	3°	46000	3.2	302	MW/1F/(3W)
854	Keith Rider Super–Speed Racer Keith Rider (Project)	1934 1 × Miller 2,535 V16/P2	8.13	8.46	12.82	5.2	5°	1360	0.5	106	LW/1F/(2W)
855	Sandberg Tsunami (Boland BB–1) Bruce Boland Pete Law	1987 1 × Packard–Rolls–Royce V–1650 Merlin 224 3,350 V12/P4	8.69	8.69	13.80	5.5	5°	3175	0.9	230	LW/1F/(2W)
856	Sanders Sea Fury (T.20 mod) (*Dreadnaught*) Sydney Camm Frank Sanders, Bruce Boland	1983 1 × Pratt & Whitney R–4360–63A 3,850 R28/P4	9.82	10.82	20.90	4.6	0°	6300	1.6	301	LW/1F/(2W)
857	Scaled Composites 21 Pond Racer PR–01 Elbert L Rutan	1990 2 × Nissan/Electramotive VG–30 2 × 1,000 V6/P4	7.71	6.80		8.7	–3°	1500	0.7		MW/3F/(2W)

United States of America (USA)

1	2	3	4	5	6	7	8	9	10	11	12	13
858	Schapel S-1275 Finesse Rodney Schapel (Project)	1985	1 × Chrysler Stake II 1,420 V8/P3	7.16	9.14			3°	862	0.6		MW/2F/(3W)
859	Stock High Speed Project John Stock (Project)	1934	1 × Rolls-Royce R 2,565 V12/P1	8.87		13.10	6.0					LW/1F/(2W)
860	Verville–Sperry R–3 Alfred V Verville	1923	1 × Curtiss D–12 510 V12/P2	9.33	7.16	13.61	6.4	14°	1124	2.2	83	LW/1F/(2W)
861	Verville-Sperry Verville (Project)	1924	2 × Curtiss D–12A 2 × 514 V12/P2									LW/1F/(2W)
862	Chance Vought VS–315 XF5U–1 Skimmer Charles H Zimmerman	1947	2 × Pratt & Whitney R–2000–2(D) 2 × 1,620 R14/P4	9.91	8.72	44.13	1.1	10° 45	7620	2.4	173	MW/2F/(2W)
863	Vultee 70 XP–54 Richard W Palmer (Project)	1941	1 × Pratt & Whitney X–1800–A4G 1,875 X24/P2×3	16.41	16.68	42.32	6.4	0°	5216	2.8	123	LW/2F/(3W)
864	Wedell–Williams No44 James R Wedell	1931	1 × Pratt & Whitney R–985 542 R9/P2	7.92	6.78	11.90	5.3	0°	1005	1.9	84	LW/1F/2W
865	Wedell–Williams No44 Wedell	1933	1 × Pratt & Whitney R–1344 810 R9/P2	7.82	7.16	11.70	5.2	0°	1100	1.4	94	LW/1F/2W
866	Wedell–Williams No44 Wedell	1934	1 × Pratt & Whitney R–1690 1,014 R9/P2	7.98	6.78	12.08	5.3	0°	1137	1.1	94	LW/1F/2W
867	Wedell–Williams No45 Wedell	1934	1 × Pratt & Whitney R–1344 810 R9/P2	7.92	7.01	11.40	5.5	0°	1215	1.5	107	LW/1F/(2W)

		Year	Engine									Config
868	Wright Flyer I Orville & Wilbur Wright	1903	1 × Wright 12 R4/2×P2	12.29	6.43	47.38	6.4	0°	340	28	7	2W/2F/2S
869	Wright Flyer II Wright Bros	1904	1 × Wright 16 R4/2×P2	12.29	6.43	47.38	6.4	0°	350	22	7	2W/2F/2S
870	Wright Flyer III Wright Bros	1905	1 × Wright 19 R4/2×P2	12.34	8.53	46.73	6.5	0°	388	20	8	2W/2F/2S
871	Wright Flyer IIImod Wright Bros	1908	1 × Wright 35 R4/2×P2	12.34	8.74	46.73	6.5	0°				2W/2F/2S
872	Wright A (France) Wright Bros	1909	1 × Barriquand & Marre 35 R4/2×P2	12.50	8.84	47.38	6.6	0°	430	12	9	2W/2F/2S
873	Wright A mod (Signal Corps) Wright Bros	1909	1 × Wright 35 R4/2×P2	11.13	8.81	38.55	6.4	0°				2W/2F/2S
874	Wright R (Baby Grand) Wright Bros	1910	1 × Wright 60 V8/2×P2	6.53	7.32	13.47	6.3	0°	390	6.5	29	2W/2F/2S6W
875	Wright F2W–1 (TX) Harry T Booth Arthur L Thurston	1923	1 × Wright T–3 760 V12/P3	6.86	6.50	16.16	5.8	0°	1295	1.7	80	2W/1F/2W

BIBLIOGRAPHY

Angelucci, Enzo: Il Caccia Americano dal 1917 ad Oggi. Roma (Italia): Arnoldo Mondadori Editore, 1985.

Berliner, Don: Victory over the Wind – A History of the Absolute World Air Speed Record. New York (USA): Van Nostrand Reinhold, 1983.

Bowers, Peter M: The Gee Bee Racers. Leatherhead (GB): Profile No 51, 1965.

Bowman, Martin W: The World's Fastest Aircraft. Wellingborough (GB), Patrick Stephens, 1990.

Buehl, Fred W; Gann, Harry S: The National Air Race Sketchbook. Los Angeles, California (USA): Floyd Clymer, 1949.

Carter, Dustin W: Racing Planes and Air Races – Volume XIII. Fallbrook, California (USA): Aero Publishers, 1978.

Cattaneo, Gianni: The S.V.A. (Ansaldo) Scouts. Leatherhead (GB): Profile No 61, 1966.

Christy, Joe: Racing Planes Guide. New York (USA): Sports Car Press, 1963.

Christy, Joe: Racing Planes & Pilots – Aircraft Competition, Past and Present. Blue Ridge Summit, Pennsylvania (USA): Tab Books, 1982.

Coggi, Igino: MC72 & Coppa Schneider – Volume I, II. Roma (Italia): Claudio Tatangelo Editore, 1984.

Cooke, David C: Racing Planes that made History. New York (USA): Putnams Sons, 1960.

Cowin, Hugh: The Junkers Monoplanes. Leatherhead (GB): Profile No 187, 1967.

Crouch, Tom D: Blériot XI – The Story of a Classic Aircraft. Washington DC (USA): Smithsonian Institution Press, 1982 (Famous Aircraft of the National Air and Space Museum No 5).

Dwiggins, Don: They Flew the Bendix Races. Philadelphia, Pennsylvania (USA): Lippincott, 1965.

Foxworth, Thomas G: The Speed Seekers. London (GB): Macdonald and Jane's, 1974 and Haynes 1989.

Friedlander, Mark P; Gurney, Gene: Higher, Faster and Farther. New York (USA): William Morrow, 1973.

Gibbs-Smith, Charles Harvard: The Wright Brothers. London (GB): Her Majesty's Stationery Office, 1963 and 1978.

Gibbs-Smith, Charles Harvard: The World's First Aeroplane Flights. London (GB): Her Majesty's Stationery Office, 1965 and 1977.

Gibbs-Smith, Charles Harvard: The Rebirth of European Aviation. London (GB): Her Majesty's Stationery Office, 1974.

Govi, Sergio: I "Reggiane" dall'A alla Z – Descrizione tecnica degli aerei Reggiane Gruppo Caproni. Milano (Italia): Giorgio Apostolo Editore, 1985.

Green, William: The Warplanes of the Third Reich. London (GB): Macdonald, 1970.

Green, William: The Augsburg Eagle – A Documentary History – Messerschmitt Bf 109. London (GB): Jane's, 1980.

Grosz, Peter M; Terry, Gerard: The Way to the World's First All-Metal Fighter. London (GB): *Air Enthusiast* No 25, 60–76.

Gunston, Bill: World Encyclopedia of Aero Engines. Wellingborough (GB): Patrick Stephens, 1986.

Gunston, Bill; Taylor, D; Ewart, A: Guinness Book of Speed. London (GB): Guinness, 1984.

Gwynn-Jones, Terry: The Air Racers – Aviation's Golden Era 1909–1936. London (GB): Pelham, 1984.

Haffke, Henry A: Gee Bee – The Real Story of the Granville Brothers and their Marvelous Airplanes. ViP Publishers, Colorado Springs, Col., USA, 1989.

Hallion, Richard P: Designers and Test Pilots. Alexandria, Virginia (USA): Time-Life Books, 1982 (The Epic of Flight).

Heimann, Erich H: Um die Wette mit dem Schall: Schwann, 1969.

Heimann, Erich H: Die schnellsten Flugzeuge der Welt – 1906 bis heute. Stuttgart: Motorbuch, 1978.

Heinkel, Ernst: Stürmisches Leben. Stuttgart: Mundus.

Hull, Robert: September Champions – The Story of America's Air Racing Pioneers. Harrisburg, Pennsylvania (USA): Stackpole, 1979.

Huntington, Roger: Thompson Trophy Racers. Osceola, Wisconsin (USA): Motorbooks, 1989.

Ishoven, Armand van: Messerschmitt. München: Heyne, 1978.

James, Derek N: Schneider Trophy Aircraft. London (GB): Putnam 1981.

Jerram, Mike: Reno 2 – The National Championship Air Races. London (GB): Osprey, 1986.

Jones, Lloyd S: US Fighters. Fallbrook, California (USA): Aero Publishers, 1975.

Jones, Lloyd S: US Naval Fighters, Fallbrook, California (USA): Aero Publishers, 1977.

Kinert, Reed: American Racing Planes and Historic Air Races. New York (USA): Wilcox and Follett, 1952.

Kinert, Reed: Racing Planes and Air Races – Volumes I–XII. Fallbrook, California (USA): Aero Publishers, 1967–1976.

Köhler, H Dieter: Ernst Heinkel – Pionier der Schnellflugzeuge. Koblenz: Bernard & Graefe, 1983 (Die Deutsche Luftfahrt 5).

Kosin, Rüdiger: Die Entwicklung der deutschen Jagdflugzeuge. Koblenz: Bernard & Graefe, 1983 (Die Deutsche Luftfahrt 4).

Laignier, G H: Livre d'Or de la Grande Semaine d'Aviation de la Champagne.

Lange, Bruno: Das Buch der Deutschen Luftfahrttechnik, Mainz: Dieter Hoffmann, 1970.

Larsen, Jim: Directory of Unlimited Class Pylon Air Racers. Kirkland, Washington (USA): American Air Museum, 1971.

Lewis, Peter: The British Fighter since 1912. London (GB): Putnam, 1965, 1979.

Lewis, Peter: British Racing and Record-Breaking Aircraft. London (GB): Putnam, 1970.

Lieberg, Owen S: The First Air Race: The International Competition at Reims 1909. New York (USA): Doubleday, 1974.

Lissarague, Pierre; Lecomte, Pierre: The Race for Speed from the Beginnings of Aviation to the Present Day. Toulouse (F): 14th Congress of the International Council of the Aeronautical Sciences (ICAS), 1984.

Mandrake, Charles G: The Gee Bee Story. Wichita, Kansas (USA): Longo, 1956.

Mandrake, Charles G: The National Air Races 1932. (USA); Speed, 1976.

Matt, Paul R: Howard Hughes and the Hughes Racer. Temple City, California (USA): Historical Aviation Album, Volume XVI, pp 4–34, 1980.

Matt, Paul R; Robertson, Bruce: United States Navy and Marine Corps Fighers 1918–1962. Letchworth (GB): Harleyford, 1962.

Mendenhall, Charles A: The Early Air Racers in 3-Views (Volumes I–III). Rochester, NY

(USA): Pylon Publications, 1971–1976.

Mendenhall, Charles A: The Gee Bee Racers – A Legacy of Speed. North Branch, Minnesota (USA): Specialty Press, 1979.

Messerschmitt, Willy: Probleme des Schnellflugs. *Schriften der Deutschen Akademie der Luftfahrtforschung*, No 31. München: Oldenbourg, 1937.

Moll, Nigel: Reno – Air Racing Unlimited. London (GB): Osprey, 1983.

Mondey, David; Taylor, M J H: Guinness Book of Aircraft. London (GB): Guinness, 1988.

Munson, Kenneth: Pioneer Aircraft 1903–1914. London (GB): Blandford, 1969.

Norden, Adalbert: Weltrekord, Weltrekord. Berlin: Drei Masken, 1940.

O'Neil, Paul: Barnstormers & Speed Kings. Alexandria, Virginia (USA): Time-Life Books, 1980 (The Epic of Flight).

Prato, Piero: I Caccia Caproni-Reggiane 1938–45. Genova (Italia): Intyrama, 1968.

Prendergast, Curtis: Aviation Pioneers. Alexandria, Virginia (USA): Time-Life Books, 1980 (The Epic of Flight).

Robertson, Bruce; Brown, K S; Heyn, E F: United States Army and Air Force Fighters 1916–1961. Letchworth (GB): Harleyford, 1961.

Schmid, S H; Weaver, Truman C: The Golden Age of Air Racing – Pre-1940 (2 Volumes) Oshkosh, Wisconsin (USA): EAA Aviation Foundation, 1983.

Schmitt, Günter: Fliegende Kisten von Kitty Hawk bis Kiew. Berlin: Transpress, 1985.

Sweetman, Bill: High Speed Flight. London (GB): Jane's, 1983.

Taylor, John W R; Munson, Kenneth: Record-Breaking Aircraft—Jane's Pocket Book 15. London (GB): Macdonald and Jane's, 1978.

Tegler, John: Gentlemen, you have a Race – A History of the Reno National Championship Air Races 1964–1983. Severna Park, Maryland (USA): Wings, 1984.

Underwood, John W: The World's Famous Racing Aircraft. Los Angeles, California (USA): Floyd Clymer, 1949.

Villard, Henry Serrano: Blue Ribbon of the Air. Blue Summit Ridge, Pennsylvania (USA): Smithsonian Institution Press, 1987.

Vorderman, Don: The Great Air Races. New York (USA): Doubleday, 1969.

Wallick, Phillip: Reno Gold – The Unlimited Elite. London (GB): Osprey, 1989.

Weaver, Truman C: 62 Rare Racing Aeroplanes from the Golden Years of Aviation. New York (USA): Arenar.

Wragg, David W: Speed in the Air. Reading (GB): Osprey, 1974.

Ziegler, Mano: Kampf um Mach I – Die Geschichte des größten Abenteuers der Luftfahrt. Stuttgart: Ehapa, 1965.

Acknowledgements

The following individuals, companies, and institutions have rendered useful assistance by providing information, photographs and drawings, for which I am grateful:

Aermacchi, Varese (I)
Bol Pond, Minneapolis (USA)
Paul A Coggan, Mansfield (GB)
Daimler-Benz A G, Stuttgart
Deutsche Forschungsaustalt, für Luft – und Raumfafist, Cologne
Deutsches Museum Munich
Dornier GmbH, Munich
Le Fanatique de l'Aviation, Paris (F)
Heinz O Göhring, Hamburg
Karl Heinz Kens, Krefeld
Lockheed California, Burbank (USA)
Messerschmitt-Bölkow-Blohm GmbH, Munich
Sergio Micangeli, Roma (I)
Musée de l'Air, Le Bourget (F)
Museo Storico dell'Aeronautica Militare, Vigna di Valle (I)
National Air and Space Museum, Washington DC (USA)
RAF Museum, Hendon (GB)
Hans Redemann, Stuttgart
Science Museum, London (GB)
Mike Stanton, Emsworth (GB)

Photograph and illustration credits

Index